A Most Singular Country

A History of Occupation in the Big Bend

D1561864

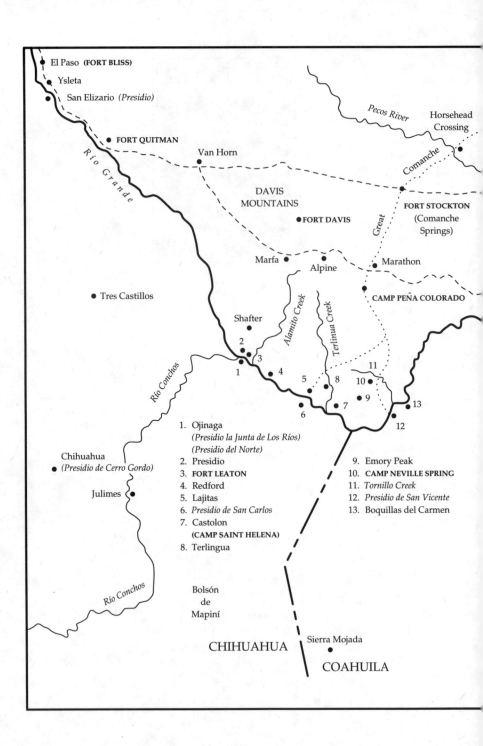

El Paso **(FORT BLISS)**
Ysleta
San Elizario *(Presidio)*
FORT QUITMAN
Río Grande
Van Horn

Pecos River
Horsehead Crossing
Comanche

DAVIS MOUNTAINS
FORT DAVIS

Great

FORT STOCKTON
(Comanche Springs)

Tres Castillos

Marfa
Alpine
Marathon

CAMP PEÑA COLORADO

Shafter

Alamito Creek
Terlinua Creek

Río Conchos

2
3
1
4
5
11
8
10
13
6
7
9
12

Chihuahua
(Presidio de Cerro Gordo)

Julimes

Río Conchos

Bolsón de Mapiní

1. Ojinaga
   (Presidio la Junta de Los Ríos)
   (Presidio del Norte)
2. Presidio
3. **FORT LEATON**
4. Redford
5. Lajitas
6. *Presidio de San Carlos*
7. Castolon
   (CAMP SAINT HELENA)
8. Terlingua

9. Emory Peak
10. **CAMP NEVILLE SPRING**
11. *Tornillo Creek*
12. *Presidio de San Vicente*
13. Boquillas del Carmen

CHIHUAHUA

Sierra Mojada

COAHUILA

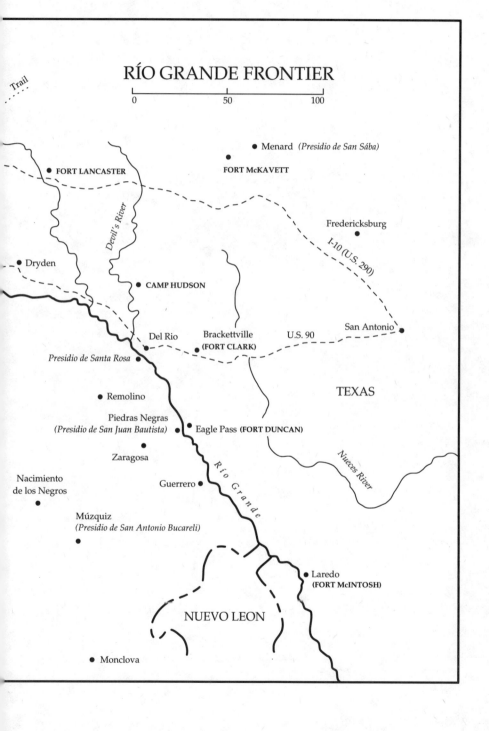

RÍO GRANDE FRONTIER

0   50   100

Trail

Menard *(Presidio de San Sába)*

FORT LANCASTER

FORT McKAVETT

Devil's River

Fredericksburg

I-10 (U.S. 290)

Dryden

CAMP HUDSON

Del Rio

Brackettville
(FORT CLARK)

U.S. 90

San Antonio

Presidio de Santa Rosa

TEXAS

Remolino

Piedras Negras
(Presidio de San Juan Bautista)

Eagle Pass **(FORT DUNCAN)**

Zaragosa

Nueces River

Nacimiento
de los Negros

Guerrero

Río Grande

Múzquiz
(Presidio de San Antonio Bucareli)

Laredo
(FORT McINTOSH)

NUEVO LEON

Monclova

Charles
Redd
Monographs
in Western
History No. 18

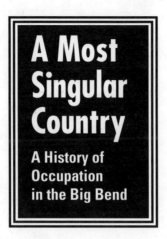

A Most Singular Country

A History of Occupation in the Big Bend

Arthur R. Gómez

National Park Service
Department of the Interior
Santa Fe, New Mexico

Brigham Young University
Charles Redd Center for Western Studies

*The Charles Redd Monographs in Western
History are made possible by a grant from
Charles Redd. This grant served as the
basis for the establishment of the Charles
Redd Center for Western Studies at
Brigham Young University.*

———

Center editor: Howard A. Christy

Library of Congress Cataloging-in-Publication Data

Gómez, Arthur R., 1946 —
   A most singular country: a history of occupation in the Big Bend
   /Arthur R. Gómez.
   235p.   cm. — (Charles Redd monographs in western history; no. 18)
   Includes bibliographical references and index.

   1. Big Bend Region (Tex.)–History. 2. Big Bend National Park (Tex.)–History.
I. Title. II. Series.
F392.B54G66   1988   976.4'93 — dc20   89–78417
ISBN 1–56085–000–0   CIP

© 1990 by Charles Redd Center for Western Studies,
Brigham Young University. All rights reserved
Printed in the United States of America

Distributed by Signature Books, 350 S. 400 E., Suite G4,
Salt Lake City, Utah 84111

Table of Contents

For my beloved sons, Paul and Chris

Acknowledgments

No publication is ever solely the work of the author; this book is certainly no exception. I have many people to thank for their time and encouragement throughout the production of the manuscript. First, I extend my deepest appreciation to Professor Gerald D. Nash of the University of New Mexico for encouraging me to undertake this project for the National Park Service though it meant a delay in completing my doctoral dissertation. He graciously offered his comments and sound advice at every turn.

I am equally grateful to Dr. Melody Webb, superintendent of Lyndon B. Johnson National Historical Park, who in her capacity as southwest regional historian expressed confidence in a hitherto unproven author to produce a publishable manuscript. It was her patience, direction, and persistent editorial scrutiny that guided this book through its formative stages. Also, to the administrative staff and colleagues of the Southwest Regional Office in Santa Fe, New Mexico, go my thanks for setting the standard of excellence that is expected of every National Park Service employee.

As is always the case in historical research, this work would not have seen completion without assistance from an army of dedicated archivists and librarians. A special note of gratitude to John A. Dwyer of the Cartographic & Architectural Branch of the National Archives; Sharon L. Roadway and her wonderful staff at the Federal Records Center in Denver, Colorado; Beverly Case and Mike Fry of Sul Ross State University in Alpine, Texas; and Kenneth D. Perry, Director of the Museum of the Big Bend.

My heartfelt appreciation goes out to the people of West Texas without whom this story would have no basis. Many of them opened their homes in order that I might share a brief glimpse into their wonderful experiences in the Big Bend. I will never forget the genuine Texas hospitality Fred and Lily Rice of Hamilton extended to me. A few selected tunes from my guitar on their front porch was hardly enough payment for such a welcome; perhaps this book will suffice. Thanks to Bennie Joe Gallego who introduced an outsider to his beloved Hispanic community of Alpine, Texas. I am forever indebted to Tom and Betty Alex as well as Vidal Davila, Jr. Their personal love for and devotion to Big Bend National Park enabled a "Colorado boy" to gain greater insight and a deeper appreciation for this compelling land.

Other federal employees did their part to facilitate the completion of this work. I wish to thank Superintendent Gilbert Lusk of Glacier National Park and Superintendent Ernesto Ortega of Wind Cave National Park for their unqualified cooperation during my research jaunts into Big Bend. No less helpful was Dr. Ross Maxwell, the first superintendent of Big Bend National Park, who cautioned me about the perils of "stick-lizards" and "knee-rabbits." His trust in me opened many doors to understanding the mystique of this curious subregion of the American West. Like so many others who visited before me, I, too, became enamored with the "spirit of the Chisos."

I can never repay the generosity of my dear friends Jim and Joyce Hyink of Los Lunas, New Mexico. They extended the warmth and hospitality of their Albuquerque home to my children while I logged countless miles on research trips. Finally, this work is dedicated to my sons, Paul and Chris, in appreciation for their willingness to adapt to new surroundings and their unfaltering belief that I would one day write a book. I love you both.

Introduction

According to local legend, after the making of heaven and earth was accomplished, the Creator took all the remaining stone rubble and tossed it into the remote corners of West Texas. Indeed, one glance at the rugged, towering peaks of the Big Bend region, contrasted to the prevailing flatness of the Chihuahuan desert, leads the visitor to logically conclude that the apparent incongruity occurred more by accident than by design.

For years scientists have endeavored to explain this fascinating inconsistency. "Depending on his viewpoint," wrote one Texas geologist in 1936, "it [Big Bend] is either a geologic paradise or a nightmare. I know of no other region in the United States where similar complicated geological conditions occur." Natural erosion and extreme temperatures are the principal agents that shaped the dramatic topographical character of the Big Bend. Varying elevations, ranging from less than 1,800 feet in the low-lying river valleys to an altitude of more than 7,800 feet at the crest of Emory Peak, provide a marvelous backdrop for what one scholar appropriately termed a "land of contrasts."[1]

Scientists tell us that two geologic ages are clearly evident in Big Bend. The oldest formations are the sedimentary or stratified Lower Cretaceous indicative of the Mesozoic Era (63–135 million years). The most notable landmarks composed of these heavy sandstone, shale, and limestone deposits are the Christmas and Santiago Mountains, which form the northern periphery of Big Bend National Park; the Mesa de Anguila overlooking the mouth of Santa Elena Canyon; and the eastern ranges known as the Dead Horse Mountains and the Sierra del Carmen, which tower in sentinel-like silence above the Río Grande.

Paralleling the gravel beds of two of the park's principal drainage systems — Terlingua Creek on the west and Tornillo Creek on the east — are the Upper Cretaceous features also representing the Mesozoic Age. These deposits, made of a softer limestone, usually cream to grayish-white in color, are more commonly referred to as the Boquillas flags. Highly accessible and readily fashioned into rectangular building blocks, these flagstone rocks are the basis for the fundamental architectural style that has prevailed throughout the region to the present day.

Unquestionably, the most prominent features of Big Bend are the volcanic formations that appeared during the Cenozoic Age (one to sixty-three million years). In simple terms, these are large masses of molten rock, which over the centuries pushed their way slowly toward the earth's surface through the softer layers of stratified limestone. The best examples of these geological compositions are found in Big Bend National Park. Foremost among the so-called "igneous intrusions" are Elephant Tusk, Backbone Ridge, Casa Grande, and the park's most celebrated landmark—the Chisos Mountains. Combined, these peaks make up an awesome spectacle that welcomes thousands of outdoor enthusiasts who annually converge upon this unique subregion of the West.

No less imposing are the precipitous canyons located at Santa Elena, Mariscal, and Boquillas. Towering limestone cliffs that rise to heights in excess of 1,500 feet punctuate the otherwise uninterrupted flow of the Río Grande. Constrained within the walls of these enormous chasms, the river twists and turns to form the familiar "V" or elbow-shaped curve from which Big Bend derived its name. The splendid ensemble of mountains and canyons so captured the interest of early travelers to the Big Bend that one observer described the geologic phenomenon as the "most amazing revelation of nature's efforts at mountain building on the continent."[2]

Dramatically contrasting with the convoluted silhouettes of the Chisos range is the seemingly endless desert that surrounds it. An unrelenting sun, with temperatures frequently in excess of 100 degrees, blisters the sandswept desert floor virtually year round. Limited annual rainfall of fifteen to seventeen inches permits only vegetation well-suited to extreme aridity to flourish in these parched surroundings. Creosote bush, mesquite trees, ocotillo cactus, lechuguilla plants, and other species of desert flora form the curious accents that are visible upon the land, except in the higher elevations where junipers and wildflowers are more common.

One notable relief from this austere desert setting are the intermittent free-flowing springs encountered throughout the area. These oases, though limited in number, were nonetheless important in attracting the earliest inhabitants to the region. First to arrive in Big Bend were the hunting and gathering peoples who occupied caves along the river or rock shelters adjacent to the freshwater springs. For the most part, these aboriginal tribes wandered through the territory en route to a more suitable living environment such as that found farther west near the confluence of the Río Grande and the Río Conchos. Still, these prehistoric visitors left ample archeological evidence to confirm their presence, which predated later arrivals by several centuries.

By the mid-1600s, a combatant and highly mobile people appeared in the trans-Pecos region. Apaches, Comanches, Kiowas, and other warriors of the Great Plains moved continuously south in pursuit of great migratory herds. As the number of buffalo diminished, however, the nomadic Indians' reliance upon food sources plentiful among neighboring agricultural tribes increased. As a result, sedentary people fell victim to incessant raiding. With the arrival of the first European settlers to the Río Grande frontier beginning ca. 1700, the frequency of such incursions became even more widespread. A network of trails, still etched across the face of the Chihuahuan desert, suggest that the influence of the Plains Indians — in a desperate struggle to sustain their existence on the open frontier — pierced deep into the heartland of an opposing Spanish empire. A clash of cultures was the inevitable consequence. For the remainder the eighteenth and most of the nineteenth centuries, subjugation of the Indians served as the pretext for the white man's persistent attempts to occupy the Big Bend. Spaniards, Mexicans, and later Americans exerted the full force of their technological and numerical superiority to eventually subdue the Indians.

For more than three and one-half centuries, the imposing canyon country of the lower Río Grande beckoned to Hispanic and Anglo settlers alike. Encompassing nearly two hundred fifty square miles of West Texas, Big Bend territory could not easily be avoided. Nevertheless, the region constituted a seemingly indomitable obstacle to all who challenged its labyrinth of canyons in search of more hospitable terrain in which to settle. During its formative years, Spanish, Mexican, and American soldiers and scientists were the earliest non-Indian occupants to reconnoitre the Big Bend. In the ensuing decades, courageous settlers from both sides of the United States-Mexico border followed them into the Río Grande valley to eke out a marginal but gratifying existence. In the opinion of many scholars of western history, the frontier phase of the Big Bend passively drew to a close with the advent of the twentieth century.

In July 1944, the year President Franklin Delano Roosevelt declared the establishment of Big Bend National Park, one of the last vestiges of

the great Hispanic and American frontier was preserved for future generations. Today, under the protective umbrella of the federal government,
represented by the National Park Service, a new episode of frontier history in the Big Bend subregion of West Texas is being written. Like many
of America's parks and monuments, Big Bend National Park stands in
tribute not only to its historic past but also as a symbol of the future — a
modern and progressive West. Though no longer reminiscent of soldier-
explorers, mountain men, and gunslingers guided by the inimitable
dogma of shoot-first-ask-questions-later, the twentieth-century West remains, in many respects, a frontier. In contrast to earlier decades, however, historic preservation laws have emerged as the code of the "New
West" while federal employees serve to enforce them.

In Big Bend today, National Park Service rangers, and the throng of
wide-eyed tourists armed only with cameras and camping gear, are the
latest in an impressive assemblage of pioneers determined to somehow
"civilize" this vast desert wilderness. The history of the occupation of this
remote subregion is as much their story as it is that of the indefatigable
adventurers who preceded them. Not unlike the descendants of Spanish
presidial troops, Mexican miners and *vaqueros,* and Anglo-American
merchants and farmers who proudly proclaim themselves residents of the
Big Bend, the employees of the National Park Service, too, remain committed to endure the isolation of this once intractable but ever-captivating
frontier of the modern American West.

CHAPTER ONE

For God and King

On this occasion, most Excellent Sir, I therefore obligate myself anew for the aforesaid expedition, and to explore and discover the North Sea and bring back detailed information about the inhabitants of these lands ... at the same time to find out the wealth of Gran Quivira and the kingdom of Texas.
—*Juan Domínguez de Mendoza, 1683*

On a crisp August morning in 1852 Marine T. W. Chandler, head of a military expedition commissioned to survey the international boundary between Mexico and the United States, paused momentarily to view the abandoned ruins of Presidio San Vicente. Perched high upon a gravel mesa overlooking the Río Grande del Norte the dilapidated fortress, once a bastion of Spanish frontier defense, stood weather-worn and decayed before the party of curious American explorers. In a detailed report to his superiors Chandler described the crumbling structure as "one of the ancient military posts that marked the Spanish rule in this country."

For almost a full decade Presidio del Paso de San Vicente,[1] established in the winter of 1774, played a significant role in the Spanish strategic line of defense imposed against aggressive Indian attacks and foreign intrusion in West Texas. Viewed by these latter-day visitors to Texas in 1852, the presidio evidenced the earliest European attempts to explore and occupy the area that Spanish cartographers labeled the *despoblado* (uninhabited lands). For more than a century and a half this parched and unforgiving expanse of Chihuahuan desert, punctuated dramatically by the enormous canyons of the lower Río Grande, represented an almost insurmountable obstacle to Spain's slow but persistent northward advance.[2]

Following Hernando Cortés's conquest of the Aztecs in 1521, the Spanish empire extended its political tentacles across the Atlantic Ocean into the valley of Mexico. By 1535 Nueva España (Mexico) became the first permanent viceroyalty established in North America. Under the legal

Soldado de Cuera or leather-jacketed soldier depicting the typical uniform of an eighteenth-century presidial soldier on the northern frontier of New Spain. The thick leather coat offered protection from Indian arrows. *(Courtesy, National Park Service, Spanish Colonial Research Center, Albuquerque, New Mexico)*

Ruins of Presidio San Vicente as they appeared in 1964. Seen here are the remains of the original chapel walls built in 1774. Note the Sierra del Carmen range in the background. *(Courtesy, Archives of the Big Bend, Clifford B. Casey Collection, Sul Ross State University, Alpine, Texas)*

authority of the viceroy, the king's direct representative in the New World, Spain underwrote the political organization of its latest colonial acquisition. Although most of the power centered around the viceroy and a judicial tribunal known as the *Audiencia,* military needs also determined that New Spain be divided into smaller administrative districts each under the supervision of a local governor. While the more settled provinces were clustered around Mexico City, a vast frontier of uncharted desert lay north of the capital. Once firmly established, the royal government wasted no time in turning attention toward the outlying territories in anticipation of expanding Spanish influence throughout the North American continent.

Dreams of increasing the wealth of the empire became the driving force for exploration in earlier years. But Spain's interminable goal to spread Christianity to native inhabitants of the New World assumed increasing importance by the mid-1600s. Imbued with the spirit of conquest and the desire to convert thousands of souls to Catholicism, the Crown sanctioned a flurry of land and sea expeditions, some of which ended in disaster. One such mission, the ill-fated attempt of Pánfilo de Narváez to reach New Spain from the west coast of Florida, resulted in the deaths of the captain and all but four members of his crew. The survivors, Alvar Núñez Cabeza de Vaca and three shipwrecked companions, were washed ashore near present Galveston Island in November 1528. For the next seven years, Cabeza de Vaca and his compatriots lived among the coastal tribes of Texas before attempting a daring overland escape back to Mexico.

In their travels across the Texas plains these adventurers became the first Europeans to penetrate, albeit marginally, the region of the Big Bend. Traveling west along the banks of the Río Puerco (Pecos River), which they reached in the summer of 1535, Cabeza de Vaca reportedly crossed the river near present Reagan Canyon, just northeast of Big Bend National Park. While scholars have yet to determine the exact spot at which the party crossed the Pecos, most agree upon the group's point of reentry into Mexico.

Cabeza de Vaca's personal account of the journey says that they crossed into Chihuahua near the confluence of the Río Grande and the Río Conchos (Conchos River), which they named La Junta de los Ríos (near Presidio, Texas).[3] Continuing westward across the Sierra Madre, they encountered Spanish troops who escorted them to San Miguel de Culiacán (in present Sinaloa, Mexico). Months later, the adventurers completed the final leg of their trek, arriving in Mexico City in July 1536. Their epic journey ended, Cabeza de Vaca and his men had successfully traversed the perilous Chihuahuan desert. In doing so, they established the first known overland route into the Río Grande valley.

The stories Cabeza de Vaca and his men told about legendary cities of gold said to be in Texas and present New Mexico prompted official response among Spanish authorities to undertake the exploration of the Río Grande frontier. In 1540 the king sanctioned an official expedition under the command of Francisco Vásquez de Coronado, the governor of Nueva Galicia (Jalisco, Mexico), commissioning him with the discovery of the new kingdoms reported to rival the grandeur of the Aztec empire. Despite a two-year search in which Coronado wandered through much of today's American Southwest, he never encountered a second Mexico City. As a result of his failure, the Spanish Crown turned its focus away from Texas and the remainder of the northern frontier for nearly fifty years.[4]

If the existence of fabulous cities of gold proved to be largely mythical, the discovery of huge deposits of silver near Zacatecas in 1546 was a certified reality. The ensuing "rush" in the mid-1500s provided a much-needed impetus to the northern colonization effort. As the mining towns of Santa Bárbara, Parral, Saltillo, and Durango became the instant cities of this remote wasteland, so too did they become the harbingers of European civilization among its inhabitants.

In time the administrative skills of frontier captains like Francisco de Ibarra, first governor of Nueva Vizcaya (Chihuahua, Mexico), and Juan de Oñate, first governor of Nuevo México (New Mexico), brought Hispanic culture face to face with the astringent and inhospitable terrain of the Chihuahuan desert region. By 1580 the limits of Spain's northern frontier were extended from the foothills of the Sierra Madre to the southern extremes of the present north Mexican states of Chihuahua and Coahuila.

The arrival of thousands of miners, merchants, and ranchers to northern Mexico during these years forced the inevitable confrontation between white intruders and native inhabitants. Indian retaliation, in fact, touched off a half-century of conflict known as the War of the Gran Chichimeca (1550 to 1600), named for the plateau country between the eastern and western Sierra Madre ranges where most of the hostility occurred. Spain's efforts to secure the roads and communities of the silver mining region against this new and formidable enemy compelled the government to establish an official military policy for the protection of its citizens along the frontier. The guerrilla tactics of the northern warriors, moreover, required substantial modifications to the Spanish defense system.[5]

One result of this experimentation was increased utilization of the presidio and the mission. Throughout the remainder of the 1500s, Spanish-Indian diplomacy vacillated between the iron fist concept of all-out warfare and the more conciliatory approach of "peace by purchase." Crucial to the success of the latter policy, the presidio and the mission served as the principal agents of frontier settlement. The presidio, which housed regular soldiers and local militia, assured Spanish colonists some measure of protection against hostile attack. Meanwhile, the mission became the vehicle for the transference of Hispanic culture and European civilization to the native inhabitants. As colonizers pressed increasingly northward toward the Río Grande del Norte, the central government guaranteed their safety through the continuous advancement of these pioneering institutions.[6]

Expansion of the Mexican mining frontier into the province of Nueva Vizcaya in 1580 prompted a renewed interest in the Río Grande valley. Mining activity necessitated Indian labor not readily accessible among the tribes of northern Mexico. Since the time of Cabeza de Vaca, Spaniards were aware of the large settlements of sedentary Indians living near the junction of the Río Conchos and the Río Grande. Unlike nomadic tribes of the northern frontier, these Indians cultivated crops and lived in well-defined communities. Not surprisingly, mine owners viewed these domesticated Indians as a source of slave labor.

Religious officials, on the other hand, perceived these settlements as targets for Christianization. Intrigued with the prospect of attracting thousands of converts to the Church, Fray Agustín Rodríguez, a zealous Franciscan friar stationed at Valle de San Bartolomé near the mining community of Santa Bárbara in present Chihuahua, Mexico, solicited permission from Viceroy Lorenzo Suárez de Mendoza to carry the word of God to these remote northern villages. His request granted in November 1579, Rodríguez solicited the accompaniment of two other Franciscans. In addition, he enlisted the services of a sixty-year-old local miner, Francisco Sánchez Chamuscado, to provide the customary military escort. Together these men prepared to penetrate the westernmost boundary of the Big Bend region for the first time since Cabeza de Vaca's adventure in 1535.

On June 5, 1581, the small band of explorers set out on a northerly course along the banks of the Río Conchos. They followed the river until reaching the point that Cabeza de Vaca had established as a landmark years before. Here at La Junta de los Ríos the party crossed the Río Grande into Texas. To their surprise, they found both the Patarabuey and Jumano Indians of that region friendly and receptive. The latter informed the Spaniards that three other white men and a black man had passed through their land years ago. The obvious reference to Cabeza de Vaca and his entourage explained, in part, the unexpected welcome of the Rodríguez party among the natives of West Texas.

At this juncture, the Rodríguez-Chamuscado expedition turned northwest following the Río Grande toward El Paso del Norte (Juárez, Mexico), eventually arriving at the broad, inviting valleys near present Bernalillo, New Mexico.[7] The mission ended tragically, however, as Pueblo Indians eventually killed all three of the priests who had elected to remain among them. Meanwhile, Sánchez Chamuscado died of a fever only days short of his arrival back in Santa Bárbara.

Upon hearing the news that three Franciscans had been left behind, a rescue expedition prepared to leave Santa Bárbara in November 1582. Under the direction of Don Antonio de Espejo, a wealthy cattle rancher and mayor of the neighboring town of Cuatro Cienegas, a complement of fourteen soldiers retraced the steps of the Rodríguez party. "After two days march of five leagues each," Espejo noted in his daily account of the journey, "we found in some rancherías a number of Indians of the Conchos nation, many of whom, to the number of more than a thousand, came out to meet us along the road we were travelling." As the march continued, Espejo estimated that the combined population of five separate pueblos, located near Ojinaga, Chihuahua (across the Río Grande from Presidio, Texas), numbered upwards of ten thousand inhabitants.

Once arrived in New Mexico, the Espejo party confirmed the rumors that Father Rodríquez and his brethren had in fact been executed. After much debate with the religious members of the expedition, Espejo decided to return to northern Mexico, but this time via West Texas and the territory drained by the Río Puerco. Arriving within sight of the Davis Mountains, Antonio de Espejo and his men crossed the Río Puerco near present Fort Stockton on August 8, 1583. The caravan then skirted past present Alpine and Fort Davis as it inched its way through the Chinati

Mountains, down Alamito Creek, and back to La Junta de los Ríos. After a brief rest, Espejo continued on his trek down the Río Conchos, arriving in Valle San Bartolomé on September 20, 1583.

While these early expeditions only marginally penetrated Big Bend country, they accomplished two things that were to have long-term significance in the future settlement of that region. First, these ventures established the Río Conchos as a natural highway for Spain's northward advance to the Río Grande borderlands. Second, the discovery of large communities of Indians near La Junta de los Ríos made that location a primary staging area for missionary efforts into the West Texas region. Nevertheless, Hispanic migration was largely restricted to New Mexico; Texas remained isolated and unsettled for nearly a century. With the advent of French, British, and Russian expansionism, beginning in the late seventeenth century, Spain sharpened its focus on Texas as the front line of defense against foreign intrusion. Correspondingly, the area known today as the Big Bend surfaced as an integral feature of the larger defense strategy of the Spanish empire.[8]

Perhaps no single event dramatized the flood tide of foreign exploration in America more dramatically than Robert Sieur de La Salle's journey down the Mississippi River in 1682. His establishment of a French outpost near Matagorda Bay two years later, moreover, alerted Spain to the fact that it no longer claimed sole possession of Texas soil. Indeed, the French foothold in the Gulf of Mexico forced a serious reexamination of Spanish attitudes toward that region. Up to now, only El Paso del Norte, which formed part of a tenuous line of communication between the more secure settlements of Nueva Vizcaya and the isolated colony of New Mexico, had been occupied. Spain's initial attempts to occupy East Texas, meanwhile, wavered in the face of increased French encroachment from neighboring Louisiana. Concurrently, nomadic Indians ravaged New Spain's northern borders beginning about 1680.

The combination of these domestic and international events prompted a sense of urgency among Spanish officials to strengthen their defensive position along the Río Grande.[9] In the process, the Big Bend region, quiescent for nearly a century, became the focus of renewed occupation. Explorations began in the fall of 1683 when Jumano chief Juan Sabeata, wearied from relentless Apache assaults targeted against the villages centered around La Junta de los Ríos, led his followers to the Spanish stronghold at El Paso.

Hoping to enter into a formal alliance with Spain to gain protection
against the raiders, the Indian leader proclaimed his desire for conversion
to Catholicism. Sabeata related an apparition that he interpreted as a
symbol of the ultimate triumph of Christianity among his people. This
extraordinary pronouncement inspired Father Nicolás López, procurator
and custodian of the Franciscan missions of New Mexico, to take action.
On December 1, 1683, Father López and two companions, Fathers Juan
de Zavaleta and Antonio de Acevado, without the usual military escort,
set out for La Junta, where they proceeded to construct the first churches
in the Big Bend.[10]

Two weeks later, Captain Juan Domínguez de Mendoza, a seasoned
veteran with over twenty years experience on the northern frontier, followed with the first expedition into the Big Bend for which there is a
detailed itinerary. Upon Mendoza's departure for West Texas, the newly
appointed governor of New Mexico, Domingo Jironza Petríz de Cruzáte,
verified the frontier commander's qualifications for the task, noting both
the loyalty and the previous accomplishments of the presidial officer. The
governor awarded the commission to Mendoza "in consideration of how
well he [Mendoza] has served his majesty in the provinces of New Mexico
from a very tender age. He was one of those who went to the conquest of
New Mexico in the year 1681."

According to royal mandate, the Mendoza expedition had a dual purpose. First, it was ordered to protect all Christianized Indians in Texas
against future depredations from raiding Apaches. Second, and perhaps
more important to the larger theme of frontier defense, Mendoza had
orders to expend every effort to determine if the French were established
in Texas.[11]

On December 15, 1683, Mendoza and a detachment of soldiers set
out from Real de San Lorenzo, the principal Spanish settlement established at El Paso. Exactly two weeks later the party reached La Junta de
los Ríos, which they named La Navidad de las Cruces in honor of the
well-placed crosses that greeted them. On his return trip, Mendoza pursued approximately the same course through West Texas that Espejo had
followed a century earlier. Once across the Davis Mountains, Mendoza
entered the wide valleys near present Alpine, Texas, which he called Los
Reyes. On January 13, 1684, the expedition struck the Río Puerco at
Horsehead Crossing, which the captain described in his journal as
"muddy and somewhat alkalined, having its source in New Mexico." Here

Mendoza met Juan Sabeata, who presented the Spaniard with a French flag, a dramatic confirmation that foreign intruders had presumably penetrated the trans-Pecos region.[12]

In February of that year, the Mendoza expedition reached the northernmost point of its journey, intercepting the Middle Conchos River where it intersects with the Nueces (near San Angelo, Texas). Changing direction toward the Río Grande, the expedition terminated its journey through Big Bend country and returned to El Paso on June 4, 1684. Several months later, Mendoza summarized the highlights of the ordeal in a report to the viceroy: "We traveled inland more than three hundred leagues toward the east, undergoing insufferable hardships of hunger and wars which the Indians of the Apache and Salineros nations waged against us." In addition to the setbacks, Mendoza also underscored the successes of his mission: "I took possession of all those lands, giving his majesty a multitude of vassals, because I made seventy-five nations under obedience to him."

Mendoza's efforts in 1683 set into motion a series of formal expeditions into the Big Bend that lasted well into the eighteenth century. Assured that the French threat in the Mississippi valley was real, the Spanish objective in Texas shifted from an exclusively missionary effort to a formalized program of frontier defense. Accordingly, when Juan Domínguez de Mendoza accepted his commission to encounter the French, he also pledged to build two "well fortified presidios in the most suitable location." The presence of these structures, officials believed, would not only provide ample protection against Apache raids on La Junta but also would serve to strengthen Spain's threatened position in West Texas.

There appears to be no record to indicate that Mendoza ever accomplished this task. An ensuing revolt against the missionaries in 1687, furthermore, suggests that the two presidios were probably never constructed. In fact, the missions at La Junta were abandoned entirely until 1714. For this reason the plan to establish a presidial line of defense in Texas assumed equal importance to that of the mission program. In the process, both objectives served as a motivating force for future Hispanic ventures into the trans-Pecos territory.[13]

The job of revitalizing the missions at La Junta fell to the acting lieutenant general of the governor of Nueva Vizcaya, Juan Antonio Trasviña Retís. Arriving on May 31, 1715, at Nuestra Señora de Loreto, the first pueblo at La Junta, Trasviña Retís supervised the reconstruction of five small churches. He entrusted the completion of the project to

Father Gregorio Osario and Father Juan Antonio García, two Franciscans who had accompanied him, before returning to El Paso. In a subsequent memorandum to the viceroy, Trasviña Retís confirmed the reestablishment of the missions and further suggested that a presidio be erected to ensure their protection. While his recommendation received no immediate response, this early petition for a presidio at La Junta de los Ríos was incorporated into a much broader design for a stronger military presence on the Río Grande frontier.[14]

As the 1600s drew to a close, Spain's internal provinces counted only twelve presidios — half of them in Nueva Vizcaya (Chihuahua, Mexico), two in Nuevo México (New Mexico) and Nuevo León (Mexico), and one each in Sonora and Coahuila. By 1725 that figure nearly doubled with Texas claiming four installations centered mostly around San Antonio and along the Louisiana border. Thus, for almost a quarter of a century the Spanish line of defense focused principally upon eastern Texas, leaving the western portion virtually unprotected.

Spain's concern for the defense of Texas occasioned Viceroy Juan de Acuña y Béjarano, the Marqués de Casafuerte,[15] to enlist the services of Brigadier General Pedro de Rivera Villalon, former commandant of San Juan de Ulua, one of Spain's coastal garrisons near Veracruz, Mexico. Rivera was commissioned to inspect the condition of the king's defenses along the northern frontier. Viceroy Acuña's detailed instructions empowered Rivera to make recommendations regarding the defensive realignment and economic reorganization of all existing frontier presidios.

On November 21, 1724, General Rivera and his entourage departed Mexico City on an unprecedented three-and-a-half-year inspection tour of the internal provinces, making Texas one of his final stops on the circuitous route. Rivera's vast military experience enabled him to quickly recognize the Río Grande as a natural barrier to would-be intruders, both foreign and domestic. His first recommendation to the viceroy, then, was to place a cordon of presidios more or less in alignment with the meandering river. Second, and more specific to Big Bend, Rivera proposed the establishment of a new fortress on the west side of Texas somewhere between La Junta de los Ríos and San Juan Bautista (across the Río Grande near Eagle Pass, Texas).[16]

Intrigued with Rivera's observations, the Marqués de Casafuerte promulgated a new directive in June 1728 to comply with the proposed improvements. Lack of funding required to implement the order, however, forced the viceroy to rescind the mandate until the following year. Nevertheless, the stated strategic importance of the Río Grande called for a more in-depth investigation of the remote territories surrounding present Big Bend. The explorations, furthermore, would enable the Spanish to identify suitable locations for future defense installations.

The demands of such a task called for a soldier with extensive military experience and an impeccable reputation for responsible leadership. Don José de Berroterán, the veteran captain of Presidio San Francisco de los Conchos, seemed more than capable to meet the challenge. With ninety well-equipped soldiers and forty Indian auxiliaries, Berroterán set out in March 1729 in an attempt to follow the Río Grande as far as La Junta. Making his way upstream to a point just south of present Dryden, Texas, the bewildered captain aborted his mission well short of completion because of extremely difficult terrain encountered throughout the journey.

Although severely criticized for his failure, Captain Berroterán defended himself, saying that the expedition was "frustrated from the beginning." If he had continued to follow the natural course of the river as instructed, he could never have overcome the imposing canyons that lay in his path; therefore, he elected not to undertake the challenge. Perhaps exasperated at his own faintheartedness, Berroterán took some consolation in merely having returned from the "labyrinth"—a fitting description for the cavernous topography typical of the Big Bend region.[17]

While fiscal and administrative problems in Mexico City postponed the full implementation of the viceroy's directive for almost a decade, the recurring Apache problem generated increased concern among frontier administrators. Repeated complaints about unyielding Indian attacks along the border from the governor of Coahuila, Blás de la Garza Falcón, demanded official response. During the fall of 1735, the viceroy ordered Governor Garza Falcón to undertake a full expedition at his expense into the northern frontier to determine a good location for the much desired fortification. In the company of Captain Joseph Antonio de Eca y Múzquiz, a soldier from Presidio San Juan Bautista, the military contingent left Monclova, Coahuila, and marched toward the Río Grande.

According to viceregal instructions, Garza Falcón was to erect the proposed Presidio del Sacramento in the best possible location. Enduring bitter north winds and constant snow throughout the winter months of 1735 and 1736, the party moved sluggishly northeast until reaching a point fifteen miles south of present Del Rio, Texas. While the main body of soldiers elected to wait out the storms in camp, a smaller contingent, under the command of the governor's son, Miguel de la Garza Falcón, reconnoitered the land as far as the vicinity of Dryden's Crossing, a

hundred miles northwest of the main encampment. Unable to continue
on his prescribed course, the governor opted to build the presidio on the
Mexican side of the Río Grande where they had camped. On January 7,
1736, the Spaniards celebrated the selection of the new site on the San
Diego River, a tributary of the Río Grande. The following week, the
Garza Falcón expedition returned home exhausted by their personal
ordeal with inclement weather and inhospitable terrain.

Although the governor derived some personal satisfaction in his
accomplishments, his superiors were not impressed with the choice of
location for the presidio. One critic argued that Garza Falcón, not unlike other provincial administrators who wanted a new military installation in their jurisdiction, had greatly exaggerated the extent of the
Indian problem in Coahuila. Further, the royal auditor contested that the
new site was too close to an already established garrison at San
Juan Bautista. He believed that Presidio del Sacramento would be more
effective if it were moved to a more advantageous position closer to the
Río Grande. While he acquiesced to the presidio's construction, the court
official was adamant that the post should not be permanent. In light of
this critical but objective assessment, the search for a suitable fortification
site along the Río Grande became more imperative.[18]

In June 1747 the official rationale for a thorough investigation of Big
Bend came in the form of a document submitted to the viceroy from the
Marqués de Altamira. The auditor of the Audiencia of México rendered
a thoughtful evaluation of the defensive posture of the Texas frontier.
Citing national defense and the needs of the church as the basis for his
argument, the colonial agent penned the following recommendations.
First, he noted that not a single presidio existed between San Juan Bautista
and El Paso del Norte, a distance of over three hundred sixty leagues
(approximately 540 miles). Second, a consequence of this oversight was
that no regular missionary work could be carried on at La Junta, an area
of considerable importance to the missionization effort in Texas. For these
reasons, Altamira concluded that an exploration of Big Bend be undertaken simultaneously from various points along the Río Grande. In con-
junction with this effort, the auditor urged that a new fortification be
established at a point which he considered to be the most strategically
significant—La Junta de los Ríos. The viceroy responded quickly and
favorably to these suggestions.[19]

According to his instructions, Governor Pedro Rábago y Terán of
Coahuila prepared to assemble the first full-scale expedition to actually

penetrate the heart of the Big Bend. Following a route similar to Berroterán's earlier excursion, the governor's party reached a point a few miles above Del Rio before turning due west toward Reagan Canyon. Unable to find a suitable crossing among the canyon's towering cliffs, the company moved steadily southwest until they located a good place to ford the Río Grande into Texas. They named this place, situated a few miles above present Boquillas, Mexico, Santa Rita.

Hoping to avoid the perils that befell Berroterán in 1729, Rábago y Terán tried to follow the course of the river, but found the task virtually impossible because of the impassable canyons located on the Texas side. When faced with formidable obstacles such as Santa Elena Canyon, the judicious officer led his men around the natural barrier. On December 13 the party passed through the Chisos Mountains into the Terlingua Creek valley before crossing back into Mexico near present Lajitas, Texas. With fewer obstructions to contend with on the Mexican side of the Río Grande, the expedition arrived in La Junta one week before Christmas.[20]

Meanwhile, to comply with Altamira's proposed multiple exploration, Captains Fermín de Vidaurre of Presidio de Mapimí and Joseph de Idyoga of San Bartolomé departed from different points in Mexico to converge upon La Junta, the latter arriving six days ahead of Rábago y Terán. Captain Idyoga gathered his contingent of troops from presidios San Bartolomé, San Francisco de los Conchos, and Cerro Gordo, all located in Chihuahua, and headed north along the Río Conchos. At the village of San Antonio de Julimes the Spanish officer added several Indian auxiliaries and continued his journey to La Junta, arriving on November 22. Once settled, Idyoga initiated a thorough reconnaissance that included the first recorded census of the area.[21]

Soon after his arrival, Governor Rábago y Terán undertook a similar investigation of the territory east of Presidio, Texas, as far as Alamito Creek. His observations prompted the governor to instruct Captain Idyoga to build the presidio at La Junta "on either bank of the Río Grande." In a follow-up report to the viceroy, Rábago y Terán listed several reasons for the decision. First, the presidio would restrain the Indians congregated around La Junta; second, it would impede Apache raids on Christianized Indians; third, it would enhance defensive communication with other military garrisons stationed along the Río Grande; and fourth, its presence would offer protection and encourage commercial mining in the Big Bend. Captain Idyoga returned to San

Francisco de los Conchos, however, before he could comply with the governor's orders.

For a full decade plans for the projected Presidio del Norte de La Junta de los Ríos lay unattended in Mexico City. Finally, on October 5, 1759, Captain Rubín de Celís set out from Chihuahua with yet another expedition into the Big Bend. Celebrating their arrival at La Junta on Christmas Eve, the party next began to build the long-anticipated presidio. In July 1760 Captain Celís reported the completion of the project. The final placement of a fortress near the junction of the Río Grande and the Río Conchos brought to conclusion an episode in Spanish Colonial frontier history that had begun with the recommendations of Pedro de Rivera Villalon in 1729.[22]

While Spanish officials acknowledged the strategic importance of the Big Bend, recurring fiscal problems and bureaucratic indecisiveness precluded the placement of a presidio in that area. When increased Apache depredations forced the abandonment of the West Texas missions, however, the defense posture of La Junta de los Ríos became a paramount concern in Mexico City. In Europe, meanwhile, France's loss to England in the Seven Years War forced a political realignment of her colonies on the North American continent. With the French threat removed from the Mississippi valley in 1763 — the result of the Treaty of Paris — Spain felt free to reevaluate its defensive position along the Río Grande. Thus, Presidio del Norte, as well as older military installations, figured prominently in a new bureaucratic reorganization effort designed to increase protection and improve defenses on the northern frontier.

If Spanish authorities were mindful of the need for a comprehensive assessment of military defenses in earlier years, the idea gained overwhelming support with the Bourbon reforms. In 1765 the viceroy issued a decree ordering the general inspection of all presidios on the frontier in an effort to evaluate their military preparedness. To complete this task he selected one of his most knowledgeable and faithful servants, Cayetano Maria Pignatelli, the Marqués de Rubí. Field Marshal Rubí, an accomplished militarist, arrived in 1764 to accept the task of reorganizing Spanish military forces in the New World. His instructions were to evaluate not only the defensive capabilities of each of the existing twenty-four presidios but also determine their cost effectiveness.

In the company of Captain Nicolás de Lafora, a designer and construction officer in the Royal Corps of Engineers, Rubí began his seven-thousand-mile trek from Mexico City in February 1766. During the three-year odyssey, the royal inspector visited every major Spanish fortification from California to Texas. Generally appalled at the deplorable state of the king's defenses, Rubí outlined his concerns in a final report dated May 4, 1768. In addition to preparing detailed maps of the journey, Lafora assessed local conditions and rendered suggestions as to the most strategic sites for the relocation of a number of presidios.[23]

Regarding Texas, Rubí found military conditions there seriously lacking, but noted that the presidios in that province were not unlike others encountered in northern New Spain. To begin, he rebuked Governor Joseph de Aguero of Chihuahua for his arbitrary decision to abandon Presidio del Norte in 1766. Rubí, in fact, was unable to conduct his inspection of that site because the governor had relocated the garrison at Pueblo de Julimes, thirty miles farther west. Rubí reprimanded Aguero for his flagrant disregard of "the orders of the present viceroy by which he was instructed to act jointly with me in deciding upon the maintenance and removal of this presidio."[24] The removal of troops from La Junta de los Ríos, furthermore, left a sizeable defense gap on the Río Grande. For this reason, Rubí insisted that the presidio be restored to its original location regardless of expense.

In addition to his recognition of La Junta as a vital defense link, Rubí made other observations in Texas affecting the future military disposition of the Big Bend. After an inspection of the presidio at San Sabá (near present Menard, Texas) in July 1767, the Marqués declared the fortress obsolete, noting that it afforded "as much protection to the interests of His Majesty in New Spain as a ship anchored in the mid-Atlantic would afford in preventing foreign trade in America." Accordingly, Rubí ordered San Sabá and all of its troops transferred to a proposed new military post closer to the Río Grande.

In his celebrated report of 1768, Rubí determined it a financial impossibility for Spain to provide a military garrison for every settlement located south of the Río Grande. With this premise in mind, he proposed the erection of a cordon of presidios situated roughly along the natural course of the river. The northern frontier, he argued, should be viewed as a single defensive unit; therefore, some measure of continuity must be present in its fortification. Up to this time, presidios were haphazardly built with no regard for a well-defined military strategy. Based upon this assessment, Rubí proposed the reduction of the presidial line from twenty-four to fifteen well-placed units along the thirtieth parallel from the Gulf of California to the Guadalupe River in Texas. The forts would be placed an average of forty leagues (about a hundred miles) apart to facilitate better communication between defensive units.[25]

Clearly, the proposed realignment implied the transfer of some presidios along with the abandonment of others. Cognizant of the vast stretch of unprotected territory found among the unexplored canyons of the Big Bend, Rubí recommended the construction of two new outposts. First, the garrison from San Sabá would transfer immediately to a proposed site on the Río Grande near San Vicente Pass. Concurrently, units from the recently abandoned post at Cerro Gordo (Chihuahua, Mexico) were to relocate forty leagues west of San Vicente at a new facility named Presidio San Carlos. Finally, the presidio at La Junta de los Ríos must be reoccupied to complete the proposed defensive chain along the river.

The viceregal regulation issued on September 10, 1772, served as the legal embodiment for the Marqués de Rubí's calculated recommendations. Divided into thirteen articles, these new laws had both a military and administrative purpose. While protection of lives and maintenance of frontier security remained the principal objective, efficient management of the presidios received equal attention. Therefore, the new legal code provided guidance for all military affairs ranging from payment of troops to the placement of a cordon of presidios along the thirtieth parallel. In response to Rubí's recommendations, the king's decree ordered the abandonment of San Sabá and the removal of its troops closer to the Río Grande del Norte.

The *reglamento* further prescribed that the territory between the presidios of La Junta and San Juan Bautista be reconnoitered for the purpose of identifying appropriate locations to build the two new installations. "I order the said commandant of Nueva Vizcaya and the governor of Coahuila separately but at the same time to proceed to execute a reconnaissance of the area," the mandate read; "The commandant is to take the necessary troops and the companies from Julimes, Cerro Gordo, and San Sabá in order that with the first of the three restored to its old presidio of La Junta, the second [Cerro Gordo and San Sabá units] can be located in new presidios to be erected along the course of the Río Grande." Appropriately, the field reports of Joseph de Berroterán and Pedro Rábago y Terán, along with Lafora's detailed maps of the area, provided guidance for one final *entrada* into the Big Bend.[26]

The orders for the proposed construction of presidios San Carlos and San Vicente brought to fruition nearly a half century of preparation and planning for the defense of the West Texas frontier. Clearly, Spain had full knowledge of the almost limitless boundaries to the north well in advance of the eighteenth century. For the most part, Spain viewed West Texas — in particular the Big Bend region — as a natural barrier to the settlement of more inviting colonies such as New Mexico.

As other European powers challenged Spain's unrivaled hegemony in the New World, the Texas frontier assumed greater strategic importance. Spain's reaction to the French presence in Louisiana occasioned plans to pacify the Río Grande borderlands by traditional means — the mission and the presidio. As the cloud of foreign intervention momentarily subsided in 1763, Spain committed its military defenses and limited financial resources to the ultimate pacification of the Indian on the northern frontier. Critical elements to the proposed Spanish line of defense in West Texas, the newly established presidios at San Carlos and San Vicente received increased attention in Mexico City during the ensuing decades.

CHAPTER TWO

The Policy of the Iron Fist

If there is a real remedy for the hostilities which the interior provinces of New Spain suffer from, it must be framed and arranged in my opinion upon Texas.
— *Teodoro de Croix, 1781*

In the solitude of his quarters at Presidio del Carrizal (located a hundred miles southeast of present El Paso), Commandant Inspector Don Hugo de O'Conor submitted his final report to Viceroy Antonio Maria Bucareli y Ursua in Mexico City. This lengthy account, dated January 30, 1776, represented a compilation of O'Conor's military accomplishments in northern New Spain since his appointment as the region's first inspector general four years earlier. O'Conor divided his summary into three parts. First, he reviewed the implementation of the king's directive regarding the placement of a cordon of presidios along the course of the Río Grande. Next, he outlined a basic plan of military operations against the Apache nation, evaluating its effectiveness to date. Finally, the colonel, plagued with failing health and wearied by years of frontier campaigns, requested a transfer from his current post to a less strenuous administrative post.

Viewed in the context of Spain's military defense plans for the frontier, this early report signified the importance of the new presidial line — in particular the proposed fortresses of the Big Bend — to the security of hundreds of colonists scattered throughout Nueva Vizcaya and Coahuila. The veteran commander not only detailed the location and strategic role of each presidio on the Río Grande, but also listed the responsibility of all troops within that jurisdiction. In addition, he delineated his plan for the defense of Spain's two-thousand-mile border against Indian attack, which by this time had become the nation's most pressing military concern. Not surprisingly, O'Conor aimed the thrust of his offensive strategy against the numerous tribes of warlike Indians concentrated in the heart of the Big Bend.[1]

In his discussion of Indian policy, O'Conor took great care to under-
score the importance of a successful military campaign against the
Crown's most implacable enemy on the Río Grande—the Apaches.
Relative latecomers to North America, most anthropologists target the
arrival of the Apaches to the American Southwest between A.D. 1000
and 1500. Linguistically linked to the southern branch of Athapaskan
speakers (e.g., Navajos), these nomadic Indians relied chiefly upon hunting and gathering for their survival. In a constant effort to find new food
sources, the Apaches soon established a notorious reputation as raiders
among the more sedentary Pueblo tribes of Texas and New Mexico. Their
name is presumably derived from the Zuni word *Apachu* meaning
"enemy." In their earliest encounters with these Indians, the Spanish
referred to them variously as Janos, Jocomes, Sumas, and Mansos. In
time, however, battle-hardened presidial soldiers also came to refer to
them collectively as "Apaches."[2]

As a southward Apachean migration, beginning about 1650, forced
early Spanish settlers out of Texas and Arizona, that area became known
as the Gran Apachería, or Apache Territory. This geographic designation
extended north from the Mexican states of Sonora, Chihuahua, and
Coahuila to the Arkansas valley in present Colorado. It ran west from the
hill country of Texas into the desert region of central Arizona. Significantly, the Big Bend region formed the nucleus of the Gran Apachería.

With the military reorganization of New Spain at the time of O'Conor's
report, the differentiation of Apachean people by name and geographic
location became more clearly defined. Apaches were divided into two
main groups: those living east of the Río Grande and those to the west.
Each tribe was then broken down into smaller subgroups or bands. The
Eastern Apaches, made up of four bands living in the Big Bend, were the
principal target of Spanish defense policy. First were the Farones, located
in the Guadalupe and Sacramento mountains between the Río Grande
and Río Puerco. From their mountain homes, these Apaches staged raids
deep into Nueva Vizcaya.

Farther southeast, the Mescaleros, who inhabited the Chisos Mountains in what is today Big Bend National Park, wreaked havoc upon the
farming and mining communities of Coahuila and Nueva Vizcaya. The
comparatively peaceful Llaneros lived on the plains between the Río
Puerco and the Colorado River in Texas. Finally, the Lipanes, recognized
as the most fearsome of the Eastern Apache bands, dominated the region
from the Panhandle to the mouth of the Río Grande. [3]

When the Marqués de Rubí returned to Mexico City from his celebrated inspection tour of the northern frontier in 1767, he rightly identified Apache resistance in Texas as Spain's foremost obstacle to the successful colonization of that region. Rubí's assessment of frontier conditions charged that the real threat to the interior provinces was not international, but domestic. The Apaches, not the French or British, presented the most imminent challenge to Spain's northern periphery.

In support of Rubí's statement, officials all along the Río Grande reported that between the years 1749 and 1763 Apaches alone had accounted for the deaths of eight hundred Spanish citizens and the destruction of more than four million pesos in property. These raids, furthermore, were all within two hundred miles of Chihuahua, the capital city of Nueva Vizcaya. Apache assaults forced many of the flourishing cattle ranches and silver mining communities into abandonment. In Rubí's opinion, Spain could not hope to occupy Texas with any measure of success until it resolved the "Indian problem."

Rubí made a second and more significant observation that would have long-term influence upon Spanish-Indian relations in Texas. While the various Apache bands rarely joined forces against the Spanish, all were united in an unyielding hatred of the northern Plains Indians — in particular, the Comanches. Competition for buffalo herds that roamed the plains region thrust these two groups into a bitter rivalry. A more powerful adversary, the Comanches were unrelenting in their effort to drive the Eastern Apaches farther south into the Chihuahuan desert. Sensing the deep-rooted enmity of this intertribal conflict, Rubí recommended that officials in Mexico City engage in a Spanish-Comanche alliance against the Apaches. While the idea was not immediately well received, Rubí's perceptions would, in time, become important in future military operations against the nomadic occupants of the Big Bend.[4]

Known to their enemies as fearless warriors, the Comanches were, without question, the "Lords of the Great Plains." By their own accounts, these hardy plainsmen began drifting south around 1700 from the Rocky Mountain country above the headwaters of the Napestle (Arkansas) valley into what is today eastern Colorado. Related to the Shoshone tribes of Wyoming and southern Idaho, anthropologists have classified the Comanches into the linguistic category of Uto-Aztecan.

The Comanches were the first among the Indians of North America to recognize the strategic value of the horse. They quickly adapted to this new form of transportation and began migrating farther south, always in

pursuit of the buffalo. In their determination to dominate the spacious
hunting grounds of the American Southwest, the Comanches challenged
and defeated the Utes, Wichitas, Kiowas, and Apaches. Comanche dominance extended from the mountainous regions of the Arkansas valley in
the north to the astringent prairies of West Texas. Appearing virtually as
one in harmony with his horse, the mounted Comanche warrior presented
himself a worthy opponent to both his Indian and non-Indian enemies.
His accuracy with a bow and arrow while riding at full gallop was
unsurpassed, and his bravery in the face of battle unparalleled. While the
Apaches tried desperately to rid their ancestral home of these fearsome
invaders, they were not successful. In time, Comanche hunting trails and
trade routes, etched across the face of the Chihuahuan landscape like
neatly woven webs, signified that Texas, too, had become part of their
uncontested domain.[5]

While Spanish officials elected to table the implementation of Rubí's
proposed alliance with the Comanches, they did proceed with the establishment of a presidial line of defense as authorized in the Regulations of
1772. In order to comply with the king's directive, Viceroy Carlos
Francisco de Croix, the Marqués de Croix, turned to Don Hugo de
O'Conor, an Irish expatriate who had once served as interim governor of
Texas. The Dublin-born refugee, nicknamed "Captain Red" for his flowing
red hair and bewhiskered face, arrived in Spain in the mid-1700s. As an
officer in the Regiment of Volunteers of Aragon, O'Conor served the
Crown in Europe as well as in Cuba before his transfer to northern New
Spain in 1765.

Major O'Conor's first assignment was to assume the temporary position
of governor of Texas, a post which he held during Rubí's inspection of
military operations in that province. When José María de Ripperdá
assumed the office in 1770, the Irish mercenary elected to remain in
Texas. He accepted a promotion to lieutenant colonel and command of
the trouble-ridden troops of Presidio de San Sabá,[6] which by this time
had been transferred from central Texas (present Menard) to Villa de San
Fernando de Austria (present Guerrero, Coahuila).

Thus, when the viceroy ordered the reestablishment of Presidio de
San Sabá—along with the placement of other defense installations—
closer to the Río Grande, Hugo de O'Conor surfaced as the best man
for the job. On December 4, 1772, O'Conor, promoted to the rank of
colonel and given the title commandant inspector of all military forces on
the northern frontier, initiated the first phase of his assignment. He left

his headquarters in Chihuahua with a company of three hundred soldiers and headed for the rugged canyonlands of the Big Bend. His first of several excursions into West Texas, the officer's main purpose on this trip was to locate appropriate sites along the Río Grande for the transfer of troops from the abandoned presidios of Cerro Gordo and San Sabá.[7]

Proceeding northeast along the Río Conchos, the expedition arrived at Presidio de La Junta de los Ríos, unoccupied since the removal of its garrison to Julimes in 1767. O'Conor observed that, although the Apaches had burned the interior of the original structure, the outer walls had not been touched. The colonel left a detachment of troops behind with orders to restore and prepare La Junta for immediate reoccupation. Continuing their journey east along the course of the Río Grande, the party followed a small tributary until reaching a spring which they named El Aguaje de San Carlos (located eleven miles southeast of present Lajitas, Texas). O'Conor determined that this site, an obvious watering place for neighboring Indians, would be a good spot for the relocation of troops from Cerro Gordo.

Christmas week found the Irish officer and his men winding their way past La Muralla de San Damáso (probably the Terlingua Fault), through the Chisos Mountains, and finally to a camp on the Mexican side of the Río Grande near the San Vicente Mountains. Rubí's report had explicitly outlined the requirements for the selection of an acceptable presidial site: ample supplies of wood, pasturage, and water were vital in this desolate environment. The graveled plateau overlooking the Río Grande, however, offered only the latter. Furthermore, the undulating land features caused by numerous natural drainages rendered construction of a presidio impractical.

Still, military engineers who accompanied O'Conor argued in favor of the strategic advantages of the location. The only point within miles that was high enough to serve as an observation post, the isolated mesa received the unqualified endorsement of the Spanish engineers as the site for the presidio. In addition to their comments, O'Conor proposed even stronger arguments for the selection of San Vicente. In his report to the viceroy the commandant noted, "This clearly is the precise point of entry of the Natagées (another name for the Llanero Apaches) and the Mescaleros." Despite some personal reservations about the inadequacy of wood and forage, O'Conor determined the location suitable for the reestablishment of the garrison from Presidio de San Sabá.

Having located the sites, O'Conor moved on to Coahuila, where he arrived at Villa de San Fernando de Austria on January 22, 1773. Four months later he returned to his headquarters in Chihuahua via the Big Bend. On this journey the commandant left two companies of men at each designated point along the river to begin construction of the proposed fortresses. "I continued my journey up the river," he later reported to Viceroy Bucareli, "marking off on its sides at suitable intervals the sites for the presidios of San Antonio Bucareli [present Múzquiz], San Sabá, San Carlos, and the one existing at the junction of the Ríos Norte and Conchos."[8] The commandant inspector and the remainder of his column arrived back in Chihuahua in June, at which time he began preparations for the transfer of all troops to their new posts on the Río Grande.

After a thorough inspection of forces to be stationed in the Big Bend, the indefatigable commander left Chihuahua in the fall of 1773 accompanied by the soldiers and their families. Those units from the abandoned fortifications at Julimes and Cerro Gordo were to be transferred respectively to La Junta and San Carlos. On October 28, 1773, Colonel O'Conor turned the command of La Junta over to Captain Don Manuel Muñoz. A seasoned combat veteran who, sixteen years later, would become governor of Texas, Muñoz accepted his charge and reoccupied the presidio with the standard complement of troops: two junior officers, one chaplain, forty-three soldiers, and ten Indian scouts. Ten days later, O'Conor placed Captain Don Manuel de Villaverde, formerly in command of the presidio at Cerro Gordo, in charge of his new post at San Carlos. Villaverde, who had campaigned on the northern frontier since the mid-1760s, also occupied his new station with fifty other soldiers and their families. On January 1, 1774, O'Conor completed the garrisoning of the presidios of the Big Bend when he placed Captain Don Francisco Martínez in command of Presidio San Vicente, which was still undergoing construction.

In March 1774 O'Conor returned to the Río Grande valley for one final inspection of the new presidios. Circumventing the traditional stopover at La Junta on this journey, he established an overland link from Chihuahua to San Carlos. This direct route to the Big Bend significantly reduced the distance between headquarters in Chihuahua and the remote outpost. Moreover, it marked a major communications improvement along the new military network. While O'Conor found the construction at Presidio San Carlos completed, his report indicated that Presidio San Vicente still lagged behind. His arrival at that post on April 14, 1774, found "seven barracks completed, work on the wall and the main bastion well underway." Nevertheless, the commandant inspector expressed personal satisfaction to the viceroy that the assigned task of fortifying the Río Grande was nearing an end.[9]

A comparison of physical characteristics reveals that Presidio San Carlos and Presidio San Vicente stood in remarkable contrast to one another. Typical of most eighteenth-century fortifications, San Carlos represented the archetype of the Texas presidio. Nearly a perfect square with sides 425 feet in length, the north and south corners were accentuated with a diamond-shaped bastion built to house artillery and serve as an observation tower. Within its thick, adobe walls the presidio contained an enlisted men's barracks, a small chapel, the captain's quarters, and several service facilities. In contrast, Presidio San Vicente presented a distorted version of the above. In order to accommodate the structure to the irregularity of the land, Spanish engineers reduced the overall length of the exterior walls and modeled them into a diamond-shaped pattern. These adjustments rotated the fortress about forty-five degrees from normal, giving it a northeast by southwest orientation. The interior design, however, was consistent with that of Presidio San Carlos.[10]

The placement of these fortifications along the Río Grande brought to fruition the strategic recommendations set forth in the Marqués de Rubí's report of 1768 and the *Reglamento* of 1772. Spanish officials, from the viceroy in Mexico City to individual presidial captains stationed along the frontier, placed great faith in the new defensive alignment as a deterrent to Indian depredations.

An iron-fist approach lay at the root of Spain's Indian defense policy in Texas. Scarcely one year after the placement of the presidios on the Río Grande, Commandant Inspector O'Conor detailed a plan of operations for the military subjugation of the Apaches. O'Conor intended to use presidial forces to drive the Apaches farther north into the Comanche-held territory of New Mexico. Pressured on two sides, the Apaches must either succumb to Spanish authority or perish at the hands of their indomitable Indian rivals.

In his report to the viceroy in January 1776, O'Conor discussed his war strategy against the Apaches. First, he assigned each of the fifteen presidios a defensive perimeter of forty leagues (one hundred miles, approximately the distance separating each installation). The jurisdiction for the units stationed at La Junta, for example, extended from Los Puliques (present Ojinaga, Chihuahua) east to El Aguaje de San Carlos.

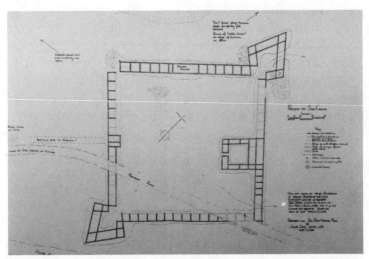

A conceptual drawing based on archeological research of Presidio San Carlos as it appeared at the time of its construction in 1773. This configuration is a classic representation of the architectural style common to most of the eighteenth-century presidios located on the northern frontier of New Spain. *(Courtesy, James E. Ivey, National Park Service, Southwest Regional Office, Santa Fe, New Mexico)*

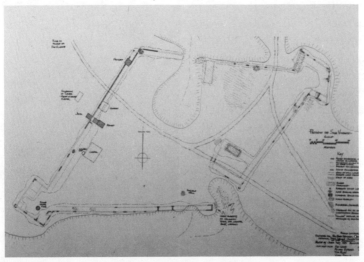

Another conceptual drawing showing Presidio San Vicente ca. 1774. Notice how the traditional diamond-shaped configuration of the presidio has been skewed to accommodate the terrain upon which it was constructed. *(Courtesy, James E. Ivey, National Park Service, Southwest Regional Office, Santa Fe, New Mexico)*

Troops from Presidio San Carlos continued the surveillance from that point to the mouth of Mariscal Canyon in present Big Bend National Park. Finally, the soldiers at Presidio San Vicente were responsible for patrolling the territory from the east end of the canyon and southeast toward present Múzquiz. According to the plan, O'Conor imposed what he believed to be an impregnable line of defense, stretching from the Gulf of California in Sonora, Mexico, to the Guadalupe River in Texas.

Frontier defense, however, was not O'Conor's sole objective in formulating the plan. The continued success of the Apaches in raiding the ranching and mining districts of New Spain underscored the need for an offensive campaign. While the crusade actually began in 1773, it reached its apex in March 1775. Just one year after the occupation of all presidios on the Río Grande, O'Conor personally directed an assault on the Apache stronghold known as the Bolsón de Mapimí. This geologic depression in the Chihuahuan desert, extending three hundred miles north to south and one hundred fifty miles east to west, lay less than one hundred miles below the Big Bend. From this desert citadel Mescalero and Lipan Apaches repeatedly staged raids that struck terror in hearts of frontier colonists. O'Conor planned to roust the enemy out of the Bolsón and drive them back across the Río Grande into the mountains of West Texas.

Concurrent with his plans for a frontal attack on the Bolsón de Mapimí, the colonel proposed a pincer-like maneuver from various points on the Río Grande to entrap all fleeing Apaches. In the spring of 1775 the commandant launched his campaign to drive the Apaches northward. Governor Don Jacobo Ugarte y Loyola of Coahuila, meanwhile, marched his troops to the Pecos River. At this juncture, support units from San Carlos and San Vicente joined Ugarte in pursuit of the escaping enemy, driving them toward the Guadalupe Mountains, northeast of El Paso. At the same time, Captain Muñoz from La Junta combined forces with the commander of the presidio at El Paso in an approach from the west. Completely surrounded, the Mescaleros took refuge in the Guadalupes. But before O'Conor ordered his army to advance, a Comanche war party swept down upon the unsuspecting Apaches killing more than seven hundred of them. This crushing defeat at the hands of their mortal enemy forced the Mescaleros to seek peace with the Spanish, who, compared with the fierce Comanches, were less threatening.

With the presidios fully operational and at least a tentative peace exacted from the Mescaleros, Hugo de O'Conor made a final entry in his report of 1776. "Everything has been accomplished that your Eminence

An early portrait of Teodoro de Croix, former commandant-general of the Interior Provinces of New Spain. *(Photo taken from Alfred B. Thomas,* ed. and trans., Teodoro de Croix and the Northern Frontier of New Spain, 1776–1783 *{1941; reprint, Norman: University of Oklahoma Press, 1968}, by permission)*

has suggested," he assured the viceroy. "All that I have stated to your Excellency has been in performance of my duty with the hope that your lordship will intercede for me with your powerful influence so that I may be granted another post in which I may regain my health."[11] Pleased with his loyal subordinate's achievements, and perhaps sensitive to the rigors that O'Conor endured during years of campaigning on the northern frontier, the viceroy granted the request for transfer. Bucareli appointed O'Conor governor of Yucatán, the position he held to the time of his death on March 8, 1779.

Thus, one brief episode in the continuing saga of Hispanic-Indian relations on the Texas frontier ended with Hugo de O'Conor's departure from Chihuahua. Perhaps more than any other commander stationed on the Río Grande, O'Conor displayed an unfaltering confidence in the utility of the presidial line. His successors, however, proved less convinced that the defensive alignment would resolve the problem of Indian unrest. The strongest critics believed that while the regulations of 1772 provided for the standardization of frontier military defense, they also lacked flexibility. Maintenance of troops engaged in reconnaissance so far from the centers of Spanish settlement left the interior of New Spain unprotected. The great distances between each fortress, moreover, made it easy for Apache war parties to evade patrols and still carry out their attacks. Indeed, it was not long before the Apaches driven from the Bolsón de Mapimí in O'Conor's 1775 campaign were back and troublesome as ever.

A second complaint against the current defense system stemmed from a lack of coordination between military leaders in the field and administrative officials in Mexico City. Most officers called for a military command independent of viceregal authority and free to respond to border crises as they occurred. While the concept of a separate frontier command in northern New Spain was not new, heightened tensions along the Río Grande by 1776 warranted some experimentation with the idea.

In that year, King Charles III, an enlightened monarch with a penchant for administrative reorganization, responded to the needs of his military leaders on the frontier. He appointed an energetic young officer with proven military experience and administrative skills to the new office of Commandant General of the Interior Provinces. Born in France, Teodoro de Croix, nephew of the former viceroy of New Spain, Marqués de Croix, had served Spain as a member of the Grenadiers of the Royal Guard since the age of seventeen. In 1765 the ambitious captain of the Viceregal Guard accompanied his uncle to the New World. Later, while in command of forces at Acapulco, the younger Croix rose to the rank of brigadier general and was awarded knighthood. On May 16, 1776, Caballero Teodoro de Croix dutifully accepted his new government post.

Croix officially began his work in Mexico City in December. His first order of business was to fill the vacancy created by O'Conor's retirement. He selected Colonel José Rubio, a loyal frontier veteran who had served with O'Conor. Next, the commandant general spent several months familiarizing himself with military conditions on the northern frontier. Poring over thousands of documents, Croix soon discovered that many of the summaries were conflicting. In his preliminary report to the viceroy, he not only assailed the military judgment of his popular predecessor, but he also maligned O'Conor's character. To begin, Croix accused O'Conor of falsifying statements regarding the military preparedness of the Río Grande presidios. Before leaving Chihuahua, the retiring Irish officer reassured Viceroy Bucareli that he was leaving the defense line fully provisioned to undertake its task. Yet, Colonel Rubio's first inspection of the region revealed that most of the presidios were woefully ill-equipped. Secondly, Croix attacked the tenuous peace agreements that O'Conor had arranged with the Eastern Apaches. While presumably at peace with the Spanish government, the Indians continued raiding defenseless colonists along the frontier.

Criticism of the highly respected O'Conor placed Croix in direct confrontation with the viceroy. The orders that defined Croix's position, however, made him responsible only to the king, and, Bucareli's personal disdain notwithstanding, Croix freely made modifications to O'Conor's strategic plans. First, Croix called for a more aggressive policy against the Apaches in Texas. Generally speaking, he believed that Spain's conciliatory attitude toward the Indians was destroying the security of the northern provinces because their raiding made colonization a risky prospect.

At present there were fewer than four thousand Spanish residents in the province. In effect, Croix's policy called for either the complete subjugation of the Apaches or total annihilation. In addition, the ardent militarist ordered a reevaluation of the defensive alignment with recommendations for improvement. The solution to peace on the frontier, Croix surmised, rested on the concept of a strong offensive and not on the constant restrengthening of an already obsolete presidial line of defense.[12]

In an effort to gain support for his plan, Croix assembled a Council of War at Monclova, Coahuila, on December 9, 1777. Present were the foremost military minds in northern New Spain. Croix presented a sixteen-point program from which these experienced soldiers were to formulate a uniform Indian policy. The most important questions raised were: (1) should Spain enter into a formal alliance with the Comanches against the recalcitrant Apaches? and (2) should they reexamine the application of the Regulations of 1772 in the light of existing conditions along the Río Grande?

Regarding the first question, Croix resurrected a notion initially advanced in the Marqués de Rubí's earliest reports of 1768. In his plea to ally with the Comanches, Croix stressed that the alliance would place the Apaches in an uncompromising position between two aggressors. Convinced that the alliance had merit, the junta determined that the Eastern Apaches would be the primary target of the combined offensive. Once the Eastern Apaches were defeated in Texas, Spain would turn next to the subjugation of the Western Apaches in Arizona and the Navajos and Utes in New Mexico. To this end, the council of war voted in favor of the Spanish-Comanche alliance as it declared all-out war against the tribes of the Big Bend.[13]

The military advisors also voted to support Croix's second recommendation. They categorically denounced the presidio system in its present design. First, there was not enough manpower to adequately patrol the vast territory paralleling the Río Grande. More important, they agreed that the relocation of some presidios from the centers of Spanish settlement left the hinterland an easy target for Apache assaults. Croix, in fact, produced an early testimony written in 1748 expressing many of these same concerns.

After his return from a second exploration of the Big Bend, Captain Don Joseph de Berroterán informed his superiors that "no suitable place existed on the banks of the Río Grande upon which a presidio could be built." The captain, a veteran of two reconnaissance missions to the area, cited a scarcity of pastures and woodlands as the main problem. But the officer's most strenuous protest lay in his firm belief that "presidios built upon it [Río Grande] twelve leagues apart could not impede the entrance of the many Indians on the northern side of the Bolsón de Mapimí." Needing no further persuasion, the council supported Croix's plan to reevaluate the usefulness of the presidial line.

With the salient features of his offensive plan carefully outlined, Croix made his first official inspection of the northern frontier. He focused on the presidios of the Río Grande in order to gauge their military effective-

ness. He left Monclova in early January 1778. Starting at San Antonio de
Béxar, the commandant general worked his way slowly upriver to San
Vicente and San Carlos.

As Croix and his entourage were returning to his headquarters in
Chihuahua via the Big Bend, a party of five hundred "daring Mescaleros"
attacked them. While the Spaniards sustained no serious injuries, the
psychological effects of the attack influenced the commandant general's
thinking about the efficacy of Spain's defense posture in Texas. If
Croix had expressed reservations about the presidial line before the
inspection, the bold Apache assault confirmed all doubts. Indeed, in one
of three comprehensive reports to the viceroy assessing the military
state of northern New Spain, Croix stressed that the presidios of the
Big Bend be abandoned. While less critical of San Carlos, Croix was
vehement in his condemnation of San Vicente and San Antonio de
Bucareli. He asserted that the isolated garrisons hardly supported themselves, as neither had adequate pasturage for their horses nor ample supplies for their troops. The Royal Treasury expended more than 100,000
pesos to maintain the two posts, though they provided no measurable
protection to the frontier.

San Vicente, Croix noted, also had serious financial problems. The
bankruptcy of two quartermasters in excess of sixteen thousand pesos
left the troops unpaid and demoralized. "Each day made visible the
uselessness of the presidios," Croix concluded. For these reasons, the commandant general ordered the closure of San Vicente and San Antonio de
Bucareli in 1781. Meanwhile, he temporarily withdrew the garrison at
San Carlos ninety miles southeast to the pueblo of Chorreas (in present
Chihuahua).

Just as Croix rearranged the presidial line to make it more efficient, he
also introduced the idea of an auxiliary defense system within the Spanish
pueblos. Croix spent most of 1782 creating a citizen militia designed to
buttress regular presidio forces in times of emergency. The towns
also provided grain and supplies to the nearest fortresses. In this way a
trained citizen's militia provided self-protection in the absence of the
soldiers, who were frequently out on patrol. By so doing, Croix hoped to
double the number of men available to carry out his offensive maneu-
vers.[14] The village of San Carlos, for example, had the capability to outfit
two squadrons and seven companies of combat-ready troops (about 300
soldiers) when called upon. After months of strengthening defenses and
preparing his forces to mobilize, Croix was at last prepared to place his

well-conceived offensive plans into action. As anticipated, the Eastern Apaches, who for centuries found sanctuary in the mountains of the Big Bend, were the principal target.

But in July 1783, before he had an opportunity to implement his strategy, Croix left the northern frontier to become the viceroy of Peru. Simultaneous with his departure the military defense on the northern frontier was restructured. The viceroy of Mexico, Manuel Antonio Flores, mandated a division of the interior provinces under two commandant generals rather than one. A western command, to include New Mexico, Nueva Vizcaya, Sonora, Sinaloa, and the Californias, came under the command of Commandant General Jacobo Ugarte, the previous governor of Coahuila, and an eastern command, to include Texas, Coahuila, and Nuevo Leon, was placed in the hands of Colonel Don Juan de Ugalde, who had replaced Ugarte as governor of Coahuila in 1777.[15]

The proposed offensive against the Apaches in Coahuila and Texas called for an experienced fighting man with unusual leadership qualities. Ugalde had proven his worth on the battlefields of Europe and North Africa, where he served until 1757. A renowned combat veteran by the age of thirty-eight, Ugalde came to the New World where he distinguished himself as the military protector of the mining region of Potosí (present Bolivia). Promoted to the rank of full colonel and awarded knighthood in the prestigious Order of Santiago, Ugalde was at the height of his military career when he received orders to transfer to the northern frontier.

Two years after his arrival in Coahuila, Governor Ugalde readied his army for the first of several extended campaigns against the Eastern Apaches. From 1779 to 1783 the vigorous commander organized four assaults upon the Mescaleros who had regathered in the Bolsón de Mapimí. His last effort, covering more than three thousand miles, drove the Apaches north out of the Bolsón and across the Río Grande — much as O'Conor had done eight years earlier — but this time further east, into the Chisos Mountains of the Big Bend. There the pursuit was halted.[16]

If Ugalde anticipated a hero's welcome when he returned to Monclova, he was sadly disappointed. Croix attacked Ugalde, just as he had previously attacked O'Conor, for failing to crush the Indian threat. In his summary report to the viceroy in 1783, he lamented the fact that six months of hard campaigning on the Río Grande had produced only marginal results. Croix charged Ugalde with military incompetence and insubordination. He reasoned that it was impractical to fight the Apaches in their mountain retreats. Entirely unsatisfied with the results of these early campaigns, Croix relieved Ugalde of his command, one of his last acts before leaving the northern frontier for Peru.

Croix's humiliations of him notwithstanding, Ugalde's forays into the Bolsón de Mapimí had exerted severe pressure on the Apaches, sufficient pressure to force at least a handful of Mescalero leaders to sue for peace in 1785. The weary Indians presented themselves to the commander at Presidio de La Junta and promised to live a reservation-like existence in the mountains of the Big Bend. Seeing that Colonel Ugalde's efforts were beginning to bear fruit, and with Croix gone and out of consideration, the viceroy reinstated the zealous officer to his post as commandant general of the Eastern Interior Provinces.

In January 1787 Ugalde launched his most ambitious campaign against the Mescaleros. For months, the determined commander tracked his foe from the Bolsón de Mapimí to the banks of the Río Grande in still another repeat of past campaigns. Scouting reports confirmed that Zapato Tuerto (Twisted Shoe) led his Mescaleros into the Chisos Mountains where Ugalde had driven his foe four years previously. On Good Friday, "camped within the shadow of the abandoned Presidio of San Vicente," Colonel Ugalde decided to follow the Indians into the Big Bend. The next day, his party of forty men climbed the perilous trails leading into the Chisos. By noon the Spanish found the main encampment "located in the opening of an arroyo which ran between the wooded slopes of two hills near a watering hole" (possibly Lower Juniper Spring). The fighting lasted all day. When the Apaches finally withdrew, hundreds had been killed and many more captured, while the Spaniards suffered only one death. Ugalde named the battleground El Aguaje de Dolores in honor of Our Lady of Sorrows.

At this juncture, Ugalde learned from one of his captives that Zapato Tuerto had formally concluded a peace treaty at La Junta. Furthermore, the presidial captain there granted the Mescaleros safe passage into Big Bend. Enraged at the prospect that Apaches were free to raid Coahuila while under government protection, Ugalde vowed to continue the campaign. He moved upriver to Presidio San Carlos where his men cele- brated Easter Sunday. On April 3 Ugalde left San Carlos and traveled to the western edge of the Bofecillos Mountains (about twenty-five miles northeast of present Presidio, Texas) where he observed several bands of Mescaleros "slipping through his fingers" en route to the safety of the military enclosure. On April 22 the presidial commander and a detachment of troops advised Colonel Ugalde to cease all hostilities against the Mescaleros, now officially at peace with Spain. Ugalde ignored the warning and pursued the Indians into the Guadalupe Mountains before returning to Coahuila.

The relentless tactics of Colonel Ugalde and others during the remainder of the decade precipitated a nominal peace with the Eastern Apaches. In March 1789 the three leading Mescalero chiefs — Patule Grande, Quemado, and Zapato Tuerto — arrived in Santa Rosa (present Múzquiz, Coahuila) to negotiate peace. The Indians agreed to gather into small communities that were to be dependent upon the soldiers at Presidio del Norte for food and protection. Confined within the windswept boundaries of the Big Bend, Spain's nomadic adversaries were reduced to a life of farming and ranching.[17]

The following year the determined Ugalde exacted a similar agreement with the more formidable Lipan Apaches. The Spaniards, however, did not simply consign the Lipan to a reservation existence as they had the Mescaleros. Rather, the army used the Lipan as scouts and auxiliary combatants in campaigns against the Navajos and Utes in New Mexico. The Lipan served Spain well in this capacity until the end of the colonial period.[18] With the termination of Juan de Ugalde's military career on the northern frontier in 1790, a century of Spanish-Indian policy in West Texas began, at last, to show positive results.

The advent of the nineteenth century signaled the demise of three hundred years of Spanish hegemony in America. In the wake of political upheaval in Europe and the New World, the Indian problems of the northern frontier seemingly dissipated. Presidial soldiers in Texas were mobilized instead to meet the onslaught of citizen armies in revolt against colonial rule. While the thrust of the independence movement centered around urban central Mexico, the northern provinces did not escape its impact. Indeed, Padre Miguel Hidalgo y Costilla and Ignacio Allende, spearheads of the revolution, escaped to Coahuila after their defeat by royalist forces in January 1811. In response, Governor Manuel Salcedo of Texas amassed troops from the presidios along the Río Grande and rushed to the defense of the empire. The capture of Hidalgo and Allende and their subsequent execution at Monclova was not enough to stem the tide of revolution. On February 24, 1821, Agustín de Iturbide boldly proclaimed his Plan de Iguala, Mexico's declaration of independence from Spain.

Transfer of power from the Spanish Empire to the Mexican Republic in 1821 also meant changes in Indian policy on the northern frontier. In theory, it appeared as if the Mexican government was prepared to follow verbatim the Regulations of 1772. Utilizing the Spanish presidial system as the blueprint for their own frontier defense policy, the Mexicans even reprinted the military code as their principal guidelines. "Everything from tactics to uniforms remained heavily influenced by Spanish tradition," wrote one scholar.[19] In addition, the provisions of Mexico's first federalist constitution, written in 1824, kept the idea of a separate military command alive. One modification, however, was to merge the remote province of Texas with the more populated and well-fortified state of Coahuila.

As northern colonists turned to the capital for military aid against Indian attacks and foreign threats, the constitution of 1824 called for greater decentralization and frontier self-sufficiency. In practice, the Spanish presidial system fell into total disarray as Mexico City became more detached from the needs of its outlying provinces. Political instability marked the tenure of the Mexican Republic. Army officers, preoccupied with the opportunity to overthrow a weak or tottering administration, concentrated their troops closer to the centers of power while they ignored conditions on the frontier. The lion's share of the defense budget, moreover, went to the maintenance of these armies. The few forces that remained stationed along the Río Grande were woefully neglected. Ill-equipped and underpaid, presidial soldiers frequently resorted to corruption and desertion, leaving the citizens of the northern frontier to fend for themselves.

In the absence of a central policy of Indian defense, individual states in the north organized their own militias. While volunteer armies had existed since the days of Teodoro de Croix, they were considered an auxiliary force. The local militia units of the Mexican period, however, became the backbone of defense along the Río Grande. Notably, they could not be deployed beyond the boundaries of the respective states. In Texas-Coahuila, two militia units operated in San Antonio, one in Goliad, one in Guerrero (formerly San Fernando de Austria), and one in Santa Rosa. San Carlos, located in Chihuahua near the abandoned presidio which dominated the region for decades, also emerged as an important military colony. One visitor to San Carlos in 1828 described the village as a "half-wild Indian and Mexican settlement on the Río Grande."[20]

The Comanches reigned supreme on the Mexican frontier during the 1830s and 1840s. Always in pursuit of horses and cattle which they traded with the Americans up north, they ravaged the Mexican villages scattered along the Río Grande. In 1828 José María Sánchez, a traveler to that province, reported fewer than four thousand inhabitants settled there. According to his observations, the Mexican colonists feared the Comanches as much as they had previously feared the Apaches. As the Mexican Period wore on, Comanche raiders struck deeper into the population centers of Mexico. In the 1840s one raid reportedly reached Zacatecas, nearly 500 miles from the Texas plains. While the Mexican Army did its best to retaliate, it was rarely successful.[21]

American expansion into Texas beginning in the 1820s was equally threatening to the residents of the north Mexican frontier. On his visit to Texas in 1828, José María Sánchez expressed great concern over the fact that American colonists were rapidly taking over that province. Rightfully, the civilian draftsman questioned the wisdom of his government's liberal colonization policies. In the employ of General Manuel Mier y Teran at the time of his visit, Sánchez witnessed first hand the unceasing wave of immigration from the United States. General Mier y Teran, a renowned engineer and Mexico's leading military authority on the northern frontier, led his inspection team to Texas to determine the seriousness of the American threat. Like his subordinate, the general voiced alarm that Mexico's hold on Texas was eroding. He proposed stronger defense measures along the Río Grande as a counter to foreign pressure. Government reaction to these proposals was exactly the opposite. President Antonio López de Santa Anna ordered the reduction of all frontier militia in his effort to centralize power in Mexico City.

The accession of a military dictator to power in 1834 fomented widespread political uprisings throughout Mexico, expressed most violently in the north. Santa Anna's weakening of the local militia not only violated the right of self-defense guaranteed in the Constitution of 1824, but it also left the north Mexican states unprotected from the virulent incursions of land-hungry Americans. In 1836 American settlers in Texas rose up in rebellion against Mexican rule. Troops under Santa Anna moving to crush the rebellion were defeated and the Texans declared their independence under the flag of the Lone Star Republic. Within a decade of that declaration, the Mexican War commenced, from which the United States wrested control of the entire trans-Río Grande region.[22]

Transfer of authority on the Texas frontier to the United States, however, did not resolve the Indian problem for Mexico. In October 1851 Colonel Emilio Langberg, a Swedish soldier of fortune in the service of the Mexican Army, prepared to make the first general inspection of the north Mexican states since the war. As commandant of all forces in Chihuahua, Langberg was to assess the extent of Indian depredations on the Río Grande. His itinerary called for a thorough reconnaissance of all territory between San Carlos and Monclova, Coahuila. Most important, he received instructions to conduct the first recorded Mexican exploration of the Big Bend.

Langberg assembled a force of seventy-four men in Chihuahua City and marched northeast toward San Carlos, arriving on October 3. After inspecting the old presidio, the Swedish officer marvelled at the accurate placement of the installation, "at the exact point where the Indians cross the Río Bravo [Río Grande]." "On this spot," he noted, "the brave inhabitants of Villa de San Carlos and their Mescalero allies withstood the Comanche assaults." While frequently the target of Indian raids, San Carlos was also a major trade center for surrounding tribes friendly to both the Spanish and the Mexicans. Impressed with the strategic attributes of San Carlos and inspired by the fighting spirit of its eight hundred residents, Colonel Langberg recommended that the site continue its role as a frontier military colony.

On October 6, 1851, Langberg continued a northeasterly course along one of the Comanche trails that led him straight toward the Chisos Mountains. While this territory now belonged to the United States, Langberg was determined to explore its uncharted boundaries. He guided his troops across high "flagstone" embankments at great risk to the horses and mules. The terrain was so difficult that the troops had to disassemble their artillery pieces and carry them on their shoulders. Always on the alert for any sign of Comanches, Langberg continued his investigation of what is today Big Bend National Park. Camped on the east side of the Chisos basin, the colonel described the range as being "like a chain of hills running uninterrupted as far as San Vicente, presenting a vision of distinct figures resembling wondrous castles and towers." The image of the Chisos, he added, remained visible to his party the entire time.

Each day at dawn before breaking camp, Langberg dispatched a patrol ahead of the main party to look for any sign of Indians. On the morning of October 7 his scouts reported that they had followed a trail as far as a place they called La Boquilla (near present Boquillas Canyon). From that point the scouts followed the Río Grande upstream to where it "squeezed between some rather high embankments," until they reached the ford near the ruins of Presidio San Vicente. The remainder of the column did not arrive until the morning of October 9. Finding it difficult to cross the Río Grande, Langberg arrived on the Mexican side late in the afternoon. "The view from above the river is so picturesque," he wrote. "The Boquilla {Canyon} rises above rich pastures on either side."

In stark contrast, the presidial site at San Vicente lacked splendor but was strikingly military in appearance. It saddened Langberg to see the old presidio — a tribute to a glorious military past — now abandoned. Like San Carlos, the ford at San Vicente had obvious strategic value. For this reason, Langberg recommended that San Vicente also be considered as a military colony. The inscriptions on the adobe walls, bearing the names of a generation of soldiers who had passed before him in search of Indians, lent credence to his recommendation.[23]

As the American government assumed sovereignty over Texas and the remainder of the arid Southwest, they inherited a multitude of problems endemic to a defenseless frontier. Westward expansionism after the Mexican War, furthermore, committed the United States Army to the protection of all citizens — Mexican and American — inhabiting the territory along the proposed Mexico–United States border. Not unlike the many Spanish and Mexican officials who came before them, American military officers viewed the Big Bend as critical to the ultimate defense of Texas.

CHAPTER THREE

Perfect Desolation

No description can give an idea of the grandeur of the scenery through these mountains. There is no verdure to soften the bare and rugged view; no overhanging trees or green bushes to vary the scene from one of perfect desolation.

— *M. T. W. Chandler, 1852*

Camped somewhere along the Río Grande, a few miles downstream from present Boquillas Canyon, Dr. C. C. Parry made the daily entry into his journal, dating it November 4, 1852. Exhausted from two weary months of travel through the trackless canyon country of the Big Bend, Parry, a field geologist assigned to one of the survey teams of the United States–Mexico Boundary Commission, penned the following statement, "We have had rather a rough time and traversed a most singular country." This brief but provocative commentary captured the emotion of all those who had accompanied Parry on his arduous journey through the lower Río Grande. Part of Mexico's cession to the United States in 1848, the newly-acquired territory indeed appeared singular and unlike any other land the American explorers had ever seen.[1]

The acquisition of a third of Mexico's national domain in 1848 provided the United States government with an opportunity to sponsor American expansion into the trans-Mississippi West. Through the untiring efforts of the War Department, the instrument of frontier settlement in these early years, Washington underwrote the cost of scientific and military explorations, internal improvements, frontier defense, and land distribution programs — all of which served to facilitate the inhabitation of its newly acquired territories. After the Mexican War, the United States government targeted most of its attention toward the opening of new lands west of the Mississippi River. During these years, the American Southwest became the principal beneficiary of federally sponsored activity. Texas was no exception.

Under the terms of the Treaty of Guadalupe-Hidalgo, the United States and Mexico agreed upon the need for a well-defined international boundary. Article V of the treaty, which articulated the instructions for the establishment of the line, called for each nation to appoint a commission to work jointly on the formation of a common border. The exactness of the boundary held particular importance to the expansionist interests of the United States. First, a number of strategic points were located on or near the proposed line of demarcation. Since the days of Andrew Jackson and James K. Polk, Americans had cast a covetous eye westward toward the natural harbor of San Diego. It was important, therefore, that the boundary survey place the harbor in United States territory. In addition, Washington diplomats desired clear access to the Colorado River as a navigable outlet to the Gulf of California. Finally, and perhaps most important to the anticipated development of Texas, the Americans desired a corridor for the construction of a southwestern transcontinental railroad to the Pacific.[2]

The Army Corps of Topographical Engineers assumed the responsibility to determine the accuracy of the international boundary. This elite team of young and highly specialized military officers had over the past decade accumulated a great deal of field experience mapping the American wilderness. The establishment of a border between the United States and Mexico, however, represented their first major project undertaken in the trans-Mississippi West. In the years that followed the war with Mexico, the vast wastelands of the Great American Desert—a popular epithet for all of the arid and semiarid lands located west of the hundredth meridian—became a veritable laboratory for these knowledgeable soldier-scientists.

Created as a separate military organization in July 1838, this small but highly significant branch of the army became the vehicle for American westward expansion. The corps never exceeded more than seventy-two officers, most of whom received their training at West Point Military Academy. From 1838 to 1863, the Topographical Corps laid out national boundaries, improved America's system of rivers and harbors, and advanced the settlement of the West with the survey and construction of wagon roads. In addition to their function as public-works specialists, these topographical officers performed a variety of scientific experiments in the field, which included data collection, astronomical observation, mapping and sketching, and rudimentary hydrology. Their training and preparation during these formative years, moreover, provided the

United States government with a core of technological experts needed to meet the demands of postwar growth.[3]

It was not surprising that after the Mexican War Texas became one of the early assignments requiring the expertise of the Topographical Corps. With the establishment of the Lone Star Republic in 1836, land-hungry Americans developed an early interest in the settlement and commercial exploitation of a sovereign Texas. As a result, Texans were not only eager but also well prepared for immediate transition to statehood. As part of the Mexican Cession to the United States in 1848, the hitherto uncharted deserts of central and western Texas demanded official government attention.

The discovery of gold in California by this time had already generated an overwhelming migration across the Great Plains to the Pacific. Hoping to avoid the harsh winters of the northern Rockies, a number of gold-seekers preferred the southerly route across Texas. It was a well-known fact, however, that the trans-Pecos region harbored Apaches, Comanches, Kiowas, and other nomadic Indians whom the army perceived as threatening to the unsuspecting horde of westward emigrants.[4] For these reasons, the federal government judiciously included Texas in its general postwar plan for frontier defense.

War Department policy in the West stressed two central objectives: first, a thorough reconnaissance for the purpose of locating suitable sites for future military installations; and second, the construction of a network of military wagon roads across the frontier. Purely civilian interests remained, however. In fact, the earliest exploration efforts in the Chihuahuan desert were civilian rather than military. Before the army could establish a system of highways across the West, local merchants in San Antonio subsidized a commercial expedition to link them with the Mexican trade centers of Chihuahua via El Paso del Norte. Their aim was to divert some of the lucrative Chihuahua-Santa Fe trade in the direction of South Texas.

During the summer of 1848 a group of San Antonio citizens collected eight hundred dollars to sponsor John C. Hays in an expedition to determine a practical wagon route to El Paso. Although hardly a menacing figure at just under five feet tall, "Coffee Jack," a seasoned Texas Ranger with field experience as a surveyor, was equal to the task. On the morning of August 27 Hays and thirty-five men under the command of Samuel Highsmith, also of the Texas Rangers, departed San Antonio for the West Texas frontier. Initially, they headed northwest to the headwaters of the

Llano River, then the party curiously reversed its course southward and crossed the Pecos River near the junction of the Río Grande. Unfamiliar with the rugged terrain of this region, they wandered aimlessly across to the Mexican side of the river, bearing generally west in the direction of San Carlos. Arriving half-starved at the little Mexican village, the party rested several days before continuing their trek upriver to Presidio del Norte.

Thus, as it had with the Spanish explorers who preceded them, the uncharted desert of the Big Bend frustrated the early American attempts. Exhausted, but safely back in United States territory, the party took refuge among American settlers living at Fort Leaton, a trading post established south of Presidio after the Mexican War. Ten days later the Hays-Highsmith party returned home rather than continue their journey to El Paso. This time they pursued a more northerly course to the Pecos, which course Hays identified as a potential year-round wagon route through the Big Bend. The weary adventurers arrived in San Antonio in late fall, no doubt disheartened by their 107-day ordeal.[5]

The need for an established wagon road across Texas remained paramount. Secretary of War William Marcy ordered the new commander of the Eighth Military District in Texas, Major General William Jenkins Worth, to commission a second reconnaissance of the Big Bend. This effort, a joint military and civilian operation, departed from Austin in March 1849. Although the civilian objectives remained essentially unchanged, the army's aim to establish a military road to El Paso added a new and important dimension to the exploration. In response to his orders, General Worth dispatched Major Robert S. Neighbors and a small detachment of troops to accompany John S. Ford, the Austin physician in charge of the venture.

Unlike their predecessors, Ford and Neighbors had a well-thought-out plan. Moving generally northwest to the headwaters of the Conchos, the party swung due west toward the Pecos. At Horsehead Crossing, a favorite fording place on the Pecos for the Spanish and Indian travelers who had preceded them centuries before, the Americans penetrated the Big Bend. Continuing on their westerly course along the Guadalupe Mountains, the group reached their destination in May. After only four days rest, Ford and Neighbors decided to return to Austin along the same route. Convinced that his party had charted a practical wagon road to El Paso, Major Neighbors boasted to a reporter for the Houston *Mercantile*

Adviser, "A better route for a wagon or railroad for an equal distance does not exist from Austin to El Paso."

The significance of these early civilian and military excursions into the trans-Pecos region was that they served to heighten interest in Washington for a more in-depth exploration of West Texas. In addition to commercial and transportation needs, there was the overriding issue of military defense. In November 1849 William Marcy's successor as secretary of war, George W. Crawford, outlined the importance of Texas in defense planning in his annual report to Congress. In addressing himself to the strategic needs of a postwar West, Crawford noted, "The additions recently made [the Mexican Cession] seem to impose the necessity of increasing the military force, in order that its strength may be adequate to the wants which the extension of our territorial limits require." The overwhelming tide of migration across Texas by this time further validated the need for expediency in formulating a defense plan for the American Southwest. The gallant attempts of John Ford and "Coffee Jack" Hays, therefore, provided the foundation for a more comprehensive national undertaking.

Colonel John James Abert, highest ranking officer in the Corps of Topographical Engineers, spearheaded the campaign for greater development in Texas. His plan, which called for the improvement of rivers and streams that emptied into the Gulf of Mexico, naturally determined the Río Grande to be especially important. Closely linked to his idea of making the rivers of the trans-Mississippi West more navigable, the colonel hoped to make Washington's dream of a railroad across Texas a reality. In the same year that Hays and Ford led their respective exploration parties into West Texas, the government sanctioned no less than a half dozen official topographical reconnaissance missions to all parts of the state. Some were designed simply to retrace the routes taken by adventurous civilians while others examined alternative possibilities for a practical military road.[6]

Responsibility for the first of these military assignments fell to a twenty-three-year-old topographical officer with no field experience on the western frontier. Lieutenant William Henry Chase Whiting, a Mississippi native who entered West Point at age seventeen but graduated top of his class in 1845 with the highest average yet attained at the military academy, eagerly accepted his assignment. On February 9, 1849, Lieutenant Whiting, and his companion from the backwoods country of Vermont,

Colonel John James Abert, the vision-
ary commander of the Army Corps
of Topographical Engineers. Abert's
personal commitment to the idea of a
transcontinental railroad had a significant influence upon the military explorations in West Texas beginning
in the 1840s. *(Photo taken from William H. Goetzmann,* Army Exploration
in the American West, 1803–1863
*{New Haven, 1959; recent reprint,
Lincoln: University of Nebraska Press,
1979}, by permission)*

Major General William H. C. Whiting in confederate uniform. As a
young lieutenant in the Army Corps
of Topographical Engineers, Whiting
established the first practical wagon
route from San Antonio to El Paso in
1849. *(Courtesy, National Archives,
Washington, D.C.)*

El Paso del Norte as it appeared ca. 1851 to a member of the
United States Boundary Survey Commission. *(Courtesy, National
Archives, Washington, D.C.)*

Brevet Second Lieutenant William F. Smith, took charge of their party of fourteen "well-versed and experienced woodsmen and hunters" and carried out their orders from General Worth. The aim of this reconnaissance was to resurvey the Hays-Highsmith route to Presidio del Norte and continue on to El Paso.

With the aid of Richard A. Howard, the scout who had accompanied Hays on his ill-fated attempt of the previous year, the military column headed west. Dissatisfied with Hays and Highsmith's initial trail, Lieutenant Whiting preferred a northwest course until reaching the San Sabá River, which provided the party with ample supplies of wood and water. At this juncture, Whiting, counting heavily upon Highsmith's reports that assured him of sufficient natural ponds along the high plains, left the San Sabá valley. As it turned out, the ponds had dried out and the San Sabá River was the last source of water the party was to encounter for the next three days. In desperation, the young army officers turned due west toward the Pecos River. The experience led Whiting and Smith to conclude that their current route could be useful as a wagon road only if wells were dug at intervals along the route.

Equally threatening were the Indians. On March 17 Whiting's party found itself surrounded by an Apache war party numbering two hundred warriors. The army officers were faced with either fighting the fearsome Mescaleros, or negotiating with them for safe passage. Apparently seeing discretion to be the better part of valor, they chose to negotiate, and that night Lieutenant Whiting and Robert Howard accompanied the Apaches to their camp where they met with Cigarito, one of the leading chiefs. After much discussion, during which Whiting and Howard argued that the reconnaissance party presented no threat and only desired to pass through Indian land, the Apaches acquiesced. Whiting noted in his journal that he considered himself fortunate that his first encounter with the Apaches only cost him a few cooking utensils. (Considering the reputation the Apaches had for being implacable in their hatred of whites, one wonders what motivated Cigarito to be generous in this instance.)

Once arrived in the Limpia Creek valley, the party made camp near the present site of Fort Davis, Texas. Next, the party turned southwest toward Presidio del Norte, where, like Hays and Highsmith before them, they refreshed themselves at Ben Leaton's Fort. On April 12 the party arrived in the parched Mexican town of El Paso, which one of the members described as a village made up of houses which were "with few exceptions little more than mud hovels."

After recounting the events of the journey with his men, Lieutenant Whiting came to some important conclusions. First, all agreed that travel through the Río Grande valley presented greater difficulties than they were prepared to deal with. Still, while the country north of the Big Bend was more passable, there was the critical problem of inaccessibility to water. Thus, on his first venture into the unrelenting heat of the Chihuahuan desert, the inexperienced frontier officer had correctly evaluated the problems that plagued generations of future pioneers in their travels across the arid West.

Less concerned with practical considerations, General Worth remained resolute in suggesting the use of the longer northern route to El Paso. He believed it to be more convenient and therefore more expedient in promoting the settlement of the area. A stable population would in turn provide the proposed military installations with a permanent source of supplies. Strategic advantages notwithstanding, Whiting and Smith decided to seek an improved route on their return journey. Proceeding downstream from El Paso, the party exited the Río Grande valley above Presidio and set a course due east to the Pecos River. They followed this stream for sixty miles, then crossed over toward the San Pedro, or Devil's River as it is known today. The party continued their easterly orientation until reaching San Antonio. In his assessment of what came to be termed the "lower route," Lieutenant Smith reported that the road, which he estimated to be 645 miles, was a vast improvement on the earlier civilian discovery.[7]

Concurrent with Whiting and Smith's return, the army began to station troops in West Texas. Brevet Major Jefferson Van Horn received orders from new Eighth District Commander, Brigadier General William S. Harney, to move the Third Infantry from San Antonio to a new garrison in El Paso. Also assigned to the column, Lieutenant Colonel Joseph E. Johnston, the ranking topographical officer in the Texas Department, prepared to leave for El Paso. His orders, dated June 1, 1849, instructed him to organize two survey parties for further reconnaissances of the Chihuahuan desert region.

While Johnston commanded one of the exploration parties assigned to Van Horn's group, Lieutenant Francis T. Bryan assumed responsibility for the other. Bryan, considered by his colleagues to be the best surveyor in the Topographical Corps, was told to retrace the Ford-Neighbors route in order to confirm its usefulness to the army. Proceeding along the exact trail Ford and Neighbors followed to the small German settlement of

Fredricksburg, Bryan's men then coursed west toward Horsehead Crossing. Once in trans-Pecos territory, the column of thirty men paralleled the Guadalupe Mountains, arriving in El Paso on July 29, six weeks after their departure from San Antonio. In his official report of the journey to Colonel Johnston, Bryan observed that there were "no obstructions to the easy passage of wagons between Fredricksburg and El Paso." Bryan added, "Grass and water may be had everyday, within marches of twenty-five miles, except from the head of the Conchos and the Pecos." Based on the lieutenant's lucid reports, the army received confirmation of the existence of an "upper" or second practical road to El Paso.

Meanwhile, assisted by Lieutenant William F. Smith, who had just returned from his first trip to West Texas, Colonel Johnston led his survey team back down the "lower route." Generally satisfied with Whiting and Smith's earlier marking of the proposed road, Johnston made some minor improvements by straightening the section between Devil's River and the Pecos. These corrections substantially reduced the overall distance traveled. Johnston's report to Colonel Abert echoed the comments of his junior officers about the importance of the San Antonio to El Paso road. But it was Captain Samuel G. French, the attending quartermaster corps officer, who recognized the broader significance of El Paso del Norte as a stopover point for thousands of emigrants en route to California. His report cited the Mexican village as "a natural resting place between the Atlantic and the Pacific."[8]

In succeeding years the officers of the Topographical Corps gained valuable field experience in Texas, which prepared them well for even greater undertakings throughout the trans-Mississippi West. Notably, Lieutenants Bryan and William Smith, by now seasoned veterans in overland travel across the Chihuahuan desert, attempted to float down the Río Grande from El Paso to Presidio. After much difficulty navigating the swift currents that ran through the canyons above the old Spanish outpost, Bryan and Smith concluded that the Río Grande could be best surveyed on land. In the meantime, two other lieutenants, Martin L. Smith and Nathaniel Michler, had similar instructions to explore the Río Grande upstream from Ringgold Barracks (near present Río Grande City, Texas) beyond the Pecos River. While the going was comparatively easier along this stretch of the river, Michler and Smith had equally disappointing results. After exploring only eighty miles beyond the confluence of the two rivers, they had to abort the expedition. The experiences that these officers shared in 1850 and 1851 foreshad-

Major General William F. Smith. As a member of the Topo-
graphical Corps of Engineers in his early military career,
Smith accompanied 1st Lieutenant William H. C. Whiting on
their epic journey across West Texas in 1849. The Whiting-
Smith Expedition was first to coin the term "Big Bend."
(Courtesy, National Archives, Washington, D.C.)

owed the problems that others soon faced in the canyons of the lower Río Grande.[9]

That these early military incursions were on the whole peripheral to the area which today encompasses Big Bend National Park in no way diminishes their overall significance. Clearly, these pioneering efforts opened the way for the permanent settlement of southwest Texas. The detailed reports of the topographical officers who visited this otherwise parched land not only acknowledged its presence but also determined its exploration vital to the successful Anglo inhabitation of the American Southwest. The perceptive Lieutenant Whiting, for example, recommended in his report that the neighboring region of the "Big Bend" be thoroughly reconnoitered as it represented the last expanse of frontier in Texas known only to its native residents.[10]

No less significant were the wagon roads that the engineers plotted. Within only a few months after the army had confirmed the desirability of the so-called "upper" and "lower" routes, they became main arteries of east-west travel through Texas. In time hopeful mining enthusiasts bound for California, and eventually the railroads and highways that represented an expanding West, followed the faint traces of the Topographical Engineers across the broad Texas plains.

If the demands of the wagon road program taxed the skills of these well-trained officers, the vast and virtually uncharted canyons of Big Bend posed challenges which were to take them to the very limits of their mental and physical endurance. In accordance with the directives set forth in Article V of the Treaty of Guadalupe-Hidalgo, both the United States and Mexico commissioned their respective survey teams in January 1849. With the understanding that the boundary as defined in 1848 was based on erroneous information, the two nations assumed joint responsibility for an accurate determination of the line.

Under the aegis of the federal government, John B. Weller, loyal Ohio Democrat and personal appointee of President Polk, brought together the U.S. boundary survey team. Andrew B. Gray, a civilian surveyor with field experience in the American Southwest, received the appointment as chief surveyor. While it might have been questionable that this position be assigned to a civilian rather than a military specialist, Gray had proved himself worthy based upon his work on the Texas Boundary Commission in 1840.

The principal scientific position of chief astronomer did, however, go to a reputable member of the Topographical Corps with considerable experience in the American West. Brevet Major William Hemsley Emory personified the professional image of the topographical engineers. His flowing red whiskers and haughty appearance seemed to magnify the character of this well-bred and highly trained soldier. Born to a Maryland family rooted in the landed aristocracy of colonial America, Emory obtained his West Point appointment through a number of firmly placed political connections. Once there, he trained in the company of other cadets who were to convert their Topographical Corps beginnings into illustrious military careers.

Lieutenant Emory began his career as a junior officer assigned to General Stephen Watts Kearny's Army of the West during the Mexican War. At that time, there were few existing accurate maps of northern Mexico. Therefore, the army's need for a good cartographic representation of the area was critical. Emory's first assignment was to provide this vital information not only to Kearny's column en route to California, but also to the War Department in Washington. The thoroughness and professionalism of Lieutenant Emory's reports and maps established for him the reputation as the "best informed individual on the area." Thus, Emory's wartime travels in the West as well as his experience as a military engineer more than prepared him to assume his new duties as chief astronomer for the United States–Mexico Boundary Commission.[11]

Not unlike its American counterpart, Mexico assembled its commission from a number of military and civilian specialists who had distinguished themselves in the field. General Pedro García Conde, the former military commander of Chihuahua, who had drawn the first geographic map of that area in 1840, headed the commission. His chief surveyor was José Salazar Ylarreguí, a civilian engineer of Basque extraction with an equally reputable background. One other notable member of the commission was Felipe de Iturbide, son of the erstwhile emperor of Mexico, who served as official interpreter and translator. On July 7, 1849, the Mexican commission joined the American survey team in San Diego, California, to officially begin operations.

Numerous financial and political problems plagued the survey from the outset; by the end of the first year the joint commission had only managed to come to an agreement on the border separating upper and lower California. Spiraling inflation provoked by the gold rush, moreover, forced the commission into unforseen expenses that depleted most of its capital outlay in the first six months. No less debilitating was the incessant arguing between the civilian and military members of the survey. The topographical officers who worked under Gray's supervision, for example, viewed him as their inferior and were in constant disagreement with his decisions.

Political machinations in Washington also had an adverse affect on the completion of the survey. In June 1849 newly elected Whig President Zachary Taylor replaced Weller with the ambitious but enormously popular John C. Frémont, known for his famous explorations of the West during the Mexican War. Official justification for this change was that Weller acted too slowly in completing the work and was much too extravagant. Frémont's association with the Topographical Corps in the 1840s should have gained him overwhelming support among the commission's military members, but his personal political aspirations placed him in direct conflict with Major Emory. Emory, who had once testified against the famous pathfinder in a court martial after the war, held Frémont in low esteem. Frustrated by numerous delays and Frémont's appointment, Emory resigned his post in December 1849, but not before he saw the completion of the western portion of the survey. Upon his departure Emory expressed his discontent: "I was quite satisfied to have nothing more to do with a mixed commission, governed by persons wholly unused to public affairs, and ignorant of the first principles of scientific knowledge."[12]

In 1850 President Taylor decided that in the interest of a successful project he would appoint a new commissioner to the second survey. In May he placed John Russell Bartlett, bibliophile, partisan supporter, and amateur ethnologist from Rhode Island, in charge of the American commission. Inasmuch as the first project began in San Diego and worked east to the Gila River, both nations agreed to start the second undertaking at San Antonio and move west along the Río Grande toward El Paso. Again, the survey suffered difficulties which precluded its advancement for most of that year. As a result, A. B. Gray became the second casualty of political vacillation that nearly brought the boundary survey to a halt. Gray's replacement as chief surveyor was none other than William Emory, who returned to his assignment in September, equipped and ably staffed to deal with the immediate problem facing the American surveyors — a complete reconnaissance of the canyons of the lower Río Grande.

Upon his arrival in El Paso, however, Emory discovered the commission to be in a state of "extreme embarrassment." Bartlett, who had absented himself in search of supplies, left the major "not one cent at my disposal to prosecute the survey." Some of the members of the party, in fact, had not received any pay in eighteen months and were reluctant to continue the project. Still, Emory found officers and men who were willing to undertake the work on credit, which enabled him to take over the project. M. T. W. Chandler headed the list of civilian members on the commission along with Arthur Schott, surveyor and artist, Charles Radziminski, cartographer, and C. C. Parry, geologist. Emory's plan was to touch the river at convenient intervals where field units would establish a supply base accessible to wagons. Next, each party would connect the intervening space between camps with a linear survey. Emory's principal military assistant was Lieutenant Michler, the topographical officer who had surveyed the portion of the Río Grande near Fort Ringgold the previous year.

Marine Tyler Wickham Chandler, a Pennsylvanian-born engineer, had worked as a surveyor for the city of Philadelphia and as a meteorologist for the Smithsonian Institution. In August 1852 the civilian scientist received his appointment to the United States Boundary Commission and orders to join Major Emory in El Paso. The major placed Chandler in charge of the survey that was to begin at Presidio del Norte and proceed downriver through Big Bend country to the mouth of the Pecos. Emory provided his field supervisor with enough rations for 110 days and furnished him with a military escort under the command of Second Lieutenant Duff C. Green of the Third Infantry, garrisoned at El Paso.

Equipped with only a crude sketch of the area, which Colonel Emilio Langberg drew on his reconnaissance of Big Bend the year before, Chandler and his men penetrated the very heart of the canyon country in August 1852.[13] The first 200 miles were accomplished on schedule, although some boats and supplies were lost. Then the party encountered the first of the "grand and imposing" canyons which interrupted the course of the Río Grande in the vicinity of the Big Bend. "It is impossible to keep along the edge of the stream in its course through the mountain," Chandler later reported, "and just as impossible to navigate it." Indeed, as he stood before the mouth of the Cañon de San Carlos (present Santa Elena Canyon) the civilian engineer had to carefully calculate his next move. He climbed the Mesa de Anguila, which loomed above the canyon on the north, for a better look downriver and saw the current "dashing with a roaring sound over the rocks." Observing further that the stream narrowed considerably as it meandered through the towering walls that bounded it on either side, he decided to detour around the obstruction.

Once past the canyon the party continued to follow the river's course.

Taking note of the peculiar topography along the way, for some time the gaze of Chandler's men had been drawn northeasterly to the highest peak of the Chisos Mountains, one of the most prominent features located in Big Bend National Park. Chandler described the significance of the peak in his journal entry for that day:

> From many places on the line it was taken as a prominent point on which to direct the instrument; and, though the face of the country might change during our progress down the river, still, unmistakable and un-changeable, far above the surrounding mountains, this peak reared its well known head. The windings of the river, and the progress of our survey, led us gradually nearer to this point of interest, and it was found to be a part of a cluster, rather than a range, of mountains on the American side, known as "Los Chisos."

Appropriately, they named the feature Emory Peak in honor of the leader of the boundary survey.

Heading in the direction of the low range of mountains the Mexicans called the Sierra San Vicente, the expedition came upon Mariscal Canyon, the second of the great river canyons along the Big Bend. This time, how-ever, Chandler decided to chance traversing the canyon, which took the party two days to complete. Emerging at the east end of the canyon, Chandler's party passed through the Sierra San Vicente where his men could see the old presidio of San Vicente a few miles downstream on the Mexican side of the river. After nearly a century of abandonment, the fortress stood crumbling before the harsh desert environment. Continu-ing their survey from Presidio San Vicente, the men crossed through the rough and broken country of the Chihuahuan desert until they arrived at the mouth of still another great chasm, which Chandler named the Cañon de Sierra Carmel (present Boquillas Canyon), which slices deeply and nar-rowly through the precipitous Sierra Del Carmen. There the party made camp and waited to be supplied.[14]

Duff Green, meanwhile, unable to follow Chandler's trail through the tortuous mountains southeast of Presidio del Norte, crossed the Río Grande into Mexico with the supply train, and, like Chandler's party before him, circumvented Santa Elena Canyon. A few miles downstream from the lower mouth of the canyon the young infantry officer reported an open area on the American side of the river that was well timbered and suitable for cultivation. Given its proximity to one of the great Comanche trails that crossed into Mexico (near present Lajitas, Texas), Green deter-

Major General William Hemsley Emory, the indefatigable scientific advisor and
military commander of the United States–Mexico Boundary Survey team that
explored the lower Río Grande valley in 1851–52. *(Courtesy, National Archives,
Washington, D.C.)*

Artist's view of the Chisos Mountains as they appeared to M. T. W. Chandler
and his survey team in 1852. The most prominent point visible is Emory Peak,
named for the soldier-scientist commander of the boundary survey team.
(Courtesy, National Archives, Washington, D.C.)

mined the site to be "deffinitely [*sic*] marked for a military post." That the location could be easily connected by a wagon route with the recently established El Paso-San Antonio road added strong support to Green's assessment of the area.[15] After several waterless days of travel through the Sierra San Vicente, on October 29 the military escort and train joined Chandler and his men at their camp near the mouth of Boquillas Canyon.

During the next several days, Chandler and Green discussed the possibility of discontinuing the survey. They agreed that any further advance would be difficult and impractical because of the shortage of supplies and the physical deterioration of the men. Some of the members, were suffering from extreme hunger, while others lacked adequate shoes and clothing. In light of these difficulties, Chandler discussed the proposition with the other men. Geologist C. C. Parry, in charge of surveying the area near Boquillas Canyon, favored discontinuing the survey. In his opinion, the difficulties they had hitherto encountered made suspension "not a matter of choice but necessity." Other members of the party concurred.

With the full support of his men, Chandler reluctantly addressed a letter to Major Emory informing him of his decision to abort the survey at Cañon de Sierra Carmel, leave the river, and lead his spent crew on the easiest route (east across Mexican territory) to Eagle Pass. The weary surveyor ended his letter on a somewhat pessimistic note: "I expect (God willing) to report to you in person with my notes in about eighteen days." Supporting the decision, Lieutenant Green's final report cited high praises for Chandler's courage in overcoming "natural obstacles almost impassible" throughout the ordeal.[16]

Despite having to terminate their river survey 100 miles short of the Pecos River, Chandler and his men achieved what others before them had failed to do. Indeed, Major Emory later expressed pleasure at what his subordinates had accomplished. That great portion of Texas which "had never been traversed by civilized man," he emphasized, had finally been surveyed and properly mapped. Months later, Dr. Parry, while "glad of a resting place after the fatiguing journey," recognized the importance of the commission's performance upon closer examination of his geological notes. Combined with the efforts of Lieutenant Michler, who sailed downstream from Reagan Canyon to the mouth of the Pecos, the success of these daring explorers of the Big Bend ranks alongside those of later, more famous, explorations of the Colorado River. By September 1853 the most difficult portion of the United States–Mexico Boundary Survey was

Artistic rendering of Boquillas Canyon as it appeared to members of the United States–Mexico Boundary Survey Commission in 1852. It was at this point that members of the expedition decided to abort their mission short of completion. *(Courtesy, National Archives, Washington, D.C.)*

successfully completed. There remained only one more reconnaissance of the Río Grande valley for the Topographical Corps to undertake.[17]

The canyon country of the lower Río Grande lay unattended until just prior to the outbreak of the Civil War. Immediately following the completion of the wagon road surveys, the army proceeded with the fulfillment of its second objective — the establishment of military defense structures in the trans-Pecos territory. Upon completion of Fort Davis, 120 miles north of the Río Grande, the army had to determine a suitable supply route through the Big Bend country to this isolated military outpost.[18] In April 1859 the War Department issued orders providing that an expedition be organized for this purpose. This mission differed from previous excursions into West Texas, however, because the army selected the Chihuahuan desert as an experimental area to test the use of Arabian camels as pack animals instead of the traditional mule. A second — though perhaps more important — objective was the location of a fort site along the Río Grande.

Second Lieutenant Edward L. Hartz of the Eighth Infantry commanded the initial expedition into the Big Bend, which left San Antonio on May 18, 1859, for Camp Hudson. While at this military fort on the Devil's River, Hartz and his assistant from the Topographical Corps, Brevet Second Lieutenant William Echols, gathered the camels, their Arabian drivers, and the necessary supplies for their journey. After nearly a month of travel in which the men experienced numerous delays because of problems with the camels, Hartz and Echols arrived at Fort Davis. On July 11, 1859, the camel train continued its southward reconnaissance from Camp Stockton at Comanche Springs (present Fort Stockton, Texas) to Willow Spring (south of Marathon, Texas). From here Hartz and Echols followed the same trail that nomadic Indians had used for centuries in their travels across Big Bend. The Comanche Trail led the party through Persimmon Gap (north of present Big Bend National Park) and down Tornillo Creek toward the crossing at the Río Grande, located opposite Presidio San Vicente. After exploring and mapping the region between Boquillas and Mariscal Canyons for about a week, the expedition returned north, satisfied that the experiment with the camels was, on the whole, a success.[19]

Hartz's superiors, however, were less satisfied with the results of his mission. In the first place, the infantry officer had failed to make any recommendations for a fort to be located along the Río Grande. "A permanent arrangement of posts on the Río Grande frontier I consider very important," wrote Colonel Robert E. Lee, then in command of the Texas Department. In his opinion, defense of the area was vital to the protection of settlers who were beginning to occupy the Big Bend. Equally important, if it hoped to maintain good diplomatic relations with Mexico, the United States had an obligation to protect the frontier against Indian depredations along the border. For these reasons, Colonel Lee ordered yet another reconnaissance of West Texas to locate the much desired site for the future construction of a fort.

This time, however, the burden of responsibility fell upon the shoulders of Lieutenant Echols, who on June 24, 1860, departed Camp Hudson and headed west with his camels and thirty-six soldiers. Echols experimented with a more circuitous route to the Big Bend that led him first to Fort Davis, then southwest to Presidio del Norte. From there he headed east until reaching the San Carlos branch of the Comanche Trail near Lajitas. From this point, Echols paralleled the Río Grande to the mouth of Santa Elena Canyon, which he named the Grand Puerta.

After a thorough examination of the "wonderful curiosity," Echols marched his men in a broad northeasterly circle around the mountains until he intersected Terlingua Creek. He then followed the stream to the point where it flows into the Río Grande on the opposite side of Santa Elena Canyon. Next, Echols turned east and followed the Río Grande to its confluence with Alamo Creek. It was this location that the engineer felt best facilitated the construction of a fort. "Satisfied that there is no better place on the river for building a post of any dimensions than that I had found," the lieutenant returned to Fort Davis to report his findings. Thus Echols — not unlike Duff Green in 1852 — was impressed with the area a few miles upstream from present Castolon, Texas, as a potential defensive position on the Río Grande.[20]

The Civil War abruptly terminated the early topographical explorations in the American Southwest, but not before the army had established a remarkable record. As military engineers, the Corps successfully surveyed and mapped thousands of miles of open territory. The network of roads charted, furthermore, laid the foundation for a more extensive system of transcontinental railroads, which fostered the settlement of the West. In their role as scientists, they observed and recorded little-known facts about the physical characteristics of the arid West which served as a compendium of knowledge for the settlers who followed them.

Regarding the Big Bend region of Texas, the efforts of the Topographical Engineers brought a hostile and uninviting territory under the protective umbrella of the federal largess. In the years that followed the Civil War, America's interminable westward thrust brought unceasing pressure upon the United States Army to protect the nation's settlers. The Indians, meanwhile, in a final desperate struggle to preserve their ancestral homeland, launched a furious assault in retaliation against the unwelcome intruders. Central to the protection of the Texas frontier, Big Bend assumed increasing importance in the War Department's comprehensive defense planning for the construction of a line of forts along the Río Grande.

CHAPTER FOUR

The Doctrine of Hot Pursuit

If the government will say that there shall be no boundary line when we are driven to the necessity of protecting our lives and property, there never will be another raid on the Río Grande.

— *Lt. Gen. Philip Sheridan, 1873*

The 1848 Treaty of Guadalupe-Hidalgo, together with the Louisiana Purchase negotiated with France in 1803, formalized the two most important territorial additions in the history of the United States. With the American victory in the Mexican War, Hispanic hegemony over the vast domain that lay west of the Mississippi River came to an end. Under the terms of the treaty, Mexico agreed to cede that area now encompassing California, New Mexico, Texas, Utah, Nevada, and portions of Arizona and Colorado. The addition of these southwestern territories altogether added 1.2 million square miles to the continental boundaries of the United States. But with the final ratification of the treaty, the United States became obligated for military defense along the Río Grande. Article XI of the agreement provided that the United States would bear the burden of responsibility for restraining Indian attacks along the international border. In accepting the terms of this document, Washington pledged to station troops in Texas to protect the northern Mexican states against Indian incursions.

As responsibility for frontier defense shifted from Mexican authority to the United States, Texas became the objective of strategic planning within the War Department. During the next decade, a perimeter of military installations roughly paralleling the course of the Río Grande served as the mainstay of defense for an advancing line of American settlement into the Southwest. If the target had a nucleus, it was the Big Bend. Long the stronghold of Apache and Comanche raiding parties, the mountain sanctuaries known as the Chisos and the Sierra del Carmen ranges enabled Indians to escape the wrath of Spanish and Mexican retaliation.

Local authorities on both sides of the border experienced only marginal success in protecting their settlements against Indian attacks, requiring the United States government to extend a forceful hand toward the security of the Texas frontier.[1]

The Great Comanche Trail, previously explored by members of the Topographical Corps of Engineers, was one feature of the Big Bend that attracted the attention of the army to West Texas. Since the late eighteenth century, the trail, actually a fan-like series of converging paths leading south toward the Río Grande, served as a major thoroughfare for Indian raiding parties en route to the population centers of northern Mexico. The trail began at Comanche Springs (present Fort Stockton), a favorite watering spot for migrating bands of Comanches, Apaches, and Kiowas. From that point, it favored a southerly orientation toward the vicinity of present Marathon, Texas, where it divided into two distinct branches.

The west branch, more commonly known as the San Carlos Trail, was the most heavily used of the two routes. Beginning at a point just above Marathon, the path ran in a southwest direction to a crossing on the Río Grande near present Lajitas, Texas. The east branch, also known as the Chisos Trail, headed due south from Marathon, piercing the Santiago Mountains at Persimmon Gap (the northernmost entrance to present Big Bend National Park). From this point it ran just west of and parallel to Tornillo Creek along its course toward the Río Grande, where it crossed near the old presidio at San Vicente.[2]

In the 1780s Mescalero and Lipan Apaches favored the Chisos Trail because it passed down a relatively easy corridor between the Chisos Mountains and the Sierra del Carmen—and which route offered a plenteous supply of water. By the nineteenth century, Comanche war parties followed this same route into Mexico. The Plains Indians used the western branch more as a trade route to San Carlos, or as a means of escaping Spanish and Mexican dragoons in hot pursuit.[3]

In December 1848 Secretary of War Marcy took steps to assure the fulfillment of United States treaty obligations to Mexico by dispatching federal troops to the Río Grande. Reports filed early the following year with the Adjutant General's Office, however, showed only 1,074 soldiers stationed in Texas. This paltry display of force could hardly defend a thousand-mile frontier that stretched from the Gulf of Mexico to El Paso. Nevertheless, the War Department established the Eighth Military Department in Texas and placed Brevet Major General George M. Brooke in command of its forces. Instructed to bear in mind that Mexican territory was as much entitled to protection against Indian attacks as that of the United States, Brooke began the task of emplacing a defense perimeter along the international border.

General Brooke's first assignment, which began in late 1848, was to oversee the construction of a cordon of border posts. Commencing with Fort Brown, the defense line inched its way up the Río Grande from Brownsville to Fort Ringgold (Río Grande City, Texas), Fort McIntosh (Laredo, Texas), and Fort Duncan (Eagle Pass, Texas), completed in 1849. Two years later, Brooke's successor, Brevet Major General Persifor F. Smith, extended the defense network across the East Texas plains from Fort Belknap (Newcastle, Texas) to its southern anchor, Fort Clark (Bracketville, Texas), located twenty-five miles east of the Río Grande. Thus, by 1852 Texas had an inner and outer defense ring encompassing its major settlements centered mostly around San Antonio and Austin. The hope that this defense system would restrain the Northern Plains Indians from assailing their victims living on the threshold of the Chihuahuan desert soon waned. Comanches and their allied brethren, the Kiowas, effortlessly slipped between the remote outposts to stage their raids with calculated success. In the first place, the army could not deter the Indians because it lacked an adequate number of mounted cavalry. A mobile enemy required swift and effective retaliatory response. The army in Texas, comprised mostly of infantry, found itself ill-prepared to meet the challenge of its mounted adversary. Even with an auxiliary force of Texas Rangers, the army was hard-pressed at this time to protect the American frontier.

Citizens of northern Mexico were clearly discouraged with the inability of American forces to halt the Indian invasion. Between 1848 and 1853, incursions into Mexico not only increased in severity, but extended farther south than ever before. Those states bordering Texas — in particular Chihuahua and Coahuila — suffered extensive property damage and loss of life. The deaths attributed to the Indians during these years for Coahuila alone numbered 191. Mexican newspapers were quick to editorialize their outrage toward the United States for failing to comply with its obligations under the Treaty of Guadalupe-Hidalgo.

In February 1852 Chihuahuan authorities sought permission in Washington for Mexican forces to cross the Río Grande in an all-out offensive against the Indians. With this unusual request, the Mexican government made clear not only its disappointment in the failure of the United States

A view of the parade ground at Fort Davis, Texas, taken from the North Ridge sometime in 1885. Fort Davis was the cornerstone of a cordon of American military forts established to protect the San Antonio to El Paso Road. *(Courtesy, National Park Service, Fort Davis National Historic Site, Texas)*

to provide adequate protection, but also expressed a desire to address Indian unrest in its own way. Using Mexican self-determination as a pretext, the State Department initiated steps to obtain a release from all commitments agreed to in 1848. The solution took the form of a second treaty, negotiated in 1853, between the two nations. The Gadsden Purchase, in which the United States paid Mexico $10 million for a strip of land north of the Gila River in the present state of Arizona, also provided for the abrogation of Article IX of the Treaty of Guadalupe-Hidalgo. No longer committed to the protection of the Mexican frontier, the War Department devoted its full attention to Texas and the remaining southwestern territories.[4]

Whiting and Smith's survey of the San Antonio to El Paso road in 1849 necessitated the positioning of a line of defense installations running west across Texas from the Davis Mountains to the New Mexico Territory. Cradled in the heart of the fertile Limpia Creek valley, Fort Davis, built in 1854, served as the linchpin for the new alignment. From this post the men of the Eighth Infantry staged a campaign against the Mescalero Apaches that resulted in their stunning defeat and removal to their present-day reservation east of Tularosa, New Mexico. In addition, the fort served as a supply depot and staging area for troop movements between San Antonio and El Paso. In 1859 Fort Davis provided rest and provisions for Hartz and Echols en route to the Big Bend country to experiment with the use of camels.

When the lower road from San Antonio to El Paso assumed importance as a federal mail route, the obligation for increased military protection became imperative. In 1859 the famous Butterfield Overland Mail established service to West Texas. The company's request that the soldiers of Fort Davis ensure the safety of the route against Comanche raiders forced a build-up of troops in the trans-Pecos region. Fort Stockton, founded in 1859 at Comanche Springs, the point at which the lower road intersected with the Great Comanche Trail, provided additional security for the overland express.

In one short decade, therefore, the War Department accomplished the first phase of its strategic operations in the American Southwest. These carefully placed military facilities shaped the perimeter of settlement destined to populate the barren territories of America's expanded national domain. While the garrisons never reached their desired troop strength, the mere presence of forts on the Indian frontier hastened the westward flow of land-hungry pioneers. In Texas the Comanches, Kiowas, and

Apaches remained steadfast in their resistance to the intruders. Their attempts to stem the tide of migration resulted in open warfare that ravaged the western plains. Their recalcitrance, moreover, forced the governments of the United States and Mexico to engage every resource available to subdue them.

For the moment, however, U.S. military advisors in Washington were preoccupied with an impending Civil War. The secession of Texas from the Union on January 28, 1861, and the Confederate bombardment of Fort Sumter later that spring, brought the first phase of the federal occupation of Texas to an abrupt halt. In that year, the United States surrendered all of its military property in Texas to the Confederacy and began the immediate withdrawal of all troops.[5] Making no distinctions between the blue coats and the gray, the Indians did not welcome Texas' most recent occupants. In fact, the absence of a well-conceived system of military defense throughout the remainder of the Civil War left Texas and northern Mexico vulnerable to increased attacks.

While the United States endeavored to maintain peace in Texas, Mexico also committed its limited resources to the defense of the Río Grande. Beginning with the strategic reorganization of the Mexican frontier in 1848, military colonies assumed the primary role of Indian defense. Notably, San Carlos and San Vicente, two colonies flanking the Big Bend on the west and east respectively, were important elements of the new protection strategy. Divided into three military districts, a total of eighteen colonies dotted the expanse of Mexico's northern frontier. Eligible male citizens within each colony received a parcel of land for cultivation in exchange for military service to the government.

The establishment of military towns on the northern frontier corresponded to the habitation of that region. While each colonist was expected to take up arms in the defense of his property, he was also encouraged to promote the permanent settlement of the Río Grande valley through the cultivation of land. In 1850 the government placed military units at El Paso, Del Norte (formerly La Junta de los Ríos), Pilares, and San Carlos, in the state of Chihuahua. The following year it authorized the military colonies of Guerrero, Monclova Viejo, Santa Rosa, and San Vicente, in the state of Coahuila. Of the 2,426 troops stationed in northern Mexico at this time, 1,715 were cavalry equipped with mounts and munitions needed for rapid deployment to any troubled spot along the border. Whether cavalry or infantry, these men were, however, farmers and not professional soldiers.[6]

Closely linked to the idea of maintaining a citizen militia, the Mexican government revived the old Hispanic tradition of utilizing Indian allies to bolster defenses along the international border. During these years, the Seminole and Kickapoo Indians made a significant contribution to the defensive effectiveness of the Mexican Army. During the summer of 1850, authorities at Piedras Negras (across the Río Grande from present Eagle Pass, Texas) were startled to find two hundred Seminoles, Kickapoos, and runaway black slaves seeking permission from the Mexican government to enter the country as colonists.

The Seminoles, a tribe indigenous to the swamplands of southern Florida, fiercely resisted American occupation of that territory until their defeat in the 1840s. During the presidency of Andrew Jackson, the Seminoles, along with several other tribes who had occupied territory east of the Mississippi River, were summarily removed to Indian Territory (the present state of Oklahoma). Accompanying the Seminoles on their epic journey west were about four hundred blacks who had escaped southern plantations to find refuge among the Florida Indians. Once arrived in Oklahoma, the Seminoles became embroiled in a power struggle with other removed tribes. The political confrontation forced some members of the Seminole tribe to leave the reservation.

One Seminole warrior, Coacoochee, a well-proportioned man of about forty years with a passion for fine jewelry, led a band of one hundred Seminoles south toward the Río Grande. Known as Wild Cat to the Americans (Coacoochee means "Wild Cat"), he became the undisputed leader of the renegade band. In addition to Wild Cat's warriors, a group of Black Seminoles, under the aegis of their leader, named Gopher John, joined the exodus from Oklahoma to northern Mexico. There they hoped to begin life anew among the inhabitants of the Río Grande frontier. While traveling through West Texas, Wild Cat and his party encountered a band of Kickapoo Indians also moving south from their reservation near Fort Leavenworth on the Missouri River. Inasmuch as the Kickapoos left their reservation under similar circumstances as the Seminoles, Wild Cat invited the them to join his party in seeking refuge in Mexico.

The Kickapoos originated in the Wabash River country of Illinois and Indiana, where they were members of the Algonquin brotherhood. Renowned militarists, the Kickapoos were the target of French and British appeals for a military alliance during the French and Indian War. The tribe's allegiance to England during the American Revolution, furthermore, fostered a deep-seated antipathy for the United States. Kickapoo hatred for Americans gained impetus with their removal in 1819 from the Wabash Valley to the Kansas plains. While they were promised uninterrupted freedom under a formal treaty with the federal government, the Kickapoos were driven farther south with each succeeding wave of westward immigrants. By 1850 three overland trails trespassed upon their territory. In addition, the pony express route from St. Louis and the military road from Fort Leavenworth cut through Kickapoo hunting grounds, forcing several tribal members to abandon these lands and migrate south into Texas.[7]

On July 12, 1850, Wild Cat appeared before Colonel Juan Manuel Maldonado, subinspector of the state of Coahuila, to petition for land, tools, oxen, and firearms. The garrison commander, beleaguered by incessant raiding from Comanches and Apaches, welcomed the military expertise of the new arrivals. He tentatively granted their request until he could obtain official word from Mexico City. Just three months later, a second group of more than a hundred blacks arrived in Piedras Negras to join forces with Wild Cat. Initially, the Seminoles and their followers were settled at various points along the Río Grande. First, they occupied Guerrero, a military colony a few miles below Piedras Negras; later they moved to San Fernando de Rosas (present Zaragosa, Coahuila), southwest of Piedras Negras.

During the next decade, Wild Cat, or Gato del Monte as the Mexicans called him, led his mixed band of Seminole and Kickapoo mercenaries into the Big Bend on numerous military forays against Comanches and Apaches. Their pursuit of the elusive enemy took them to San Carlos and San Vicente, both of which served as staging areas for offensive expeditions into the Chisos mountain country. On one occasion, the tireless Seminole chief tracked a band of Mescalero Apaches for three hundred miles, finally forcing them to seek refuge with the commandant at San Carlos. Granting their request for protection, Captain Don Diego Elguezábal refused to allow Wild Cat entrance into the presidio. Unable to carry out his mission to conclusion, Wild Cat returned to his headquarters in Coahuila and informed his superiors that he had found the Mescaleros, but that they were "in great harmony" with the Mexican officer at San Carlos.

The military successes of the Seminoles and the Kickapoos won them high praise from Mexican officials. In late 1851 President Mariano Arista rewarded Wild Cat and his followers for their contribution to the defense of the northern frontier by granting the Seminoles four parcels of irrigable land in the Santa Rosa Mountains of Coahuila. The townsite, to be named Nacimiento de los Negros, was situated a few miles northwest of the military colony of Santa Rosa (present Múzquiz). Colonel Emilio Langberg, commander of all forces along the Río Grande, personally distributed provisions and farm implements to the highly regarded warriors. Considered to be "the finest agricultural region in Coahuila," Nacimiento served as the permanent home of the Seminoles and their black kinsmen for the remainder of their stay in Mexico. The Kickapoos, meanwhile, were granted a similar concession of land farther north at Remolino, near the military colony of Monclova Viejo.

The Seminole presence in Coahuila proved to be a mixed blessing to the Mexican government. On one hand, their skilled tactics and military prowess brought peace to the border frontier. During their tenure at Nacimiento, these seasoned warriors participated in no fewer than forty campaigns against the Southern Plains Indians. Relentless trackers, the Seminole-Kickapoo army frequently pursued their enemy for weeks at a time until there was no alternative but to engage in combat.

On the other hand, the ongoing relationship between the Florida Indians and the runaway slaves who lived with them proved to be a long-term liability to Mexico. Beginning in 1851 Texas slave owners organized a series of filibuster campaigns into Mexican territory designed to recapture the Black Seminoles and return them to bondage. Although never entirely successful, armed Texans crossed the Río Grande at least once every year until the outbreak of the Civil War.

Under growing pressure from the Mexican government to return to the United States, compounded by Wild Cat's death during a smallpox epidemic in the spring of 1857, the Seminoles abandoned Nacimiento. On March 23, 1859, the state of Coahuila issued an official decree providing for the removal of all Seminole Indians and Black Seminoles from their lands. Under new leadership, the Seminoles elected to return to their reservation in Oklahoma. The combat-seasoned veterans of the Mexican frontier returned to join their tribal kinsmen in support of the Confederacy against the Union. The Black Seminoles, meanwhile, refused to reenter United States territory while slavery remained in effect. Instead, their new chief, John Kibbits, led them across the north Mexican desert where they served the Mexican Army as scouts and mercenaries. Significantly, the experience gained from fighting Apaches and Comanches over the next decade made this handful of black frontiersmen a valuable asset to the United States Army in future years.[8]

The Union victory over the Confederacy in 1865 hastened a mass migration of pioneers away from the war-torn battlefields east of the Mississippi toward the land of opportunity in the West. The population of the isolated southwestern territories soared with the addition of more than three million newcomers between 1870 and 1880. With the arrival of the nation's first transcontinental railroad, the native inhabitants of the Great Plains experienced a rapid disappearance of their ancestral homeland. Pressured on the north by an advancing white man's frontier, the Kiowas, Comanches, and Apaches of West Texas pushed deeper into the southern extremities of the Chihuahuan desert. Again, the Big Bend region became the focal point of military activity along the Río Grande.

The military reoccupation of Texas began in earnest by mid-1867. Under the guidance of Major General Philip H. Sheridan, commander of the Fifth Military District (which included Texas), the army revitalized its prewar defense system. First, the quartermaster department rehabilitated forts along the Río Grande that had been abandoned at the outbreak of the Civil War. The defense cordon from Fort Brown to Fort Clark reinstated a protective network along the United States-Mexico border. Next, the army assured the security of the San Antonio to El Paso road with the reoccupation of Forts Stockton and Davis. The addition of new outposts such as Fort Concho (near present San Angelo, Texas) bolstered the defenses within the interior. By late 1868 a dozen military detachments in as many installations stood poised to protect the ever-increasing citizenry of Texas.

The election of General Ulysses S. Grant to the presidency in November 1868 assured military leaders that a forceful Indian policy would be imposed in the West. Central to the success of the army's offensive strategy against the guerrilla tactics of the Indians, the concept of "total war" pervaded the thinking of most military planners. If the Indians were to be subdued, they argued, their lines of supply had to be completely destroyed, their villages attacked without warning, and all who openly resisted, whether men, women, or children, were to be considered combatants and dealt with accordingly.

In its effort to meet these objectives, the army enlisted the services of "friendly" Indians as well as seasoned frontiersmen skilled in the wilderness arts of tracking and land survival. In the ensuing years these auxiliary forces served as scouts, forging the way for the army in an unyielding pursuit of the enemy. For this reason, perhaps, when a party of Black Seminoles appeared before the commanding officer at Fort Duncan,

Texas, and offered to assist the United States Army in its war against the Plains Indians, their services were readily accepted.

On the morning of March 17, 1870, Brevet Colonel J. C. DeGress, commander of the Ninth Cavalry stationed at Fort Duncan, mustered his all-black enlisted personnel for reveille. Much to his astonishment, a band of one hundred Black Seminoles, just arrived from Piedras Negras on the opposite side of the Río Grande, greeted him. Their leader, John Kibbits, informed Colonel DeGress that his party was returning to the Seminole reservation in Indian Territory. While living in Mexico, the chief learned that a treaty concluded between the United States government and the Seminole tribe in 1866 guaranteed "all the rights of native citizens" to his people. With slavery no longer an issue, Kibbits determined it was time to leave Mexico after twenty years of self-imposed exile and return his people to the reservation.

Once arrived at Fort Duncan, the Seminole spokesman agreed to enlist the services of some of his men as scouts. In exchange, the tribe received cash payments and provisions of food. Eager to accept the services of the Black Seminoles, DeGress wrote to his superiors applauding "their ability as good trailers and their awareness of the habits of the Indians." With approval from Washington, these hardy survivors of numerous Indian campaigns on the northern Mexican desert prepared to embark upon a new and illustrious military career as scouts for the United States Army.

Never numbering over fifty men at any time, the Seminole Negro Indian Scouts, which became their official military designation, were initially attached to Fort Duncan. By the fall of 1871 the army stationed a second unit of Seminole scouts under the leadership of Elijah Daniels at Fort Clark. Some years later, this latter element of Black Seminole scouts staged their final military reconnaissances from Camp Neville Spring, located in the heart of present Big Bend National Park.[9]

The appearance of the Black Seminoles at Forts Duncan and Clark at this time was more than just coincidence. Perhaps aware of lingering prejudices toward blacks during the postwar period, Kibbits sought help among his own kind. It was common knowledge that these forts along the Río Grande headquartered elements of the Ninth Cavalry and the Twenty-fifth Infantry, known more popularly on the western frontier as the "Buffalo Soldiers." These units were unique as components of the United States Army because they consisted of black enlisted personnel commanded by white officers. Assigned to some of the most remote outposts in West Texas throughout the latter half of the nineteenth century,

"Buffalo Soldier" as he may have appeared in field dress in the 1870s. This trooper was a member of the all-black Tenth Cavalry unit stationed on the West Texas frontier. *(Courtesy, National Archives, Washington, D.C.)*

"Buffalo Soldiers" in parade dress at Fort Davis in 1875. These all-black fighting units of the United States Army earned considerable fame on the West Texas frontier and later in Arizona. *(Courtesy, National Park Service, Fort Davis National Historic Site, Texas)*

the Buffalo Soldiers proved themselves time and again worthy of recognition in the army's struggle against the Indians. Appropriately, the addition of the Seminole scouts represented a unique but welcome complement to these seasoned regiments.

Not unlike other black units, the Seminole scouts assigned to Fort Clark were placed under the command of a white junior-grade officer. Lieutenant John Lapham Bullis, a vigorous, wiry little man with a pencil-like mustache, enthusiastically accepted his new command in early 1873. A combat veteran of the Army of the Potomac during the Civil War, Bullis developed a desert-wise acuteness for the West Texas frontier beginning in 1869 with his first assignment to that region. His capacity for physical endurance, particularly in the harsh desert environment, not only prepared the officer for his latest assignment, but also endeared him personally to his subordinates. Suffering alongside his Seminole scouts, Bullis survived many days without food or water tracking Indians across the Texas plains.

Since their arrival in 1850, the Kickapoo presence in Mexico created a new set of problems for American defense forces stationed along the Río Grande. Civil unrest in Mexico during the 1870s, coupled with the weak leadership of President Sebastian Lerdo de Tejada, caused that government to turn its back on the security needs of the Río Grande district. The result was relative lawlessness along the border that enabled a loose confederation of Kickapoos and Apaches to plunder the surrounding territories without reprisal. Unsuspecting cattle ranchers in the Big Bend and other areas of West Texas became favorite targets of the Indians. While the Mexican government focused its attention on political instability within the capital, the Indians disposed of thousands of stolen cattle, horses, and other contraband to merchants and traders living in the numerous border towns.

In addition to the Kickapoos, the Apaches continued to plague the inhabitants of the Río Grande frontier. Although few in number, the Lipan Apaches, living near the Mexican community of Zaragosa, Coahuila, enjoyed remarkable success under the capable leadership of Chief Washa Lobo. Meanwhile, Mangas Coloradas, leader of the Warm Spring Apaches, preferred to inhabit the territory near the Mexican village of San Carlos, where his band terrorized the Big Bend. Most numerous, however, were the Kickapoos living on the outskirts of Nacimiento (near present Múzquiz) and on the upper Río San Diego at Remolino. Estimated at more than thirteen hundred strong, the Kickapoos crossed

One of two Seminole Negro Indian Scout Units stationed at Fort Clark near Brackettville, Texas, in the 1880s. Some of these men may have been detached to Camp Neville Spring under the command of 2d Lieutenant Charles Grierson. *(Courtesy, Museum of the Big Bend, Alpine, Texas)*

the Río Grande virtually at will to carry out their attacks on Texas citizens. Responding to the desperate appeals of these victims, the State Department pressed Mexico to allow American troops to cross the international border in hot pursuit. Their pleas, however, fell upon deaf ears.

In January 1873 President Grant divulged his plans for a more assertive policy directed against the Kickapoos. He enlisted Colonel Ranald Slidell Mackenzie, whom the president considered to be "the most promising young officer of the army," to lead a strike force against the Indians that would presumably take U.S. troops deep into Mexican territory. The spring of 1873 found Lieutenant Bullis and his Seminoles preparing for the first of many military offensives against the Kickapoos. Mackenzie assembled his punitive force of four hundred well-armed troops at Fort Clark, which included Bullis and twenty-five of the Black Seminole scouts. Their objective was a group of Kickapoo villages concentrated near Remolino. At seven o'clock on the morning of May 18, Mackenzie's command attacked the villages swiftly and decisively.[10]

While the Battle of Remolino dealt a crushing blow to Kickapoo supremacy on the Río Grande, it also raised serious diplomatic questions about the violation of Mexico's territorial sovereignty under the pretext of border security. Heated arguments between Mexico and the United States centered around the doctrine of hot pursuit. General Sheridan, voicing support of Mackenzie's action, assured Secretary of War William Belknap that "if the government will stand firm we are near the end of all difficulties on the Mexican frontier." The Mexican government, however, rebutted that the raid was a flagrant assault on the unsuspecting Kickapoos; therefore, the doctrine of hot pursuit was clearly inapplicable in this case.[11]

Violation of the international boundary remained a diplomatic problem between the two governments for the next several years. Unquestionably, Mackenzie's raid into Mexico was an affront to its territorial sovereignty. Still, it would not be the last time that United States or Mexican troops ignored the international line while attempting to resolve the "Indian problem." The sworn testimony of one Mexican soldier, Eustaquio Garza, confirmed that the Mexican Army crossed the Río Grande in June 1874 with a hundred men and chased Indians as far north as the Guadalupe Mountains.[12] Similarly, the U.S. Army, usually with Lieutenant Bullis and his Seminole scouts leading the way, crossed the Río Grande whenever they felt it necessary.

Brigadier General Ranald Slidell Mackenzie who, according to President Ulysses S. Grant, was one of the fastest rising officers in the United States Army. He led the campaign against the Kickapoos at Remolino, Coahuila, Mexico, in 1873. *(Courtesy, National Archives, Washington, D.C.)*

Interior of a troop barracks at Fort Clark ca. 1875 near Brackettville, Texas. It is typical of those on the West Texas frontier. *(Courtesy, National Archives, Washington, D.C.)*

The accession of revolutionary strongman Porfirio Díaz to the presidency of Mexico in 1876 brought a solution to the diplomatic stalemate between the two governments. Unlike the weaker administrations of the past, the Díaz regime assured the United States that it would employ tougher measures to prevent lawlessness along the Río Grande. Hoping to gain diplomatic recognition for his government, Díaz made good his promise by dispatching General Geronimo Treviño north to inflict punishment on all violators — Indian or Mexican — of the international boundary.

Improved cooperation between U.S. and Mexican forces paved the way for a joint military operation against one of the last remaining Apache threats to the Texas-Mexico frontier. Washington's policy of concentrating all Apaches onto a single, miserable reservation at San Carlos, Arizona, proved to be a regrettable decision. In September 1877, Victorio, the capable and aggressive leader of the Warm Spring Apaches, convinced more than three hundred followers to leave the reservation. For the next three years the daring Apache field general led the army on a bewildering chase that eventually terminated on the fringes of the Big Bend. In the fall of 1880 components of the Twenty-fourth Infantry, the Ninth and Tenth Cavalry (Buffalo Soldiers), and the Seminole scouts from Fort Clark joined forces with the Mexican Army in a desperate maneuver to recapture the elusive renegade.

Colonel Benjamin Henry Grierson commanded the black forces of the Tenth Cavalry dispatched from Fort Concho to aid in the campaign. Grierson, a quiet, unassuming man, commanded the Tenth Cavalry since its creation in August 1866. In the decade that followed, the former music teacher and Civil War hero led his troops on a circuitous military excursion across the West that finally brought the unit to Texas. The Victorio War afforded Grierson and his underrated soldiers an opportunity to prove themselves in battle. With orders from General Sheridan to engage the enemy, Grierson's army departed Fort Concho in July 1880 and proceeded to Big Bend country.

Grierson's strategy was simple. Rather than exhaust his forces in a fruitless chase across the Texas desert, he decided to position his men at key watering holes in anticipation of meeting Victorio in combat. The uncomplicated plan proved successful. Desperately in need of water, Victorio and 150 warriors tried to drive off the men of the Tenth from Tinaja de las Palmas in Quitman Canyon (northwest of present Fort

General Benjamin Henry Grierson, the quiet but efficient commander of the all-black units at Fort Davis. He spearheaded the United States campaign against renegade Apaches to help bring peace to the Big Bend. *(Courtesy, National Archives, Washington, D.C.)*

Victorio, leader of the Warm Springs Apaches and chief adversary of the U.S. Army in Texas, New Mexico, and Arizona. An able field general, Victorio eluded capture for many years before his death at the hands of Mexican troops in 1880. *(Courtesy, National Archives, Washington, D.C.)*

Davis). Grierson's troops, however, forced the Apaches into retreat. On August 6 the determined renegade chief crossed the Río Grande once again only to have the American soldiers drive him back from Rattlesnake Springs. This time, however, New Mexico cavalry units chased Victorio across the border and into the hands of Colonel Joaquin Terrazas and four hundred Chihuahuan soldiers at Tres Castillos. On October 15, 1880, Terrazas attacked the Indian camp by surprise. Among those killed was Victorio (Indian survivors claimed that he took his own life when he saw that all was lost), and the epic saga of one the most notorious Apache chiefs in the history of the Southwest was brought to a dramatic conclusion.[13]

Victorio's death by no means ended hostility in the Big Bend. On the contrary, while his uprising may have been the last serious Indian threat to the Texas frontier, citizens along the Río Grande still had to contend with Mexican and Anglo bandits. In 1882 President Díaz at last agreed to a reciprocal treaty between his country and the United States. While both signatories agreed to the doctrine of hot pursuit as it applied to Indian raids, they made no provision for local bandits. With no legal provision for pursuit, crossing the Río Grande back into Mexico gave cattle rustlers and horse thieves immunity from punishment.

Fear of recurring Indian unrest, coupled with increased Mexican banditry in the Big Bend, caused such concern among military officials at Fort Davis that they authorized the establishment in 1879 of a sub-post closer to the Río Grande. Camp Peña Colorado, located four miles south of present Marathon, Texas, housed elements of the Tenth Cavalry, and the twenty-fifth infantry recently transferred from Fort Concho to Fort Davis. In addition, the new camp served as an outpost for one unit of twenty Seminole Indian scouts detached from Fort Clark. The scouts, who with Lieutenant Bullis had once chased Apaches out of the Sierra del Carmen into the vicinity of Boquillas Canyon, were already familiar with the rugged terrain of the Big Bend.[14]

In 1884 an incident involving Mexican bandits again created diplomatic tension between the governments of Mexico and the United States. In November officials at Fort Davis received word that a band of Indians raided Brough's mining camp, located about thirty miles southwest of the Rosillos Mountains (near present Government Spring in Big Bend National Park). The Indians reportedly killed all the members of the Petty family, said to be employed at the camp. On the morning of November 17, Captain Robert G. Smither assembled Troops A and B of the Tenth

Infantry unit ca. 1880 engaging in target practice near Fort Concho, Texas. *(Courtesy, National Archives, Washington, D.C.)*

Fort Duncan, located on the Río Grande near present Eagle Pass, Texas. It was here that the Black Seminoles first arrived from Piedras Negras, Coahuila, Mexico, in 1870. *(Courtesy, National Archives, Washington, D.C.)*

Cavalry and set out for the Big Bend. According to his official report, he was bound for the Chisos Mountains "to thoroughly scout that section of the country with a view of finding and destroying a band of depredating Indians." Two days later Smither arrived at Camp Peña Colorado only to discover that Lieutenant M. F. Eggleston, with a company of men and the Seminole scouts, had already left the post in pursuit of the raiders. On November 22 Smither arrived at the mining camp, located "west of Tornillo Creek about six miles south of Nevil [*sic*] Spring." After burying the Petty family, the soldiers followed an easterly course down "Willow Canyon" to Tornillo Creek. They followed the creek to the "gravelly foothills" near the Río Grande where Lieutenant Eggleston was camped (near San Vicente crossing). It was at this point that Eggleston informed Smither that Mexican bandits, not Indians, had murdered the Petty family. His scouts tracked them to the Río Grande, where he was awaiting permission from headquarters to cross the river to give chase. Cognizant of the fact that the doctrine of hot pursuit did not apply to Mexican bandits, Captain Smither decided to reconnoiter the area while waiting for authorization to cross the Río Grande.

While Eggleston remained in camp, Smither took the scouts and a company of men upstream and scouted the western and northwestern slopes of the Chisos Mountains. Finding the terrain "almost impossible," he returned to Eggleston's camp. On December 2 the commander at Camp Peña Colorado issued orders for the patrol to pursue the bandits across the international border. After crossing the river, Smither led his troops past the Sierra San Vicente, through "a tortuous and precipitous cañon" (probably Mariscal Canyon), and on to San Carlos. On December 6 Smither recovered eight horses that had been stolen from the camp and left abandoned near San Carlos crossing. Convinced that he could not catch the bandits, he returned to Fort Davis and reported that "there is no doubt in my mind that these marauders are Mexicans and not Indians."

Captain Smither's entry into Mexico was in clear violation of the reciprocal treaty of 1882. Major General John Schofield, the adjutant general of the army, reminded the commander of the Texas Department that the doctrine of hot pursuit applied only to Indians and not to Mexican bandits. Brigadier General David S. Stanley countered that Captain Smither and Lieutenant Eggleston presumed the raiders to be Indians and could not be certain until the last moment that they were Mexicans. Despite their claim to the contrary, Secretary of War Robert T. Lincoln concurred

Second Lieutenant Charles H. Grierson shortly after his arrival to Fort Davis, Texas. "Charlie," son of General Benjamin Grierson, established Camp Neville Spring in 1885 with the Seminole Negro Indian Scouts, and served as the first commanding officer for the Big Bend outpost. *(Courtesy, National Archives, Washington, D.C.)*

Ruins of the Officer's Quarters at Camp Neville Spring, located in the heart of present Big Bend National Park, taken in 1984. The date "1888" etched into the headstone above the fireplace is still visible today. *(Courtesy, Vidal Davila, National Park Service, Big Bend National Park, Texas)*

with the Mexican government that Smither and Eggleston had violated the agreement.[15]

In the army's view, the Petty incident justified the construction of still another military post in the Big Bend. On January 2, 1885, General Stanley issued orders for the Seminole scouts to join Troop A, Tenth Cavalry, of Camp Peña Colorado in locating a suitable site for the new post. Initially, the camp was located at Willow Springs, just south of Camp Peña Colorado. Charles H. Grierson, a second lieutenant in charge of the detachment and the son of the famous commander of the Tenth Cavalry, expressed concern about the shortage of wood and the sulfurous taste of the water at Willow Springs. He requested permission to search for a more acceptable location for the camp.

Young "Charlie" had not had an easy time following in his father's celebrated footsteps. A victim of mental illness, he nearly was forced to resign his appointment to West Point after suffering a nervous breakdown. Still, the determined cadet received his commission in the United States Army and reveled in his latest assignment to Fort Davis, then under Colonel Grierson's able supervision. His orders were to establish the post. On February 22 Lieutenant Grierson sent a dispatch to his father informing him that he located the ideal spot with "the best water I have yet seen anywhere in this part of the country." Neville Spring, "located eight or ten miles west of Tornillo Creek," officially became a subpost of Fort Clark (near present Brackettville, Texas) on March 5, 1885, just weeks before Lieutenant Grierson and the entire Tenth Cavalry received transfer orders from Texas to the Department of Arizona.[16]

General George Crook's campaign against Geronimo in Arizona in 1885 lent new military importance to Camp Neville Spring. Afraid that the skillful Chiricahua Apache leader might escape into Texas, the general ordered all forces in the Big Bend to be especially alert. Drawing upon the army's experiences against Victorio in 1880, Crook ordered the Seminole scouts stationed at Neville Spring to "cause all crossings of the Río Grande between Presidio del Norte and Presidio de San Vicente to be closely watched by continuous scouting so as to prevent their [Apache] crossing from Mexico to Texas." For the next several months, the Seminole scouts patrolled the Big Bend, reporting back to headquarters that several Chiricahuas were seen attempting to cross the Río Grande near Presidio del Norte. While the appearance of the Apaches on the Río Grande kept Big Bend troops vigilant, there is no record to indicate that the Indians actually crossed into Texas.

Geronimo's surrender to General Nelson Miles on September 3, 1886, reduced the Seminole scouting activities at Neville Spring to little more than routine patrols. Monthly reports from the post for the remainder of that year revealed that the Seminoles saw no Indians between San Vicente crossing and San Carlos. On December 19, 1887, Second Lieutenant J. M. Cunningham, commander of the camp at that time, filed his end-of-year report to Fort Davis. The Seminole scouts attached to his command, he noted, reconnoitered an area of 150 miles surrounding Neville Spring, but without a single sighting. Significantly, the officer informed his superiors that the entire Big Bend area, including the most important watering holes, was "completely covered by cow-men camps." For this reason, Cunningham decided it was no longer necessary to continue sending out Seminole scouting patrols. Indeed, there was to be no more trouble with Apaches. With the surrender of the Chiricahua Apaches under Geronimo, and the imprisonment (in Florida) of Geronimo's band and other Chiricahua and Warm Springs Apaches in September 1886, open warfare along the Río Grande ceased forever.

On April 7, 1891, the commanding officer of the Seminole Negro Indian Scouts at Camp Neville Spring received instructions to abandon the camp and transfer his troops to Polvo (present Redford, Texas), closer to the Río Grande. While they remained an official military unit until 1914, the Seminole scouts enjoyed their last active assignment in the Big Bend in the 1890s. Their first commander, John Bullis, retired from service with the rank of brigadier general after spending several years as the Indian agent at San Carlos, Arizona. Many of the Black Seminoles returned to live out their lives near the familiar setting of Forts Duncan and Clark. Others, meanwhile, chose to remain in the barren habitat of the Chihuahuan desert, where many had contributed to the military pacification of the region.[17]

When the United States assumed jurisdiction over the American Southwest in 1848, it necessarily accepted the problems that accompanied an unsettled frontier. Nevertheless, for more than fifty years the American government did its best to overcome the Indian challenge, which previous to this time had frustrated Spanish and Mexican authorities. In establishing a perimeter of fortresses along the Rio Grande, the United States Army met its commitment to protect an advancing wave of pioneers determined to settle in the Big Bend. Constantly undermanned, the frontier army employed "Buffalo Soldiers" and Seminole mercenaries to hasten peace on the West Texas plains.

The use of Indian against Indian in frontier warfare, however, was not an American innovation. Spanish and Mexican military leaders were first to recognize the strategic importance of Indian alliances. Just as Spain employed Comanche and Pueblo auxiliaries to subjugate the Apaches and the Navajos, Mexican military leaders enlisted the services of the Kickapoos and the Black Seminoles. With the aid of these latter warriors, the United States Army maintained the tradition and staged an all-out military offensive that resulted in the subsequent defeat of the Southern Plains Indians. The Red River War (1874–1875) broke the strength of the Comanches and Kiowas in West Texas. With Victorio's defeat at Tres Castillos in 1880 and Geronimo's surrender in 1886, even the formidable Apaches succumbed to military authority.

The Plains Indians were the inevitable victims of Hispanic and American determination to dominate the trans-Pecos region. As exploration gave way to military assertiveness, Indian resistance to the white man's advance faltered in the wake of an advancing westward migration. Meanwhile, the parched, desolate surroundings of the Big Bend stood in unyielding opposition to all who challenged it as new occupants penetrated its mountainous barriers in search of land and livelihood. In time, Hispanic and Anglo cattlemen, miners, and farmers, who arrived in the final decades of the nineteenth century, replaced the mounted soldiers and hastened the permanent European settlement of the West Texas frontier.

CHAPTER FIVE

No Winners, Only Survivors

The Terlingua was a bold running stream, studded with cottonwood timber and was alive with beaver. Today there is probably not one tree standing on the Terlingua that was there in 1885.

                 —James B. Gillett, 1933

In his annual report of 1887, it was significant that Second Lieutenant J. M. Cunningham, then in command of the detachment of scouts stationed at Neville Spring, noted the appearance of an increasing number of cattlemen in the Big Bend. Their arrival marked a turning point in the occupation of that region as American military presence gradually gave way to a more permanent form of settlement. Accessibility to water soon became the barometer for the cattleman's success in the arid West Texas domain. Not surprisingly, early ranching centered around numerous natural springs that dotted the sunbaked landscape. For centuries these oases provided welcome relief from the desert sun to all newcomers.

Interest in the trans-Pecos region as a potential cattle kingdom, however, took several years to evolve as the harsh climate held little appeal to most settlers. Before 1890 the Nueces River country reigned supreme as the cradle of the American cattle industry. In the 1830s an estimated 100,000 head of cattle, mostly a hardy Mexican variety that were the forerunners of the Texas longhorns, roamed wild throughout the lush grasslands of central Texas. Early American arrivals to that region realized the economic potential of this untapped resource. They soon developed a market for beef in the population centers of the United States. The discovery of gold in California in 1848 provided a healthy but limited stimulus to the industry. Also, for the remainder of the 1850s, Texans trailed their herds north to Missouri, where they provisioned thousands of immigrants en route to the Pacific slope. Still other herds were driven to New Orleans, where cattle were transshipped to American port cities lining the Atlantic seaboard.[1]

Fort Leaton, near Presidio, Texas, taken ca. 1964. This rambling fortress, which has undergone restoration, was once used by the U.S. Army as a defense outpost along the lower Río Grande. *(Courtesy, Archives of the Big Bend, Clifford B. Casey Collection, Sul Ross State University, Alpine, Texas)*

Despite encouraging response to a nascent industry before 1880, the cattle business remained slow to develop in Texas. The seemingly inexhaustible supply of cattle available exceeded the demand for beef in the United States. Walter Prescott Webb, a noted authority on early Texas history, estimated that herds increased nearly 1,500 percent between 1830 and 1850. In addition to an obvious economic imbalance between supply and demand, early cattlemen confined their activities to the eastern portion of the state. Mindful of the problems of environment and Indian unrest common to West Texas, the cattlemen left that region largely unoccupied.

Early American economic interests in the trans-Pecos region focused more upon a lucrative trade system that developed before the Mexican War. The establishment of a wagon route between the city of Chihuahua, Mexico, and Independence, Missouri, in 1840 lured would-be entrepreneurs into the area. Ben Leaton, a veteran of the Mexican War, who had emigrated to the West from the backwoods country of Kentucky, was among those early arrivals to the Río Grande valley. Leaton, a freighter on the Chihuahua Trail before the outbreak of the Mexican War, was well acquainted with West Texas.

While Leaton may have been the first American to breed cattle and sheep in the Big Bend, stock raising was second to other commercial interests. In August 1848 he purchased El Fortín de San José, an old Mexican fortress located south of present Presidio, Texas. Juan Bustillos, owner of the property since 1831, had refurbished the original structure. Leaton enlarged the house into a rambling fortress that enclosed twenty-two rooms, two large granaries, and a small chapel within its three-foot-thick adobe walls. Centrally located to Indian, Mexican, and newly-arrived Anglo-Americans living along the Río Grande, Leaton's fort soon became a major trade center. With the discovery of gold in California in 1848, the facility also served as a favorite resting place for weary travelers who crossed the Texas desert to reach the Pacific gold fields.[2]

In addition, Leaton's fort assumed military importance as it represented the only major fortification on the American side of the Río Grande between Eagle Pass and El Paso. On his visit to Presidio del Norte (present Ojinaga, Chihuahua) in 1849, Lieutenant William H. C. Whiting likened Leaton's facility to a baronial fortress more likely encountered on the highland plains of Scotland. Yet the young topographical officer noted the bastion's potential as a fortification against neighboring Indians. In a report to his superiors in November 1849, Major Jefferson Van Horn, commander of American troops recently dispatched to El Paso, suggested that the fortress be used as an outpost for troops assigned to patrol the Río Grande.[3] These observations persuaded the U.S. Army to capitalize on the strategic position of El Fortín. After Leaton's death in 1851, the trading post remained in private hands. Leaton's successors, however, invited the army to station patrol units in the well-fortified enclosure. With the establishment of Fort Davis in 1854, troops sent to patrol the Río Grande frequently accepted the welcome extended to them by the residents of Fort Leaton. This informal arrangement and the army's use of the facility continued until the outbreak of the Civil War.

The presence of permanent military installations on the Río Grande frontier after 1850 provided the first dependable market for cattle in the Big Bend. With the establishment of Forts Davis, Stockton, and Quitman along the San Antonio to El Paso road, beef speculators soon realized the potential for sales to the army. Contrary to the belief of most East Texans, the rich gramma grasses that carpeted the watered areas of the trans-Pecos region and consistently mild winter climates made the Big Bend a natural environment for stock raising. The arrival of American soldiers, moreover, not only offered the pioneer ranchers an outlet for fresh meat, but also protection for their herds against Indians.

Milton Faver, an eccentric easterner said to be fluent in several languages, including Spanish, was the first significant large-scale cattleman to arrive in the Big Bend. An imposing figure of a man with a flowing waist-length beard, Faver quickly capitalized upon the military presence in West Texas as a market for his cattle. In 1857 he settled in the area northeast of Presidio del Norte where he established his fortress-like headquarters on Cíbolo Creek. Over the next twenty years he amassed a ranching empire that spread across 2,800 acres. For nearly two decades Faver's Mexican longhorns, emblazoned with his famous "Lazy F" brand, supplied the mess halls of the United States Army in Texas with much-needed beef.

The birth of the cattle industry in the Big Bend was not limited to Anglo-American settlers. In 1855 Manuel Múzquiz, a political refugee, escaped to Texas from his home in northern Mexico and settled in the canyon that still bears his name (six miles southeast of Fort Davis). With the help of his large family and a half-dozen Mexican cowboys, Múzquiz also contracted with the commander at Fort Davis to supply beef. Notably, Múzquiz replenished his own herds with Mexican longhorns which he purchased near Presidio del Norte. The practice of buying Mexican cattle, then driving them north for grazing, established a tradition among Big Bend ranchers that existed well into the twentieth century.

Ironically, the Civil War, which created unprecedented demands for beef in the northern states, brought the burgeoning cattle industry of West Texas to a virtual standstill. Withdrawal of Union troops from Texas in 1861 caused the cattle market to collapse. More importantly, the resurgence of Indian hostility in the absence of the soldiers virtually wiped out most of the small ranchers. Left unrestrained to resume their attacks on vulnerable stockmen, Apache raiders dealt a fatal blow to ranching on the Río Grande. In the summer of 1861, for example, Manuel Múzquiz abandoned his place and returned to Mexico. While Milton Faver enjoyed greater success in repelling the Indians, he, too, lost most of his stock. Thus, not unlike their Confederate brethren in the Deep South, West Texans suffered the sting of economic hardship characteristic of the final years of the Civil War.[4]

Several factors combined to foster the revival of the Texas cattle industry after the Civil War. To begin, years of Indian raids in northern Mexico nearly denuded the range of all livestock. Mexico, therefore, provided a healthy market for American cattle in the postwar years as they were used to breeding new herds. The late 1860s and early 1870s marked the beginning of major drives from central Texas into northern Mexico via the Chihuahua Trail. Names like W. A. Peril and W. O. Burnam — forerunners of ranchers who later settled Big Bend — pioneered the drives. In Chihuahua, wealthy Mexican landowners bought thousands of head of American stock to replenish their expended herds.

The most profitable market for Texas cattlemen, however, lay in the northern United States. The phenomenal postwar growth of urban America created an insatiable appetite for beef. In 1865 cattle purchased in Texas at three and four dollars per head were valued at ten times that amount on the northern markets. At this rate of profit it did not take long for western ranchers to calculate a small fortune — if they could get their cattle to the buyer. In 1867 Joseph G. McCoy, a livestock dealer from Chicago, devised a plan to bring Texans in contact with northern cattle buyers. McCoy established Abilene, Kansas, as the first major cattle town in the West. Centrally located along the Kansas Pacific Railroad, Abilene surfaced as a convenient meeting place for drovers from Texas who sold their cattle for shipment to the east for processing. Between 1866 and 1880 more than four million cattle were marketed in the East. As Walter

P. Webb later observed, "Through Abilene passed a good part of the meat supply of a nation."[5]

The return of the U.S. Army to West Texas after 1865 also contributed significantly to the resumption of the cattle industry. In the first place, successful military campaigns against the Comanches and the Apaches brought long-desired peace to the Big Bend. During the 1870s and 1880s pioneer stockmen such as Daniel Murphy, Deidrick Dutchover, Carmen Ramírez, John Beckwith, and Francis Rooney prospered under contracts to supply beef and mutton to the army. Rooney and Beckwith were the chief suppliers to Camps Peña Colorado (1879) and Neville Spring (1881), both subposts of Fort Davis, which were established in the Big Bend for reconnaissance purposes. Murphy, meanwhile, promoted the townsite of Murphyville (present Alpine, Texas) as a major West Texas cattle town.

Technological improvements after the Civil War also helped to promote a healthy cattle industry. The invention of the Bates Process, a method of refrigeration for railroad cars and boats, stimulated an overseas market for dressed beef. As a result, animals were slaughtered in Midwestern packing houses and the meat shipped directly to consumers. In addition, Agustus Swift and other pioneer industrialists experimented with new canning techniques which revolutionized the industry. These innovations, which enabled packers to preserve meat for longer periods, combined to increase the demand for processed beef.

Without question, the national mania for expanding the railroads after the Civil War had a profound impact on the growth of the western cattle industry. Claiming only thirty-five thousand miles of track in 1865, railroad companies increased their mileage to nearly two hundred thousand in less than two decades. With the completion of the first transcontinental line in 1869, industrial tycoons raced across the country in their obsession to link East and West. An arterial network stretching like tiny fingers across the face of America, the railroads touched even the remotest corners of West Texas.

Ruthless competition in the 1880s between Collis P. Huntington, owner of the Southern Pacific, and Jay Gould, the hard-nosed president of the Texas and Pacific, first made the railroad accessible to the cattlemen of the Big Bend. The Galveston, Harrisburg, and San Antonio Railroad (G. H. & S. A.), the first major railway to extend west from the Gulf of Mexico, preceded the Southern Pacific into Texas. When the line

reached San Antonio in 1880, Collis Huntington entered into negotiations with T. W. Pierce, president of G. H. & S. A. He wanted Pierce to
continue building to El Paso where Huntington's Southern Pacific, running east from California, could join it to form the first transcontinental
route across Texas. Meanwhile, Jay Gould, the new owner of the Texas
and Pacific, vowed to block Huntington's plan. Gould later relented in
exchange for an agreement to share traffic along the proposed route.

Gould's withdrawal from the race enabled Huntington and Pierce to
proceed across Texas. In July 1881 construction began on both ends of
the San Antonio-El Paso line. Roughly paralleling the same course that
the topographical engineers established in the 1850s, the G. H. & S. A.
reached Marfa and Alpine, Texas, in late January 1882. One year later,
on January 12, 1883, President T. W. Pierce ceremoniously joined the
two lines on the west bank of the Pecos River. "In the majestic presence of
these great canyons of the Río Grande," he uttered solemnly, "I proceed to
drive this spike which connects by rail the waters of the Pacific Ocean
with those of the Gulf of Mexico." Within months, the first through train
traveled across the shimmering tracks loaded with passengers eager to
start life anew in the rugged West.[6]

The industrialization of the United States in the late nineteenth century
attracted thousands of immigrants in search of economic opportunity.
While the majority of foreign visitors to America journeyed across the
Atlantic and the Pacific, a significant number also drifted north across
the Río Grande. When contrasted with the meteoric growth of the United
States at the turn of the century, Mexico's internal development appeared
painfully slow. Decades of political instability frustrated national growth.
Increasingly, Mexican citizens were lured to an industrializing American
Southwest. By 1880 Mexican immigrants displaced Irish, Italian, and
Chinese track laborers on all major railroads in Texas. Utilizing El Paso
as a collection center for incoming workers, railroad officials redistrib-
uted them to all parts of the state. By 1900 all West Texas towns — Marfa,
Alpine, and Marathon — harbored a sizeable Mexican population.[7]

The arrival of the railroad to the trans-Pecos region marked the beginning of land speculation throughout the Big Bend territory. In 1880 the
country between El Paso and San Antonio encompassed 43,726 square
miles of land but numbered less than 20,000 inhabitants. The railroad
held control over most of this acreage. Texas land laws dating from 1854
provided that sixteen sections of land be set aside for every mile of track
built, and the railroad companies were responsible for their own sur-

veys — an open invitation to fraudulent claims. In 1883 Texas established a state land board to ensure the proper reclassification of all lands. As a result, the board recovered some of the land from the G. H. & S. A., which was resold to interested buyers. If isolation and obsolete land laws discouraged the settlement of West Texas in earlier years, a population rush was clearly in progress by the mid-1880s. The new land redistribution program proved to be a major attraction to settlers in the Big Bend.[8] One scholar noted that 90 percent of all ranches still in operation in the 1930s were started between 1880 and 1890. Other factors made West Texas a favorable choice for the cowman during these decades. In 1885, for example, northwestern cattle-producing states imposed a quarantine on East Texas cattle suspected of carrying a variety of tick fever. Notably, the quarantine did not apply to stock raised in the Big Bend.[9]

The opportunity to amass huge tracts of land attracted men like John T. Gano and E. L. Gage to West Texas. Gano, the son of a former Confederate general, first arrived in the Big Bend in 1879. He worked as a deputy surveyor for Presidio County, accepting title to small parcels of land as payment for his professional services. Over a period of several years, Gano personally accumulated more than fifty-five thousand acres in what is today Big Bend National Park. His property holdings, moreover, served as the foundation for the ranching industry in that area. Recognizing the potential to convert his property into ranch land, Gano initiated a profitable cattle business with his brother.

In 1885 John and Clarence Gano formed the Estado Land and Cattle Company with headquarters in Dallas, Texas. Inasmuch as most of their land was located in Survey Block G4 in southern Brewster County,[10] the Ganos registered their Big Bend enterprise as the G4 Ranch. The company's holdings extended from Agua Frio Mountain on the north to the Río Grande on the south, and from Terlingua Creek on the west to the Chisos Mountains on the east. In the summer of 1885 the Gano brothers purchased three separate herds of cattle totaling six thousand head and brought them to graze in the Big Bend. Five years later, the G4 brand claimed more than thirty thousand head. They established three line camps in the Big Bend: one near Agua Frio, a second at the mouth of Terlingua Creek near Santa Elena Canyon, and the main camp at Chisos Spring (present Oak Canyon Spring).[11] According to James B. Gillett, former Texas Ranger and manager of the new operation, "At that time not a single human was living in the country mentioned, and not one head of cattle grazing in that territory. The Ganos had it all to themselves."

By the 1890s other cattlemen were well-established in the Big Bend. Most gathered their herds around the numerous natural springs that once abounded in the Chihuahuan desert. E. L. Gage, also a former land surveyor, located his herd in the shadow of the Sierra del Carmen at McKinney Springs, named for his foreman and longtime employee, T. Devine McKinney. Gage remained several years in what is today Big Bend National Park, but eventually moved his operation closer to the railhead at Marathon, Texas. Tom Pulliam owned property at Government Springs. He herded his cattle throughout the Chisos near Pulliam Bluff, the mountain that still bears his name. Southwest of the Chisos, Newt Gourley settled his stock around Tule Spring, where he ranched for the next thirty years.

Cheap grazing land and abundant spring water also attracted Mexican cattlemen into the Big Bend. Renowned for their horsemanship and knowledge of cattle, the Mexican *vaqueros* had engaged in cattle raising along the Río Grande since the 1830s. Their familiarity with the dry desert climate caused the Mexicans to raise exclusively a rugged, thin-blooded variety of longhorn that could adapt to arid conditions. Attracted to the virgin grazing lands of the Big Bend, Mexican cowboys drove their herds north across the border where some established successful ranching operations that compared favorably with those of their Anglo counterparts.

Martín Solís was perhaps the most influential of these early Mexican pioneers. A wiry little man with fair complexion and a prominent roman nose, Solís registered his brand in Alpine in 1894. He and his four sons — Benito, Juan, Tomás, and Francisco — built their ranch approximately two miles upstream from Boquillas Canyon. Three years later the Solís family purchased more land near Mariscal Mountain, which proved to be excellent range for horses and cattle. For more than a decade the Solís family enjoyed a successful ranching operation that supplied beef to the thriving mining communities that appeared along the Río Grande by the turn of the century. After Don Martín's death, Benito extended the family holdings to include land around Glenn Springs, where he ranched until 1916.

Other Mexican cattlemen left their mark on the Big Bend in the 1890s. Félix Domínguez, for example, grazed his cattle along the southeastern base of the Chisos, near the mountain named in his memory. Fredrico Billalba, a native of Aldama, Mexico, owned fifteen sections of land adjacent to the Gano ranch which he worked until the 1920s. Félix Gómez

Mexican *vaqueros* were vital to the success of cattle ranching in the Big Bend. Many worked as laborers for Anglo ranch owners. Others, such as Ramon Molinar shown here, owned their own ranches and were recognized throughout the region as successful businessmen. *(Courtesy, Archives of the Big Bend, Clifford B. Casey Collection, Sul Ross State University, Alpine, Texas)*

owned and operated his own spread on upper Alamo Creek for several years. Lesser known pioneer Mexican stockmen included Roman de la O, whose ranch was located due west of present Castolon, and Santiago Baisa, who ran his herd along the lower section of the Río Grande near what is today called the Woodson Site.

The days of the open range, however, were short-lived in the Big Bend. By the late 1890s two second-class roads were cleared to allow for an even greater influx of settlers into the region. Built to facilitate the development of mining in the area, the first of these roads extended from Marathon to Boquillas via Fort Peña Colorado, Persimmon Gap, and Tornillo Creek to a point just north of the little Mexican village. A second road, from Alpine to Terlingua, skirted the G4 Ranch, then headed south to the river. Thus, by the turn of the century, cattle ranching no longer remained unchallenged as the mainstay of the Big Bend economy. The emergence of a mining industry, however, created an excellent local beef market.

By 1900 the Big Bend beckoned to a new breed of Texas cattleman who saw even greater opportunities for success.[12] Improved ranching methods and increased markets for leaner beef made the years 1900 to 1918 a peak period of cattle production in the Big Bend. This was "cow-calf" country, cow-calf being the practice of breeding cattle solely to produce calves for sale to feedlot owners located in the Midwest. The "feeders" in turn fattened the cattle for slaughter, then distributed the meat to various markets. West Texas stock did so well on the lush grasses of the Big Bend that most yearlings weighed anywhere from five to seven hundred pounds upon delivery. The ultimate goal of the Big Bend cattleman, therefore, was to produce calves that could be sold directly to feeders. Cross-breeding among West Texas herds during these years, moreover, produced a more standard quality of Hereford that was highly regarded on the Midwestern market.

With the advent of World War I the demand for beef once again skyrocketed. During the war years American beef exports rose from a meager six million pounds per year to an astounding five hundred million by 1918. Notably, the federal government, chief purchaser of beef during this time, preferred leaner, grass-fed, cattle — common to the Big Bend — for overseas shipping. Grain-fed beef from the Midwest had a tendency to spoil because of its high fat content. Finally, the creation of the cattleman's association, designed to standardize beef marketing practices among local ranchers, did much to promote a healthy economic climate for

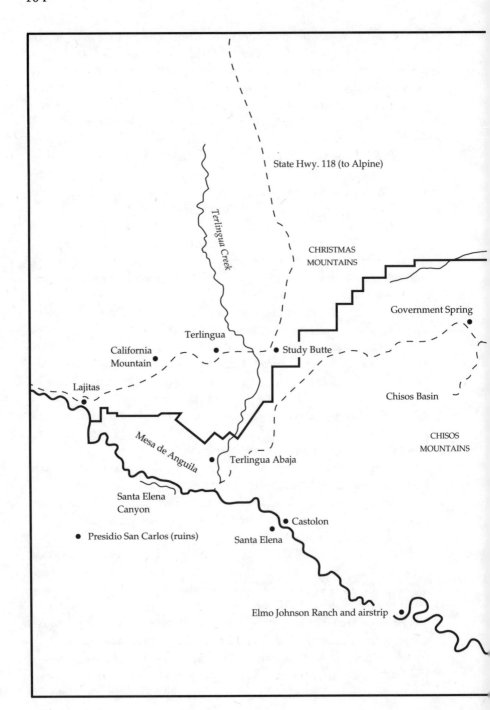

State Hwy. 118 (to Alpine)

CHRISTMAS
MOUNTAINS

Government Spring

Terlingua Creek

Terlingua

California
Mountain

Study Butte

Chisos Basin

Lajitas

CHISOS
MOUNTAINS

Mesa de Anguila

Terlingua Abaja

Santa Elena
Canyon

Castolon

Presidio San Carlos (ruins)

Santa Elena

Elmo Johnson Ranch and airstrip

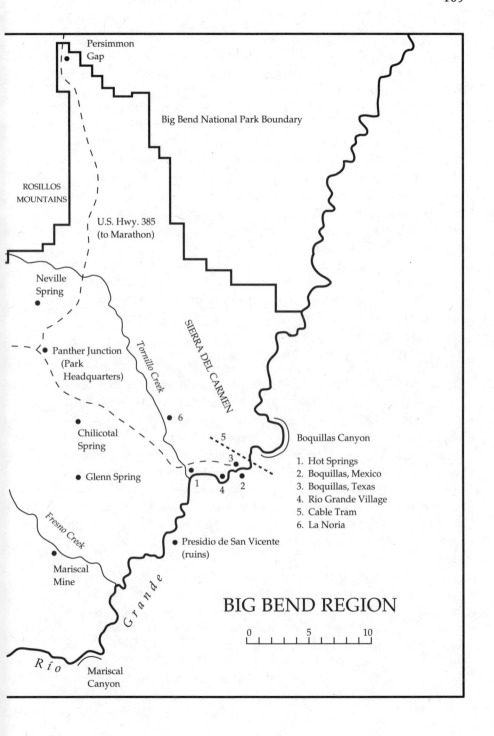

Persimmon Gap

Big Bend National Park Boundary

ROSILLOS MOUNTAINS

U.S. Hwy. 385 (to Marathon)

Neville Spring

Panther Junction (Park Headquarters)

Tornillo Creek

SIERRA DEL CARMEN

6

Chilicotal Spring

Glenn Spring

5

3

1

4

2

Boquillas Canyon

1. Hot Springs
2. Boquillas, Mexico
3. Boquillas, Texas
4. Rio Grande Village
5. Cable Tram
6. La Noria

Fresno Creek

Presidio de San Vicente (ruins)

Mariscal Mine

Río Grande

BIG BEND REGION

0   5   10

Mariscal Canyon

trans-Pecos stockmen during the war years. Thus, a combination of several factors brought even greater success of the cattle business in the Big Bend to fruition. It was not long before stockmen from other parts of Texas began to look to the west.[13]

A thriving cattle industry in West Texas from 1900 to 1920 paralleled closely a gradual population increase in the Big Bend. In the early 1900s, John and Fred Rice, two brothers from Barstow, Texas, were among the first of the new breed of ranchers to arrive. Like many newcomers to the area, the Rice brothers worked on other ranches until they could start their own herds. Fred Rice found employment on the Lou Buttrill ranch, a large operation just north of the Rosillos Mountains. After a few years the Rice brothers purchased stock from Félix Gómez and Pablo Baisa and entered into the cattle business for themselves. In time, the Rice brothers decided to raise a hardier Brahma-type of cattle, breaking away from the tradition of the Mexican cattlemen who raised mostly longhorn stock, and the Anglo ranchers who preferred Herefords. John located his herd on the east side of the Chisos near present Chilicotal Spring. His brother, meanwhile, established his range in the north, closer to Tornillo Creek at Grapevine Hills Spring.

Others who followed the Rices into the Big Bend, however, brought Hereford stock from East Texas. In 1908 Waddy Burnham, whose father had driven cattle from Menard, Texas, through Big Bend country in the 1870s, established his own ranch at Government Spring (northwest of present Big Bend National Park Headquarters). Not long after, Burnham bought more acreage in order to expand his herd. Closer to the more temperate climate of the Chisos Mountains, Burnham insisted on raising Herefords rather than relying upon the more traditional southern breeds. Relative latecomers such as Sam Nail and his brother Jim, who located their ranch west of the Chisos near Oak Canyon in 1916, experimented with Black Angus for a short time, but eventually turned to raising Herefords.

If the early ranchers of the Big Bend could not agree upon which variety of cattle could best survive the desert environment, all recognized the need for a good water supply. The attraction of cold running streams and natural ground springs present in the early 1900s contrasted sharply to the astringent conditions found in Big Bend National Park today. "Water was never really a problem in those early days," Waddy Burnham's son, Bill, recalled. "There is probably more water out there [Big Bend] than most people realize. You just have to clean out the springs once a year."

Indeed, Waddy Burnham had a chain of free-flowing springs and shallow wells that stretched from the base of the Chisos all the way to Neville Spring. The Rice's, too, had ample water. In fact, they built a large surface tank for storage, using a windmill to pump water from nearby springs. This method of conserving water through the use of ground tanks became a popular practice among many of the ranchers of the Big Bend.[14]

Experienced Mexican labor was also available in abundance to the West Texas cattlemen throughout the early decades of the twentieth century. During the Mexican Revolution (1910–1930), ten percent of Mexico's national population emigrated to the American Southwest. More than one million homeless refugees poured into Texas. Driven from the war-torn states of Chihuahua and Coahuila, many Mexican Nationals settled along the Río Grande in present Big Bend National Park to raise goats and practice subsistence farming. Still, others sought employment among the Anglo and Mexican ranchers who, by now, were well established in the area. Local ranchers openly welcomed the seasoned *vaqueros*. In the beginning, Anglo ranchers employed mostly "wet" labor, *vaqueros* who were not legal citizens of the United States. In time, however, the stockmen came to rely upon local Mexican residents of the Big Bend living on both sides of the present park boundary. Cresencio Sánchez and Liberato Gamboa of San Vicente, for example, became permanent employees at the Fred Rice place. In later years, Fred Rice, Jr., remembered the Mexican cowboys as outstanding horsemen.

Similarly, Viviano Castillo, well known for his skill in masonry, built the large surface tank at Chilicotal Spring while working as a hired hand for John Rice. Pedro Sálas and Carlos Picasso, also from San Vicente, lived at Government Spring where they worked for Waddy Burnham. Other Mexican cowboys served as utility laborers on ranches in the area. Simón Celaya, a native of San Luis Potosí, worked for Coleman Babb, owner of the K-Bar Ranch (just east of Big Bend National Park Headquarters). Like many foreign arrivals to the Big Bend, Celaya immigrated from central Mexico in search of better employment opportunities in the West Texas cattle country.[15]

Economic stability and growth during the 1920s not only assured a stable market for beef to the cattlemen of West Texas, but also allowed diversification of the entire stock-raising industry. During those years, sheep and goat ranchers began to look at the trans-Pecos region as a promising area for their trade. To be sure, Mexican residents of the Big Bend raised goats for years to feed their families, yet only a handful en-

Librado Iniguez, one of many Mexican goatherds who thrived in the Big Bend. Iniguez worked for Elmo Johnson and marketed a few of his own goats. This photo was taken in 1930. *(Courtesy, Photography Collection, Harry Ransom Humanities Research Center, University of Texas at Austin)*

Gilberto Luna, local Mexican goatherd and a virtual legend among Hispanic residents of the Big Bend. He was one of only a handful of self-employed Mexican ranchers in the region. *(Courtesy, Archives of the Big Bend, Clifford B. Casey Collection, Sul Ross State University, Alpine, Texas)*

Gilberto Luna's jacal as it appeared at the time of its occupancy probably in the 1940s. The building is typical of most Mexican dwellings scattered all through the Big Bend. *(Courtesy, National Park Service, Big Bend National Park, Texas)*

gaged in commercial goat raising. Brijador Holguin and Librado Iniguez were two Mexican goatherds who prospered from the sale of their animals to local mining camps. They located their ranches along the river in the area known today as Sierra Chino (a few miles downstream from present Castolon). Gilberto Luna, who herded his goats on upper Alamo Creek (about four miles northeast of Santa Elena Canyon) also raised his stock for sale to local consumers. These operations were, however, small as well as local.

Homer Wilson, a mining and petroleum engineer from Del Río, Texas, was the first large-scale sheep and goat rancher in the Big Bend. His interest in mining first attracted him to the area, but shortly after his arrival in 1929 Wilson began to purchase prime grazing land west of the Chisos Mountains. He spent nearly $60,000 over a five-year period to amass a sheep ranching empire that covered forty-four sections of land, which included most of the old G4 Ranch. With his ranch headquartered at Oak Spring, Wilson conducted a successful sheep business until the 1940s.

Wilson's innovative sheep ranching practices, coupled with his concern for water conservation, promoted unusual harmony with the cattlemen of the area. Considered a friend to his neighbors, Wilson spared no expense in protecting his flocks against predator animals that were a menace to all ranchers.[16] His introduction of a net-wire, wolf-proof fence won him wide acclaim throughout West Texas. The fence not only protected his stock from predators, but also kept his sheep from grazing on the cattleman's range. Wilson also used his engineering talents to design improved methods for gathering water for storage. He built a small reservoir, dug shallow concrete wells and even designed a pipeline system to pump fresh water to remote sections of his property. His line camp located on Blue Creek was the most up-to-date facility of its day. In the truest sense, Homer Wilson best represented the new breed of stockmen; he was prepared to use all of his skills to overcome the stringent environment of the Big Bend.

While the Great Depression caused an economic downturn throughout most of the nation, combined with drought conditions it virtually devastated the cattle industry in West Texas. The decade of the thirties was the worst in the history of the Texas cattleman, and that industry never recovered in West Texas. "We were unprepared for the Depression," recalled Hallie Stillwell, whose husband, Roy, had ranched in Big Bend country since 1903. In 1933 President Franklin D. Roosevelt initiated the Federal Emergency Relief Administration program in an attempt to buy large quantities of beef to be distributed to the urban poor. Conditions by this time were so severe in the Big Bend, however, that most of the ranchers had to shoot their stock because they could neither feed them nor move them. "We did not have good roads, our tank water ran out, and our wells went dry," Mrs. Stillwell remembers.[17]

The Great Depression and dust bowl conditions forced most of the cattlemen to give up their struggle in the Big Bend and find work elsewhere. However, despite these hardships, Sam Nail, Waddy Burnham, Coleman Babb, Félix Gómez, Roy Stillwell, and some others elected to stay in the cattle business beyond 1936. But it was the conservation policies of the New Deal Era that followed, however, that actually brought down the curtain on open ranching in West Texas.

Instead, the modern cowboy sought new methods of maintaining his stock, conserving his rangelands, and getting his beef to market. "Improved transportation was the biggest change in the 1930s," notes Bill Burnham. "Now the stock owners can truck their cows to market." Indeed, the efforts of New Deal programs, such as the Civilian Conservation Corps, did much to improve roads and other communication systems in the Big Bend. If future droughts occurred, the rancher now had the means to transport his cattle to different locations.

Since the 1850s, the struggle to survive in the Big Bend pitched the West Texas cattleman against Indian attacks, inhospitable climate, and unpredictable economic conditions. Yet, in his determination to replace the frontier soldier as the permanent occupant of this territory, the cowman challenged all natural obstacles in his gallant attempt to domesticate an untamed land. Adaptation and technological know-how were crucial elements in the cowboy's formula for success. These qualities enabled him to utilize all of the available resources — land, labor, and water — necessary to endure his rugged existence in the Big Bend. Notably, the rancher's determination to occupy the region sustained most of them through the droughts and the economic instability of the 1930s.

The Great Depression, however, left an indelible mark on the minds of most Americans. To those who experienced the dust-bowl conditions in Texas, Oklahoma, Kansas, and other agricultural states, poor conservation practices were to blame. Not surprisingly, concern about decades of overgrazing of rangelands in the West influenced the thinking of New Deal conservationists in Washington as well as in West Texas. Their efforts in later years to conserve and preserve the natural splendor of the

Big Bend from excessive use marked the end of the cattle industry in what would eventually be designated Big Bend National Park. Mindful only of their need for economic survival, the cattlemen failed to foresee the long-term consequences of the conservationist movement. Like the Indians and the soldiers who preceded them, the cowmen soon came to realize that their struggle against nature allowed them to survive only temporarily in the Big Bend. In the end, they did not promote the final occupation of this land, and others followed. Indeed, despite their determination to succeed, the cattlemen were not the winners. Rather, they were just more of the many survivors.

CHAPTER SIX

The Rainbow Seekers

Boquillas is a widely divided settlement that owes its existence to a nearby silver mine in the adjacent mountains of Mexico. Two miles below the smelting works is a densely crowded village of two thousand Mexican inhabitants.

—*Robert T. Hill, 1899*

The appearance in October 1899 of three flat-bottomed, wooden row-boats floating down the Río Grande must have been a wondrous curiosity to residents of the dilapidated village of Boquillas, Texas. Assigned to a United States Geological Survey exploration team, the boats carried a crew of weary passengers who were nearing the completion of a trek through the canyons of the lower Río Grande. Robert T. Hill, the bewhiskered and articulate leader of the expedition, recorded his early impressions of the remote mining community, which he distinguished as the only American settlement encountered throughout the exploration. "There is no sign of stucco, whitewash, or ornamentation of other kind," the geologist remarked somewhat disappointingly; "Streets and walls and interiors are all a continuation of the dirty adobe soil of which the houses are built." Though seemingly unimpressed, the veteran scientist determined that Boquillas, Texas, and its Mexican counterpart, were active mining camps with a combined population of nearly two thousand people.

Unlike most other border towns that lay along the sinuous course of the Río Grande, Boquillas was neither dependent upon agriculture nor ranching for its livelihood. Rather, mining was the principal enterprise to which the bustling river community owed its existence. The residents of Boquillas, Texas, and Boquillas, Coahuila, mined silver in the nearby Sierra del Carmen. Soon after his arrival, Hill noted that a quarter-mile long cable tram physically linked the two settlements. Mine owners, in fact, used the cable, which originated in Mexico, to transship ore to the American side for smelting and processing.[1]

Rising to a gentle arch high above the Chihuahuan desert, the Sierra del Carmen lured would-be rainbow seekers to its bosom for more than a century. Legend claimed that Presidio San Vicente, located a few miles upstream from Boquillas, once served as a prison for slave miners. The story told of Spanish soldiers who forced Indian slaves to produce silver from a mythical mine high in the Chisos Mountains. According to one version, the mine was located along the summit of present Lost Mine Peak in Big Bend National Park. At sunrise on Easter Sunday the entrance to the shaft was clearly visible, but only from the courtyard of the old presidio. Spaniards guarded the mine's location so well, legend states, that they blindfolded their captives before marching them to work its silver-laden veins. Some say that when Spanish troops abandoned Presidio San Vicente in 1781, the Apaches sealed the entrance to the mine, erasing it from memory for all time.[2] While the existence of the Lost Mine has never been documented, the legend has become one of the fascinating contributions to the rich folklore of the Big Bend.

Legends notwithstanding, early Hispanic visitors realized the potential for mining in the Big Bend. On his exploration of the Chisos Basin in October 1851, Colonel Emilio Langberg described the region as visibly rich in mineral ores. "Evidence indicates that several mines had once been in operation," Langberg observed, "but, because they lacked adequate labor for exploitation and they lived in constant fear of Indian attack, the Spaniards abandoned these early mining efforts." The Mexican officer also noted that neighboring Indians appeared regularly in San Carlos to trade precious metals for weapons and supplies. These metals, he concluded, were mined in the Chisos. In his final report of 1851, the colonel expressed his firm conviction that the mountains of the Big Bend were laden with valuable gold and silver.[3]

In spite of these promising reports, the economic development of the northern frontier evolved slowly. Political revolution in Mexico left the border states of Coahuila and Chihuahua unattended until the 1880s. With the rise of Porfirio Díaz to the presidency, the Mexican government took calculated measures to industrialize the nation. Under Díaz's guidance, and an entourage of bureaucratic elites known as the *científicos,* Mexico made an ideological commitment to modernization.

The government viewed foreign investment as an efficient way toward achieving its goals. Over the next two decades the Mexican economy came under the dominance of French, German, British, and American investors. The mining industry—once the mainstay of the Spanish Colonial economy—enjoyed a spectacular revival under the new Mexican regime as foreign entrepreneurs vied for the unrecovered mineral resources of Mexico's northern provinces. Beginning with a silver strike in the Sierra Mojada range of southwestern Coahuila in 1880, American mining interests were soon attracted to the Río Grande country near Big Bend.

Within five years of these discoveries, thirty American companies produced more than a thousand tons of silver-rich ore per week. The need to process the ore surfaced as the most pressing concern within the nascent industry. Robert Safford Towne, an Ohio-born mining engineer, journeyed to Texas to resolve the problem. In August 1887 Towne supervised the construction of a smelting facility at El Paso. Next, he financed the establishment of the Mexican Northern Railroad, Coahuila's first modern transportation system. In doing this, Towne assured himself that the mines at Sierra Mojada would keep his smelter well supplied. Towne, who enjoyed tremendous financial success as a result of the El Paso operation, attracted one of the nation's leading processing companies to West Texas. In 1888 Consolidated Kansas City Smelting and Refining Company (KSARCO), a New York-based corporation with smelters in Kansas and Colorado, expressed an interest in buying the El Paso plant. Company officials noted that El Paso lay at a crossroads where American ore moved east and Mexican ore moved north. In addition, the prevalence of cheap labor in Texas offset transportation costs for shipping the ore to the border. These advantages, KSARCO officials determined, "assured the financial success of the plant." On March 22, 1888, Towne transferred ownership of the El Paso smelter to KSARCO, and joined the firm's management staff.

Meanwhile, the quest to discover new sources of precious metal pushed Mexican prospectors into the northernmost extremes of Coahuila. Not surprisingly, legends of abandoned silver mines attracted a new generation of rainbow seekers into the Big Bend. The discovery of silver in the Sierra del Carmen in the early 1890s resulted in a new mining operation known as La Mina de la Fronteriza. Shortly after that find, hundreds of miners from Durango, Zacatecas, and Sierra Mojada converged upon the Río Grande frontier in hope of quick wealth. Virtually overnight, the once desolate military district in northern Mexico transformed into a thriving mining community. On April 2, 1897, Federico Martínez, the town's first elected magistrate, declared La Villa de Boquillas del Carmen an official village.[4]

Concurrently, American miners, hoping to capitalize on the latest "silver rush," founded a second community on the Texas side of the border. Because of the significant increase in mining activity along the Río Grande, the United States Customs Service appointed its first officer to the area. In 1894 D. Edward Lindsey established his headquarters across the river from Boquillas del Carmen (present Boquillas Canyon overlook in Big Bend National Park). In addition to his official duties for the government, Lindsey built a small store to service the Mexican and American miners. By 1899 the Texas community grew to include the store, a customs house, a post office, and several small adobe huts to house local prospectors. Dependent solely upon the mining operations at Boquillas del Carmen, residents called the village Boquillas, Texas.

Shortly after it purchased the El Paso smelter, KSARCO expanded its holdings in West Texas to include property near Boquillas. In 1897 KSARCO bought land from Charles Sherwood, a real estate speculator from Madison, New York. The company bought Block G–19, Section 7 (site of present Barker Lodge in Big Bend National Park), with the intention of building a cable tram across the Río Grande. In this manner, KSARCO planned to transport ore from the Coahuila-based mines to the American side for processing. Company officials, in fact, specified in the deed their intent that a tramway be "extended across the Río Grande."[5]

In addition to the construction of the cable tram and a small processing plant, county records credit KSARCO with the sponsorship of numerous internal improvements in the Big Bend. When the mining company arrived in Boquillas, they learned that Ed Lindsey already had graded a crude road to Marathon. Needing supplies for his business, Lindsey ordered the goods shipped by rail from San Antonio. Next, he hired Mexican freighters to deliver the merchandise from Marathon to his store. It was imperative, therefore, that Lindsey establish a dependable link to his suppliers in Alpine and Marathon. Not long after KSARCO began operations in Boquillas, the company spent $75,000 to upgrade the road to a second-class highway. The Marathon-Boquillas highway not only assured KSARCO easier acquisition to equipment and supplies but also it enabled more laborers to move into the mining district.

The establishment of a network of roads associated with mining in the Big Bend also stimulated the growth of the freight industry. It was not uncommon to see two to three hundred wagons hauling supplies back and forth between the mines and Marathon. While some Americans engaged in the business, Mexican freighters virtually monopolized the industry in West Texas. In the first place, Mexican mules were considered superior in strength and endurance to most American breeds. Second, mine owners valued Mexican drivers because they were familiar with the animals and their performance in the desert environment. Each wagon required a minimum of twelve mules to transport loads sometimes weighing more than one hundred thousand pounds. The Gonzales brothers, headquartered in Saltillo, Coahuila, and the Ben Gallego family of Alpine, Texas, dominated the industry along this portion of the Río Grande. Employing only the best Mexican drivers, these men provided an invaluable service to the mine owners.[6]

The twentieth century brought significant changes to the Boquillas mining industry. Most important was the transference of all KSARCO properties to one of America's leading financial giants. In 1899 Robert Towne negotiated a merger between KSARCO and Daniel Guggenheim of New York. The Guggenheims, wealthy American industrialists with mining investments throughout Latin America, were especially interested in KSARCO's smelting facilities in Texas and Colorado. In April 1899 eleven independent companies merged to form the American Smelting and Refining Company (ASARCO) with the Guggenheim family as principal shareholders. As a result of the consolidation, Kansas City Smelting and Refining Company relinquished all of its property to ASARCO— including the cable tram and processing plant located in Boquillas.[7] The outbreak of the Mexican Revolution in 1911, however, forced the Guggenheim family to temporarily abandon all mining activity along the Río Grande.

The advent of World War I brought new demands for industrial metals from Texas as well as other western states. Long noted for its deposits of lead, zinc, and mercury, the Big Bend made a notable contribution to the war effort. In 1914 a group of San Antonio and Houston businessmen, hoping to make good their claims in Texas lead and zinc production, renewed interest in the Boquillas mining district. Their plans focused on the Puerto Rico Mining Company, a promising Mexican-owned operation near Boquillas del Carmen.

While Mexican engineers supervised the actual mining, the Americans designed an expensive and complicated plan for processing the ore. ASARCO's closure of the small smelting plant in Boquillas in 1911 made its El Paso facility the only one in West Texas. This required that ore produced in Mexico be transported across the Río Grande and hauled by

Mexican miners employed at the Puerto Rico Mining Company near Boquillas, Coahuila, Mexico. The mining industry attracted thousands of laborers to the Río Grande border beginning in the 1890s. *(Courtesy, National Park Service, Big Bend National Park, Texas)*

Cable tram that stretched from the Puerto Rico mine in Coahuila, Mexico, across the Río Grande to La Noria, Texas. The huge wooden struts that supported the cable are still visible today. The tram, built in 1914–15, was an engineering marvel for its time. *(Courtesy, National Park Service, Big Bend National Park, Texas)*

wagon to Marathon, where it was loaded on Southern Pacific cars and shipped to its final destination.

To accomplish this task, the Texas investors built a second cable tram a few miles downstream from KSARCO's earlier model. A more elaborate undertaking, this tram spanned six miles of desert terrain including the Río Grande. The designers placed the American terminus near La Noria, a small community located along the southern extreme of Tornillo Creek. This way local residents would supply the wagons needed to freight the ore to Marathon. While contracting Mexican teamsters was not a problem, the success of the undertaking demanded that a road be built from La Noria to the Boquillas-Marathon highway (probably the Old Ore Road). The Texas businessmen hired Farmer Jennings of San Antonio to supervise both construction of the road and the tram. The latter demanded a great deal of engineering know-how as well as plenty of muscle. The design of the aerial tramway called for a line of 75-foot towers spaced at close intervals. The towers, made of timber, supported a ¾-inch steel cable extending the entire distance from the terminal to the mine and back. The tram carried ninety iron buckets, each capable of transporting ore at the rate of 7.5 tons per hour. Built at an astounding cost of $100,000, the cable tramway experienced short-lived success because the Puerto Rico Mine remained open until shortly before the end of World War I.[8]

The discovery in North America of mercury — or "quicksilver" as it was more commonly called — accelerated man's interest in silver mining throughout the west. Since the days of Spanish Colonial America, mercury was a valued commodity among silver producers. For centuries, European metallurgists relied upon the rare element to separate silver from its natural quartz state. Spain, one of the few mercury producers in the world, monopolized the quicksilver industry throughout the remainder of the Colonial period. During Spain's three-hundred-year tenure in America, there were no new discoveries of mercury to rival those of the famous Almaden Mine near Madrid. In 1845, however, Captain Andres Castillero, a young Mexican cavalry officer and trained metallurgist, uncovered huge deposits of mercury-bearing cinnabar while on a routine mission near San Jose, California. His accidental find resulted in the opening of the New Almaden Mine, one of a handful of sources for quicksilver known to exist in the Western Hemisphere.

The establishment of the New Almaden Mine on the eve of the greatest mining rush in American history was nothing short of providential. In

Terlingua, Texas, as it appeared about the time that quicksilver mining was on the decline, ca. 1930. Note the traditional adobe-style architecture common throughout the Big Bend. Today, the ghost town of Terlinqua is a popular tourist attraction. *(Courtesy, Archives of the Big Bend, Clifford B. Casey Collection, Sul Ross State University, Alpine, Texas)*

Remains of the sprawling mercantile store in Terlingua Abaja that was owned and operated by Cipriano and Guadalupe Hernández. Terlingua Abaja was a thriving, predominantly Mexican community. *(Courtesy, Archives of the Big Bend, Clifford B. Casey Collection, Sul Ross State University, Alpine, Texas)*

full production by 1850, the mine contributed immeasurably to the mass processing of precious metals in the American West. Increased demands for the exotic, oilylike substance stimulated an active search for new deposits of cinnabar. Thirty years elapsed, however, before the next major discovery. In 1884 Ignatz Kleinman, a Hungarian Jew and owner of Presidio's lone general mercantile, made what appears to be the first significant recovery of quicksilver in the Big Bend.[9] Kleinman's discovery, coupled with a later find in 1900 by Martín Solís, attracted hundreds of prospectors into the trans-Pecos region. For many early arrivals to the Big Bend, the Chisos Mining Company of Terlingua, Texas, was their ultimate destination.

Terlingua, a corruption for the Spanish *tres lenguas* (referring to either the three forks of a nearby creek or the three languages spoken in the area), had its origin long before the Chisos Mine opened for business in 1903. In 1890 Mexican immigrants to the area established a small village a few miles below the famous latter-day mining boom town. When the new community sprang up around the Chisos Mine the original Mexican village assumed the name Terlingua Abaja, or lower Terlingua. The latter community, clustered around the general store of Cipriano and Guadalupe Hernández, remained for the most part exclusively Hispanic. Arrivals from Mexico, finding employment in the Chisos Mine, eventually settled amid the familiar surroundings of the older, more established Mexican community.

Curiously, the earliest prospectors to develop quicksilver production in Terlingua were neither Mexican nor well-trained mining engineers. Rather, they were local cowboys without practical mining expertise. The Normand brothers of Marfa, Texas, for example, were prosperous ranchers and the first Anglos to mine cinnabar in Terlingua. In 1898 Bert and James Normand, in partnership with two others, purchased twenty-five thousand acres of land in the area they called "California Hill" (four miles west of present Terlingua, Texas). They christened their enterprise the Marfa and Mariposa Mining Company. Two years later a second pair of cowboys, T. Devine McKinney and J. M. Parker, stumbled onto a huge outcropping of cinnabar a few miles east of California Hill. Unaware that their discovery was destined to become the largest single area of quicksilver in the region, the novice cowboys tried unsuccessfully to mine the ore.

Nonetheless, encouraged by these early recoveries, others staked their claim in Terlingua. The Gleim family of Shafter, Texas, after enjoying enormous success in silver production, tried their hand at mining quicksilver. Other operations established during the early 1900s included the Lindheim-Dewees Mine, the Texas Almaden Mine, and the Colquitt-Tigner Mine. The "rush" to Terlingua began in earnest by 1910. Combined, these mining enterprises produced nearly one thousand flasks of mercury, thus proving that Terlingua was a reliable source of quicksilver.

Despite indications of early economic success, Stuart T. Penick, a member of the United States Geological Survey, registered the following negative impression of the West Texas boom town: "Terlingua was a sprawling camp of temporary sheds and shelters composed of various kinds of material, such as tin, canvas, old sacks, sticks, and adobe bricks." The smelter and the general store were the only permanent buildings. Most of the village's population of three hundred, Penick observed, represented "the lowest class of Mexicans."[10]

Although Terlingua appeared dismal and desolate to Stuart Penick, its potential for economic prosperity became an irresistible attraction to Midwest entrepreneur Howard Everett Perry. Perry, a wealthy Chicago industrialist who amassed his fortune in the shoe manufacturing business, inherited his parcel of Brewster County, Texas, as compensation for an unpaid debt. A frenetic little man, imbued with the ruthlessness not uncommon to other turn-of-the-century industrial tycoons, Perry was not one to let a business opportunity go unattended. First, he filed suit against T. D. McKinney and J. M. Parker, and won a court decision to develop his claim exclusively. Next, he purchased several sections of surrounding property and initiated full-scale exploration for mercury-bearing ore. With the assistance of Eugene Cartledge, a prominent Austin lawyer, Perry secured a $50,000 loan to capitalize the Chisos Mining Company, which the two partners incorporated on May 8, 1903.

At first, most Big Bend residents found it difficult to take Perry seriously. His diminutive stature hardly conveyed the image of a forceful, competitive businessman. One neighbor remembered him as "a little-bitty short feller, couldn't have been over five feet." The miner likened him to Charlie Chaplin because of the manner in which he walked with his feet at forty-five-degree angles. Mexican residents in the area nicknamed Perry "El Perrito," in honor of his bulldog-like demeanor.[11] Once the Chisos Mine was in full operation, however, all realized that Howard E. Perry, exuding self-assurance and energy, intended to call Terlingua to the attention of the entire mining world.

Unlike his predecessors, who employed a haphazard approach to mining the valuable metal, Perry appointed a renowned mining engineer,

Dr. William Battle Phillips, of the University of Texas, as the company's first superintendent. Thus, Perry relied upon expert advisors as well as his own personal experience in the business world to forge an industrial empire.

Soon after its opening in 1903, the Chisos Mining Company produced 5,029 flasks of mercury valued at more than $200,000. This figure represented about half of the total production in the state for that year. Under Phillips's able management, the Chisos Mining Company supplied 20 percent of the nation's quicksilver after two years of operation.[12] In 1905 Perry bought the Scott Furnace from the defunct Colquitt Tigner Mine (five miles west of Terlingua). This purchase enabled his company to convert cinnabar into mercury at the rate of fifteen tons of ore every twenty-four hours.

The early success of the Chisos Mine attracted hundreds of Mexican nationals as well as local residents to work in the mine. One early arrival recalled "1,000 to 1,500 Mexicans living in tents and stone huts of almost every size and description imaginable." C. A. Hawley, an accountant for the company store, remembers only four or five Anglo families besides his own living in the town. Only the assayer, smelter foreman, company doctor, and mine superintendent were non-Hispanic. The majority of the Mexican males worked as laborers in the mine. The company maintained an around-the-clock schedule of two ten-hour shifts. Adult miners received $0.90 to $1.25 per day, while boys, old men, and inexperienced laborers earned $0.50 to $1.00. One mining official, writing about the Big Bend mining activities, noted, "Of the six states producing quicksilver, Texas ranked lowest in wages paid to employees."

Mexican workers at Terlingua were also subject to a double standard that was common throughout the mining industry in the Southwest. Miners rarely — if ever — were paid in cash. Rather, the foreman distributed a punch card redeemable for merchandise only at the company store. Hawley, in fact, admitted that the goods in the store were priced "exceedingly high," which led local residents to quip that while the Chisos Mine was in itself a prosperous endeavor, the "store was a gold mine." Perry was not above firing an employee who showed an inclination to "live economically" rather than spend his entire earnings at the store. In contrast to common laborers, management personnel — all of whom were non-Hispanic — received an actual paycheck.[13]

Not all Mexican workers, however, were indentured to the Chisos Mining Company. Those who were fortunate enough to own their own wag-

Freight wagon with mule team as they appeared during the peak of mining activity in the Big Bend. These wagons belonged to Jesús and Dario Cobos, two of the many Mexican wagoneers employed at local mines. *(Courtesy, Archives of the Big Bend, Clifford B. Casey Collection, Sul Ross State University, Alpine, Texas)*

A typical Mexican wood hauler with mules. The wood was vital to local mining operations because it fueled giant furnaces around the clock. *(Courtesy, Archives of the Big Bend, Clifford B. Casey Collection, Sul Ross State University, Alpine, Texas)*

ons and mules profited as freighters. Mexican teamsters enjoyed greater social status within their own community, moreover, because they were considered independent contractors. Marfa, located about a hundred miles north of the mining camp, was Terlingua's link to the outside world. Each day, freighters hauled their Studebaker wagons filled with supplies, water, mail, and passengers across weather-worn trails to and from the bustling cow town. Transporting flasks of mercury from the mine to the railhead at Marfa proved even more profitable. Each eighty-pound container was worth a dollar in shipping charges to the freight operator.

As a result, some Mexican wagoners accumulated sufficient wealth to purchase their own land and expand their businesses. Among the Mexican elite who thrived in the Terlingua district, Felix Valenzuela and Paz Molinar were the largest contractors. Valenzuela owned four wagons and a herd of thirty to forty mules. After only a few years in the business, Valenzuela rarely drove the wagons himself. Instead, he subcontracted younger, more steady-handed drivers from Terlingua Abaja to haul the shipments. Conversely, Paz Molinar hired his brothers, Juan and Vicente, to help meet his contract obligations to the mine. The three brothers owned property along the Río Grande, known to local residents as Rancho Molinar, just below Terlingua Abaja. In 1905 the Molinar brothers contracted to supply the Terlingua mining community with fresh water at a rate of one cent per gallon. They transported the water in a 350 gallon tank.[14]

Mexican wood haulers, too, provided much-needed services to the Chisos Mining Company. Inasmuch as the furnace burned twenty-four hours a day, it required enormous supplies of firewood. In the early years, abundant cottonwood groves growing along Terlingua and Alamo Creeks satisfied the demand, but after only a decade of operation, the once plentiful sources of fuel near Terlingua were exhausted. In response, Perry contracted wood haulers from across the border to supply the company's needs, thus providing gainful employment to neighboring Mexican residents. In their zeal to meet the requirements of the Chisos Mining Company, Mexican wood haulers virtually denuded the banks of the Río Grande of cottonwoods. The subsequent scarcity of firewood in the Big Bend forced Perry to experiment with coal, which he found in good supply near the mine. By 1911 the Chisos Mine completed its conversion from a wood to a coal-burning furnace.[15]

During the early 1900s, quicksilver operators in the Big Bend ranked among the top producers in the world. But fluctuations in a world mar-

ket beginning in 1919 hastened the demise of quicksilver mining in
Terlingua. Not unlike the rest of the nation, the West Texas mining industry struggled through the Great Depression. Even the seemingly invin-
cible Chisos Mining Company, bolstered throughout the 1930s by
massive federal subsidies, failed to recover and closed its doors forever on
October 1, 1942. Two years later, Howard E. Perry, the patriarch of the
Terlingua mining district, succumbed quietly in his sleep.

Other quicksilver operations flourished — albeit briefly — in the Big
Bend. Among the more important enterprises was one that developed in
the vicinity of Mariscal Mountain, some thirty miles southeast of
Terlingua. Realizing the importance of Martín Solís's curious discovery of
cinnabar near Mariscal Mountain, in 1900, U.S. Customs Officer Ed
Lindsey quickly filed mining claims to the area. While Lindsey's Mine
functioned less than five years, the enterprising federal agent proved that
the Mariscal district harbored a substantial vein of quicksilver ore.

Lindsey, however, apparently could not afford to ship the ore to
Terlingua for processing. For this reason, he sold his mining claims to
Isaac Sanger, who with a group of Dallas, Texas, businessmen, formed
the Texas Almaden Mining Company in November 1905. Under the su-
pervision of H. M. Nesmith, the company mined cinnabar at Mariscal
Mountain and announced plans to build a furnace similar to the one at
Terlingua. A nationwide economic depression in 1907, however, forced
mercury prices to plummet. Consequently, the Texas Almaden Mining
Company ceased all operations the following year.

During the early decades of the twentieth century, scientists developed
myriad uses for mercury. The metal proved useful as a conductor of elec-
tric current, as an ingredient in medical and dental preparations, as an
additive to pesticides, and most importantly, as an explosive. When converted to a crystalline substance known as mercury fulminate, quicksilver
becomes highly volatile. In this state, the most common use for mercury is
to detonate gunpowder in cartridges and shells.[16] Not surprisingly, the
increase in the market value of quicksilver corresponded with the advent
of the First World War.

Such potential for profit stirred renewed interest in the southern
mining districts of the Big Bend. W. K. Ellis, a Midwestern businessman
who journeyed to West Texas to operate a wax production plant near
Mariscal, purchased all claims and mineral rights to the Texas Almaden
Mining Company. From July 1917 to May 1919 the Ellis Mine processed
nine hundred flasks of quicksilver. Each flask, with a capacity of

approximately three quarts of liquid mercury, sold at the standard war-time rate of $100 to $125 per flask. Understandably, when the price for mercury dropped to less than $50 per flask after the war, Ellis liquidated his holdings.[17]

In 1919 William D. "Billy" Burcham, a Oregon mining promoter and a recent graduate in engineering from Leland Stanford Jr. University, ex-pressed an interest in the Mariscal claims. Burcham brought a colorful mining background to Big Bend. Shortly after leaving Stanford, regarded by some as the most prestigious mining school in the West, Burcham found employment in Shafter, Texas. Easily the largest silver producer in the state, the Shafter Mine provided Burcham useful practical experience until about 1915. Soon thereafter he assumed management of the Dallas Mining Company in Study Butte, Texas (near the present west entrance to Big Bend National Park). In the summer of 1919 Burcham invited a group of New York financiers to organize the Mariscal Mining Company. With Burcham as president of the corporation and general manager of all mining operations, the mine reopened in August 1919. Burcham modernized the outdated facility and installed the long-needed forty-five-ton Scott furnace, judged capable of handling all of the company's pro-cessing needs.

Investment in the most up-to-date equipment during a time of declin-ing markets for mercury spelled imminent disaster for the Mariscal Min-ing Company. In 1921 the trustees authorized the issuance of 200,000 shares in the mine at ten cents each in an effort to offset expenses. As quicksilver prices plunged even further, Burcham borrowed $20,000 from the bank against a deed of trust for all property at Mariscal Mine. The following year, the company borrowed an additional $40,000, but the depressed postwar market eventually forced the closure of the mine in the fall of 1923. During its brief tenure, the Mariscal Mining Company produced only four hundred flasks of refined mercury—less than half the output of the previous Ellis Mine—that sold for an average of $46 per flask. Clearly, Burcham was equipped with unusual technical expertise that should have made Mariscal Mine a successful mining operation. Yet, it appears he underestimated the consequences of a fluctuating consumer market. Burcham, despite his technical abilities, overinvested at the worst possible time.

For all of its shortcomings, the mine served as an important means of employment for Mexican nationals who immigrated to Texas in unprece-dented numbers. During the 1920s, the bloodiest period of the Mexican

A graphic illustration of the demanding labor required of Mexican mine workers. These are two miners in the Waldron Mine near Terlingua, Texas, in 1916.
Each of the sacks of cinnabar averaged about eighty pounds. *(Courtesy, Photography Collection, Harry Ransom Humanities Research Center, University of Texas at Austin)*

Ruins of Mariscal Mine taken in 1970. Note that the remains shown in the
foreground present a historical evolution of the structure; these are the ruins of
earlier operations. The main structure in the background, built in 1942, are the
remains of the Viviana Mining Company. *(Courtesy, National Park Service, Big Bend
National Park, Texas)*

Revolution, a flood of homeless refugees headed north to escape the carnage. Most of those attracted to the mining districts of the Big Bend came
from the Sierra Mojada region of northwestern Coahuila. Experienced in
mining, Mexican migrant workers proved invaluable to local mine owners as a source of cheap but highly efficient labor.[18]

Many Mexican laborers who arrived at Mariscal during these years
brought with them a variety of indispensable skills. Filberto Marufo, for
example, made a notable contribution to the mining community despite
rumors that he had deserted from the Federalist army. Trained as a
blacksmith while serving in Mexico, Marufo offered unique technical
abilities to Mariscal Mine operators. Others who did not work under-
ground also provided vital services, and foremost among the contributors
were the freighters. As in the case of Terlingua, Mexican teamsters proved
invaluable to the Mariscal mining operation as well as to the neighboring
community. Located several miles from the main road to Boquillas on the
east and Terlingua on the west, Mariscal residents relied totally on freight
wagons for all of their daily needs. More important, the nearest source of
fresh water was at Glenn Springs, ten miles north across rugged desert
trails. Mexican freighters made frequent trips to supply the Mariscal
community with water. Given the level of dependence of both skilled and
unskilled Mexican labor on mining at Mariscal, the unanticipated closure
of the mine in 1923 devastated the local economy. Most of the unemployed moved west to Terlingua.[19]

The mining industry left an indelible mark not only upon the land, but
also upon the illustrious history of the trans-Pecos region. Previous to the
discovery of quicksilver, this remote corner of Brewster County, Texas,
harbored only a handful of courageous occupants. The lure of instant
wealth enticed hundreds more to settle along the banks of the lower Río
Grande. Technology, courage, and determination were the hallmarks of
these enterprising pioneers. Unlike some of their earlier Spanish and
American predecessors, the latter-day mining population of Big Bend
built communities, improved transportation systems, and—alongside the
cattlemen—forged the first semblance of long-term occupation. By this
time the Plains Indians, who for centuries dominated the West Texas
scene, were gone. Only meager traces of their material culture remained
to evidence their former presence. In the years that lay ahead, Mexican
revolutionaries, fueled with an implacable anti-American sentiment, presented yet another formidable barrier to the final occupation of the Río
Grande frontier.

CHAPTER SEVEN

Wings and Saddles

I've been riding on the border, many, many long years. I've been riding on the border, to quiet the Texas fears. Did you ever see an outlaw, from Brownsville to Calexico? No. I'm still riding on the border, waiting to see the show. (Sung to: "I've Been Working on the Railroad")

—*U.S. Army, Eighth Cavalry, 1916*

On October 5, 1910, Francisco I. Madero, a soft-spoken little man born to a prominent landholding family in Coahuila, Mexico, declared his *Plan de San Luis Potosí*. This brief but emotional proclamation officially marked the beginning of the Mexican Revolution. Aimed at the political overthrow of Porfirio Díaz, a self-proclaimed despot who had ruled Mexico with an iron hand for more than three decades, the Mexican Revolution disrupted the lives of all those who inhabited land on either side of the international border. From 1910 to 1930 every man, woman, and child in Mexico became embroiled in a brutal and seemingly endless civil war that threatened to destroy the entire nation. Just months after Madero's dramatic announcement, military leaders, especially those located in the north Mexican states of Sonora, Chihuahua, and Coahuila, pledged the full support of newly assembled peasant armies to the revolutionary effort.

The chaotic atmosphere generated by the revolution also had an adverse effect on American citizens living along the Río Grande. West Texans in particular suffered the consequences of a lawless frontier at the hands of Mexican bandits who conveniently exploited the political rebellion for personal enrichment. For the most part, these outlaws were deserters from the ranks of the revolutionary armies who no longer claimed partisan loyalty. Instead, they gathered into renegade bands and terrorized defenseless farmers and ranchers living within the desolate stretches of desert between northern Mexico and Texas.[1]

The Wood-Ellis wax factory while it was still operating at Glenn Springs, Texas, in 1917, one year after the famous bandit raid. Note the piles of fibrous candelilla plant from which the wax is derived. *(Courtesy, Photography Collection, Harry Ransom Humanities Research Center, University of Texas at Austin)*

A candelilla wax plant worker with his family in front of their home at Glenn Springs, Texas. The factory attracted Mexican immigrants who were experienced in wax production. The dwelling in the background is constructed from the candelilla plant. *(Courtesy, Photography Collection, Harry Ransom Humanities Research Center, University of Texas at Austin)*

Naturally, the civil unrest that intensified conditions along the border during these troubled years aroused concern among Big Bend residents. J. O. Langford, owner of a bathhouse and health spa located at Hot Springs, Texas (about two and one-half miles upstream from Boquillas), voiced an early complaint to the federal government that the region needed increased military protection. In the spring of 1912 Langford received news via one of his Mexican neighbors from San Vicente, Coahuila, that bandits were planning to stage an attack on their tiny farming community. Convinced that there was nothing to prevent the desperados from carrying their raid into Texas, Langford appealed to the commander of Troop C of the 14th Cavalry, which was garrisoned in Marathon, for assistance.

Concerned about the threat to American mining operations in the area, the army stationed twenty-five cavalrymen, under the command of First Lieutenant James L. Collins, at La Noria, the American terminus for the new cable tram in operation for a little more than a year. The troops arrived in March 1912 but remained in the Big Bend only a few months. While it appears that the presence of armed American soldiers averted the raid on San Vicente, their return to Marathon in early 1913 left the border region vulnerable to other bandit incursions. As a consequence of the army's early departure, Langford and his family were forced to abandon their home to seek refuge in El Paso.[2]

There was good reason for local residents to fear that the Mexicans might consider the Big Bend a prime target for an assault. In the first place, the distance and extreme isolation of the area from surrounding West Texas communities made it difficult for the army to provide adequate protection. Only a handful of soldiers, assigned to guard the federal post offices located at Boquillas and Glenn Springs — each a center of regional commercial activity — were available to defend against potential bandit attacks. Secondly, it was common knowledge that mining operations at Boquillas supported hundreds of employees with a sizeable monthly payroll. Thus, the attraction of the thriving community, enhanced by the town's vulnerability to attack, made Boquillas a prime target for Mexican bandits, who crossed into Texas with impunity.

The presence of a candelilla wax factory a few miles west of Boquillas also increased the probability of a raid. In 1913 Captain C. D. Wood, a retired infantry officer with campaign experience in Cuba and the Philippine Islands, built his wax processing plant at Glenn Springs. Wood and his partners, W. K. Ellis, a Midwest businessman, and Oscar de Montel,

Major General Frederick "Fighting Fred" Funston, who in 1916 was assigned the seemingly impossible task of patrolling a two thousand-mile stretch of the Río Grande border. *(Courtesy, Photography Collection, Harry Ransom Humanities Research Center, University of Texas at Austin)*

another veteran of the Spanish American War, enjoyed financial success with the operation. The company produced wax from the candelilla plant, which to the present day grows in abundance throughout the Río Grande valley. Inasmuch as the process required a good supply of water, Wood located the factory at Glenn Springs. Used as a waterproofing agent for tent canvas, candelilla wax was a highly valued commodity during the First World War. However, wax production required laborers with experience and highly specialized skills. For this reason, the factory at Glenn Springs employed a sizeable Mexican population. In addition to the wax works, the three businessmen maintained a post office and a well-supplied general merchandise store.[3]

The period 1913 to 1916 was especially turbulent on the Río Grande. Texas law enforcement files overflowed daily with reports of killings and robberies. One incident resulted in the murder of a U.S. Customs officer at the hands of Chico and Manuel Cano, two notorious local agitators. The unrestrained violence along the border prompted a flurry of protests from local citizens as well as state officials demanding federal intervention. Much to their surprise, the army did not retaliate. One irate citizen complained to his congressman that his neighbors were abandoning their homes for lack of adequate protection. Congressman W. R. Smith forwarded the grievance to the War Department, appending his own warning that unless federal troops were deployed to Big Bend more serious trouble could be expected.[4]

Citizen discontent forced Governor James Ferguson to make an official appeal to President Woodrow Wilson. In his letter dated June 11, 1915, the Texas chief executive stressed the need for American soldiers in the Big Bend. "The preservation of property rights has become exceedingly difficult," wrote Ferguson; "Marauding bands from Mexico make raids almost daily upon the property of our citizens." In a desperate appeal for protection, Governor Ferguson proposed some alternatives. First, he requested a congressional appropriation of $30,000 for the maintenance of thirty Texas Rangers to provide the needed security on the border. If money was unavailable, the governor suggested a detachment of fifty army regulars be placed at the disposal of the Texas Adjutant General's Office for the same purpose.

President Wilson forwarded Ferguson's appeal to Major General Frederick Funston, commander of the army's Southern Department, who promptly denied the request. Known to his colleagues as "Fighting Fred," the former Medal-of-Honor winner boasted an illustrious career that took him from the woodlands of the Alaskan frontier to the West Texas plains. Funston assured the governor that the army was doing its best to protect the border. He noted, however, that his command labored under two major handicaps. First, troop limitations in Texas reduced the number of men available for duty on the Río Grande. Placing additional troops in Texas, therefore, could not be achieved without jeopardizing other sections of the border. "The army is not big enough for the job at hand," Funston explained.[5]

Secondly, Funston cited the legal restrictions that prevented the army from deeper involvement in Texas. In the War Department's view, bandit raids on the Río Grande did not constitute a threat to the security of the United States. Rather, the army believed banditry should be considered a local disturbance requiring the attention of state law enforcement agencies. Furthermore, War Department regulations expressly prohibited the army from serving as a police arm of the state of Texas. While General Funston conceded that conditions in Big Bend had worsened to a point that "justified martial law," he underscored the legal dictates that left the army powerless to take action at this time. Notably, the general suggested that much of the lawlessness in the Big Bend existed in part because of collusion between the bandits and the growing number of Mexican nationals living on the Texas side of the border.

Funston's reluctance to comply with the governor's request was not unreasonable. In the past the Texas Rangers assumed the burden of responsibility for policing the border against local agitators. The early decades of the twentieth century, however, found the illustrious law enforcement agency in a state of decline. Recruitment of new rangers was unsuccessful. In short, the state was ill-prepared to defend its citizens against Mexican depredations.[6]

In spite of these circumstances, the federal government was adamant in its belief that banditry was a state responsibility. In a letter to President Wilson, Secretary of War Lindley M. Garrison clarified the War Department position, saying, "the particular conditions that the Governor [Ferguson] has in his mind have nothing to do with the situation in Mexico." In short, the United States government made a clear distinction between armed revolutionaries and common bandits. Banditry was, in the War Department's view, the basis for instability in the Big Bend. Accordingly, military officials considered the border unrest "a matter within State jurisdiction" and were thus hesitant to respond.

Less than a year after Garrison's declaration, a series of international incidents occurred to provoke the War Department into rethinking its defense policy on the Río Grande. In January 1916 followers of the famous Chihuahuan rebel leader, General Francisco "Pancho" Villa, detained a train near the mining town of Santa Ysabel, Chihuahua, and summarily executed eighteen American mining engineers. Scarcely three months later on the morning of March 9, 1916, 485 rebels under orders from General Villa crossed into United States territory to attack the dreary little adobe town of Columbus, New Mexico. In the aftermath of a six-hour battle, seventeen Americans lay dead as fire destroyed the town.

Some historians argue that Villa was in collusion with German agents who hoped the assault would occupy the United States in a full-scale war with Mexico. Most scholars believe, however, that Villa staged the event largely out of desperation. After his resounding defeat at the hands of government forces, Villa retreated to his familiar Chihuahuan mountains demoralized and badly in need of food, clothing, and munitions. Villa's motive for the attack on Columbus, therefore, was to acquire money and arms to continue the revolution.[7]

Led by Senator Albert B. Fall of New Mexico, American interventionists clamored for a half-million U.S. troops to invade Mexico. President Wilson, on the other hand, consented only to dispatching a small force under the command of Brigadier General John "Black Jack" Pershing to punish the offenders. Pershing, a West Point graduate who earned his nickname after years on the frontier with the all-black Tenth Cavalry, in late March 1916 led an expeditionary force of six thousand men across the border in pursuit of Villa. Familiar with practically every convolution of his Chihuahuan mountain domain, the wily Mexican general avoided capture. While the American expedition remained in northern Mexico until January 1917, they returned to the United States after their failed attempts to capture the illusive rebel leader.

Villa's murder of the Americans at Santa Ysabel and his subsequent raid on Columbus confirmed the worst fears of those residents in Texas desirous of military protection. It made little difference if the outrages were carried out by revolutionary soldiers or bandits; all armed Mexicans presented a threat to the security of the Río Grande border. After the Columbus incident, panic-stricken citizens blamed Pancho Villa and his men for virtually every incident of banditry. One scholar, however, noted that most of the border trouble during these years stemmed from "bandit

Lieutenant Colonel Natividad Álvarez shortly after his capture on May 5, 1916, near Boquillas, Texas. The former Villista was held responsible for the raids on Glenn Springs and Boquillas. *(Courtesy, Archives of the Big Bend, Clifford B. Casey Collection, Sul Ross State University, Alpine, Texas)*

Store owner, Jesse Deemer, one of the Americans taken captive during the Mexican bandit raid on Boquillas, Texas, in 1916. *(Courtesy, Photography Collection, Harry Ransom Humanities Research Center, University of Texas at Austin)*

Monroe Payne, son of one of the Seminole Negro Indian Scouts who served with U.S. Army in the Big Bend, was the other captive taken from Boquillas, Texas. Payne was fluent in Spanish and a well-known figure on the Río Grande border. *(Courtesy, Photography Collection, Harry Ransom Humanities Research Center, University of Texas at Austin)*

gangs [who] simply took the opportunity to line their own pockets, gladly giving the blame — or the credit — to Villa."[8] Nevertheless, two months after the infamous assaults, one more incident, which finally forced the War Department to assume a more assertive posture in Texas, occurred in the Big Bend.

Coincidentally, the event took place on the night of the Mexican celebration of Cinco de Mayo. Shortly after eleven o'clock, on the evening of May 5, 1916, Captain Wood awakened to the sound of heavy gunfire in the distance. He grabbed his rifle, and with his neighbor and business partner, Oscar de Montel, set out to investigate the commotion. Wood soon realized that the barrage came from the direction of his candelilla wax plant at Glenn Springs, three miles from his home in present Robber's Roost. Upon their arrival at the scene, the two men witnessed "sixty or more" Mexican raiders plundering the little village adjacent to the factory. The raiders killed four Americans, looted the general store, and set some of the buildings ablaze. When the fighting stopped at dawn, Wood and de Montel tallied three of the seven U.S. soldiers stationed at Glenn Springs dead along with young Tommy Compton, the store manager's son.

While the main body of assailants pillaged Glenn Springs, a second group of bandits headed for the mining camp at Boquillas. At daybreak, the Mexicans, led by a former Villista officer, Lieutenant Colonel Natividad Álvarez, raided the general store. Store owner Jesse Deemer, and Monroe Payne, his supply clerk, offered no resistance as the outlaws took money and supplies. The raiders retreated across the border with the two Americans as hostages. As they crossed the Río Grande, the Mexicans robbed the Puerto Rico Mining Company of its payroll, then made their escape across the open desert.[9]

Not surprisingly, West Texans blamed Pancho Villa for the raids at Glenn Springs and Boquillas. The army's preliminary reports of the incident were exaggerated and confused. One report read "two hundred Mexicans yelling 'Viva Villa' " attacked the garrison at Glenn Springs, although Captain Wood, who witnessed the carnage, reported seeing only about sixty men. Meanwhile, William Blocker, American vice consul at Piedras Negras, Coahuila, wrote to Secretary of State Robert Lansing informing him that Jesse Deemer and a second man "have been found dead with their throats cut from ear to ear." At the same time, the army reported to the Secretary of War that the two Americans had been taken into Mexico as hostages. In effect, there appeared to be no reliable information about

Lieutenant Colonel George T. Langhorne (on the left) shown here in 1919 with Major General Joseph T. Dickman, then commander of the Southern Department. In 1916 the flamboyant Langhorne led a punitive expedition into Mexico in pursuit of the Glenn Springs–Boquillas raiders. *(Courtesy, Photography Collection, Harry Ransom Humanities Research Center, University of Texas at Austin)*

The caption reads: "Adobe cook house at Glenn Springs, Tex, in which 9 U.S. soldiers made their defense against Mexican bandits." The bandits burned the structure after killing three American soldiers. *(Courtesy, Archives of the Big Bend, Clifford B. Casey Collection, Sul Ross State University, Alpine, Texas)*

the raid except that the bodies of the three dead soldiers had been transported to Marathon for burial.[10]

Inasmuch as the War Department believed Pancho Villa to be responsible for the raids in Big Bend, a full-scale military retaliation was ordered. General Funston wasted little time in mobilizing units of the 14th Cavalry under the command of Colonel Frederick W. Sibley at Fort Clark, and troops from the 8th Cavalry at El Paso led by Major George T. Langhorne. The two detachments combined forces at Marathon to form the Second Punitive Expedition under Sibley's command, which proceeded directly to the Big Bend. Funston's instructions to his subordinates were explicit. They were to track down and engage the men who committed the "Glenn Springs outrage," and, if necessary, "to follow them into Mexico." Major Langhorne, the dapper and flamboyant West Pointer noted for his courage and decisiveness, was ordered to lead the main pursuit force into Mexico. On May 11, 1916, Sibley gathered his troops at Jesse Deemer's place in Boquillas, where he initiated the campaign.

Because the Mexicans had at least a three-day head start on the Americans, Colonel Sibley divided the main force and ordered the more lightly equipped detachment under Langhorne to march out immediately, the remainder of the force to follow in trace.[11] Major Langhorne's advance across the Río Grande on the evening of May 11 marked the second major American military intervention into Mexico in the same year. With eighty men, two wagons, and Langhorne's personal chauffeur-driven Cadillac touring car, the Americans crossed the Río Grande at San Vicente. On May 13 Sibley followed with the slower-moving main column. In one week the expeditionary unit advanced about two hundred miles south of the Río Grande.

Cognizant that the U.S. Army was in hot pursuit, the Mexicans tried to negotiate with Major Langhorne. A few miles outside of Sierra Mojada, Coahuila, the American officer received a note from Jesse Deemer. Deemer said he and Monroe Payne had been well treated, and that the bandits wanted to exchange them for Colonel Alvarez and others captured at Boquillas. Confident that the outlaws were only a few miles ahead, Langhorne piled a dozen sharpshooters into his limousine and headed for the little town of El Pino, Coahuila. Before they arrived, an American journalist, reporting on the events of the expedition, informed Langhorne that the bandits had scattered, leaving the two hostages behind with a local rancher. On May 15 the major dispatched a message to

Colonel Sibley reporting that Jesse Deemer and Monroe Payne had been "liberated."

Determined to punish the offenders, Major Langhorne made El Pino an advanced base from which to continue the chase. He split his detachment, sending First Lieutenant Stuart Cramer with "B" Troop to the southwest. Desperately short of food and water, Cramer's patrol scouted the outlying area for only a brief time before returning to El Pino. En route, Lieutenant Cramer engaged a small group of the bandits. After the firing ceased, the young officer reported wounding six Mexicans, taking two prisoners, and recovering a "considerable [amount] of the loot taken from Deemer's store."

Colonel Sibley's arrival at El Pino with the main column was somewhat anticlimactic since the remaining bandits had already escaped. Nevertheless, Sibley advanced his troops south an additional twenty-five miles to Cerro Blanco, Coahuila. On May 18 the colonel received a dispatch from General Funston instructing him to withdraw all of his forces from Mexico "as soon as you have accomplished [the] purpose of your mission." Convinced that the Mexicans were too badly scattered to continue the campaign, Sibley considered his assignment successfully completed and turned his forces northward. On the morning of May 21, 1916, Sibley's men reentered the United States, thus bringing to conclusion the Second Punitive Expedition.[12]

On the surface, the U.S. Army's retaliation against the Glenn Springs-Boquillas raiders was seemingly uneventful. But a second military expedition across the Río Grande so soon after the departure of Pershing exacerbated the already tense international situation between Mexico and the United States. In the first place, the War Department's response nearly disrupted high-level diplomatic negotiations that coincided with the military campaign. Government officials on both sides were appalled at the flagrant disregard for territorial sovereignty.

More importantly, the assault on West Texas forced military leaders to question American vulnerability on the Río Grande. "Funston is sick with apprehension over the safety of the border in which I consider he is justified," wrote General Hugh Scott, commander of U.S. forces at Fort Bliss in El Paso. In anticipation of future invasions, Scott requested of the Secretary of War that all munitions stored near the border be moved to interior points not subject to attack.

The punitive expeditions ordered in response to Villa's raid on Columbus and the bandit incursions in the Big Bend heightened tension between the neighboring countries to the brink of war. Since 1876, when Colonel Ranald Mackenzie led his cavalry against the Kickapoos at Remolino, American interventionism in Mexico surfaced as the preeminent diplomatic issue between the two nations. The American military campaigns of 1916 produced a similar reaction. As expected, President Venustiano Carranza vehemently protested American violations of his country's territorial sovereignty.

As the army assumed a more assertive policy against Mexican invaders, the State Department worked to ameliorate the volatile conditions prevalent on the Río Grande. Shortly after the United States authorized the Pershing campaign in 1916, American diplomats feared the possibility of an armed confrontation with Carranza's forces. For this reason, Secretary of State Robert Lansing made overtures to negotiate. In an effort to circumvent the full-scale retaliation of the Mexican government, the State Department ordered James L. Rogers, the United States Consul in Mexico City, to arrange a conference between Mexican and American military leaders to discuss border problems. In his report to Washington, dated April 26, 1916, Rogers informed his superiors that General Alvaro Obregón, commander of all forces in northern Mexico, was en route to El Paso to attend the proposed meeting. General Obregón and "some other high officer of the Mexican Army" convened with Generals Funston and Scott on May 2. In his summation of the first meeting, General Funston noted that the Mexican delegation arrived in the West Texas city with an attitude of "hostility and uncertainty."[13]

The American generals were hardly intimidated, however. Indeed, they reminded Obregón of the "deplorable consequences" Mexico would suffer if there was an attack on Pershing's troops. Such action, Scott warned, "could only result in the destruction of his [Obregón's] government and loss of his country." Perhaps swayed by the American hard-line stand, the Mexican general requested a private meeting with Scott. After twelve hours of intense negotiations, the two military commanders struck a verbal accord that promised to resolve the issue of American military intervention in Mexico.

The thrust of the agreement focused principally upon the protection of the Río Grande against future invasion. First, General Obregón agreed that under no circumstances would his army engage the punitive forces. Subject to the approval of his government, the general agreed to withdraw all troops along the northern frontier that threatened Pershing's advance. Secondly, the Mexican representative committed his government

Companies "A" and "B" of the 6th Cavalry in the summer of 1916, just after their arrival at Glenn Springs from San Antonio. Glenn Springs was just one of several defense outposts located along the lower Río Grande. *(Courtesy, National Park Service, Big Bend National Park, Texas)*

Army tractor pulling artillery across the West Texas desert, which illustrates some of the strategic problems arising from the defense of the United States-Mexico border in 1916. *(Courtesy, National Park Service, Big Bend National Park, Texas)*

to a vigorous campaign against all known bandit elements in the border area. In return, the Americans promised the gradual withdrawal of all of Pershing's forces from Mexico, beginning with the immediate recall of all auxiliary units. In his report to Secretary of War Newton D. Baker, General Scott wrote:

> The decision of the American Government to continue the gradual withdrawal of the troops of the punitive expedition from Mexico was inspired by the belief that the Mexican Government is now in a position and will omit no effort to prevent the recurrence of invasion of American territory.

President Carranza was generally satisfied with the agreement concluded at El Paso. He expressed some concern, however, that the Americans had not fixed a date for the complete withdrawal of Pershing's military expedition. Washington diplomats countered that no date would be set until the United States had some assurance from Mexico that the Río Grande border was safe from bandits. In response, Obregón submitted to an oral agreement with Scott and Funston that he would dispatch his personal troops to police the border area in Sonora, Coahuila, and Chihuahua. Obregón's pledge, in effect, enabled the United States to commence an immediate recall of American soldiers from Mexico.[14]

The conference at El Paso was a concerted effort on the part of the United States and Mexico to resolve a long-standing diplomatic issue through amicable negotiations. Clearly, the territorial sovereignty of both nations had been violated. While American interventionists endorsed a declaration of war on Mexico, the official position of the Wilson Administration was to seek a peaceful solution. Near the conclusion of the conference, the U.S. consul at El Paso, George Carothers, expressed guarded optimism that a workable solution was at hand.

Despite the seemingly good intentions of the Carranza government, Generals Funston and Scott voiced their concern to Secretary of War Baker that Mexico was ill-prepared to meet the terms of the agreement. "We feel that the whole proposition is redolent with bad faith," they reported. Obregón was only buying time "to keep the United States troops quiet until Mexican troops are in position to drive them out of Mexico by force." The American generals reinforced their statement by insisting that military units stationed near the Río Grande were dangerously undermanned. The distribution of troops at present was so weak, they cautioned, the army could not withstand an attack in force.

Funston and Scott's skepticism was not unwarranted. Just when American diplomats believed they were nearing a workable accord on the mutual defense of the Río Grande, news of the Big Bend raids reached Washington and El Paso. Upon hearing the news, General Obregón pledged the support of his government in pursuing the raiders. He assured Generals Scott and Funston that Mexico was equally outraged by the Glenn Springs tragedy, and that the perpetrators were bandits and not partisan soldiers. Similarly, Venustiano Carranza tried to persuade Secretary of State Lansing that the attack on West Texas was "beyond the control of the Mexican Government." He even suggested the possibility that the bandits may have been organized on the American side of the Río Grande. The entire incident, he surmised, was an attempt by American interventionists to provoke an international conflict.[15]

Clearly, the Glenn Springs-Boquillas raids lent credence to the critical appraisal Generals Scott and Funston had earlier expressed about their agreement with Obregón. In their report to the Secretary of War dated May 8, they referenced the assault on Texas, saying, "We expect many attacks along the whole border similar to the latest attack in Big Bend Río Grande." As a precautionary measure, they appealed to Washington to call out National Guard units from Texas, Arizona, and New Mexico to help bolster defenses in the Big Bend against the probability of future invasion.[16]

Without question, the attacks on Big Bend served the interests of border residents desiring a reevaluation of U.S. border defense policy. Since the beginning of Mexico's civil war, West Texans lived in fear of attack from either bandits or revolutionary soldiers. They appealed for increased military protection, but were denied all requests until after the Glenn Springs raid. Contrary to Carranza's theory, however, it would not have been in the American's best interest to provoke an international incident. Nevertheless, blaming Pancho Villa for the raids on Glenn Springs and Boquillas rather than fixing the blame on common criminals — where it rightfully belonged — tended to generate the desired response from the United States Army.

While the murder of the Compton boy and three American soldiers may have warranted military intervention, there was some question as to the danger that Jesse Deemer and Monroe Payne faced as hostages. Both men were well known to Mexicans living on the border, and each spoke fluent Spanish. Monroe's father, a descendent of one of the Black Semi-nole scouts, spent many years in Mexico. In addition, Deemer reportedly knew his kidnappers. One author writes, "Deemer probably would have been killed immediately had not several of the bandits urged that he be spared because of his many kindnesses to Mexican families around Boquillas." Still, in the army's view, the murder and kidnapping of Texas citizens demanded a swift and appropriate response.[17]

The appearance of the Sibley-Langhorne expedition in Mexico on the heels of the Pershing campaign placed the Carranza government in an extremely embarrassing position. According to the understanding between Obregón and Scott at El Paso, no additional U.S. troops were to be sent across the border. Sibley and Langhorne's presence clearly abrogated that agreement. Carranza accused the United States with "intent upon rendering [a] situation unnecessarily difficult for Mexico and adding to [the] perplexities of international relations."

Mexican newspapers, meanwhile, placed increased pressure on Carranza to respond militarily. Newspapers such as *El Democrata* challenged the chief executive to "maintain the dignity of the nation and defend the autonomy of her soil." Reporters pleaded with Mexican military leaders at the El Paso conference to not give in to American demands. Finally, editorialists assured their readers that "if an attempt were made, owing to the assault at Big Ben [*sic*], to send another expedition into Mexico, the Government would prevent it at any cost." In light of this public outcry, Carranza believed that he had no recourse but to meet the American presence with armed force.[18]

Alerted to the possibility of a clash between Mexican and American soldiers, William Blocker, U.S. Consul at Piedras Negras, Coahuila, reported on May 11 that one thousand cavalry were heading north from Saltillo and Torreón. Blocker also expressed his belief that the Mexican troops had orders to attack if they encountered Sibley and Langhorne. A second State Department official based in Saltillo voiced a similar alarm. In an interview with the governor of Coahuila, the magistrate declared his commitment to oppose all Americans who had crossed into Mexico unless they retreated. Finally, a telegram from James Rogers in Mexico City dated May 23 confirmed that top-ranking Mexican commanders on the northern frontier received orders "to attack the American force unless it retired at once."[19]

If the War Department had not taken measures to recall the Sibley-Langhorne expedition, it appears that Mexico was prepared to engage

American troops. Perhaps Carranza personally never intended to confront the United States. His official response may only have served to mollify an outraged public. Whatever his motives, President Carranza issued the orders to halt the American advance. Faced with a second incident of U.S. military intervention, the frustrated leader had an obligation to uphold Mexico's territorial integrity. Carranza's best hope for a resolution to the dilemma rested with the outcome of the El Paso conference. The Glenn Springs raid and the military response that it provoked threatened to disrupt the international talks before they were successfully concluded. Thus, when the War Department ordered Colonel Sibley to withdraw his column to the United States, it not only prevented a disastrous clash between Mexican and American forces, it enabled diplomacy to prevail over armed conflict.

The Mexican intrusions on American soil in 1916 forced profound changes in the U.S. military defense posture on the border. Over a two-year period thousands of armed American soldiers were dispatched to the Big Bend. Included in the troop buildup were National Guardsmen from Texas, New Mexico, Arizona, Pennsylvania, and New York. In his report to Washington, General Funston recognized the problem of defending a one-thousand-mile border with only six available regiments of cavalry. The battle-hardened commander saw no viable option other than to patrol the border with the cavalry while maintaining a reserve of infantry to protect against an impending attack. "I fully realize that the people of the country and the War Department expect me to give the very best protection possible to every town and every industry," the general pledged, knowing full well the limitations on his ability to provide such protection.

Funston determined that the Big Bend Military District would be divided into ten isolated outposts. Company I of the 4th Texas Infantry, which constituted part of the reserve, was transferred from Marathon to La Noria, the American terminus for the cable tram. Concurrently, Troops A and B of the 6th Cavalry, headquartered at Fort Sam Houston in San Antonio, established a base camp at Glenn Springs in the summer of 1916. The following year some of Pershing's 8th Cavalry, recently returned from Mexico, replaced the 6th, which was transferred to France. Other soldiers were dispersed along the Río Grande at Castolon, Lajitas, Polvo (present Redford, Texas), Presidio, Indio, Ruidosa, Candelaria, and Porvenir. Concurrently, the army based artillery squadrons at Marfa and Alpine, the major railroad outlets for the entire Big Bend.[20]

Castolon assumed particular importance in the army's defense planning. Located between Santa Elena and Mariscal canyons, Castolon was one of only a few crossover points on the United States–Mexico border. More importantly, a handful of well-placed soldiers at Castolon could protect the Terlingua mining district—where lucrative mining payrolls and the Chisos Mining Company store were inviting targets. On October 15, 1916, the War Department leased from Clyde Buttrill approximately four acres of land at Castolon overlooking the Río Grande valley.

Next, the army established a new military outpost named Camp Saint Helena, which it occupied with elements of the 5th, 6th, and 8th Cavalry. While most of the soldiers lived in tents, they constructed a number of wooden buildings in the camp between 1916 and 1917.

In 1919 the War Department revamped its military strategy in the Big Bend. The idea was to strengthen the Mexican border patrol system by replacing the smaller, remote outposts with a number of larger, permanent facilities. Camp Saint Helena was one of approximately forty new military posts targeted for expansion. The so-called Mexican Border Project called for substantial modifications to the post. From September 1919 to August 1920, the army's Construction Division expended $22,000 on internal improvements. Among the changes were a new electrical distribution system and modernized water and sewage facilities. Once construction was completed, the new post consisted of nine structures: an officer's quarters, a noncommissioned officer's quarters, barracks with mess hall, lavatory, recreation hall, canteen, grain shed, stable, and water tower and storage tank.[21]

Ironically, the army never fully utilized the updated facility. It appears that American military occupation of Big Bend after the Glenn Springs raid effectively curbed further bandit activity in the immediate area. Accordingly, the strategic importance of Camp Saint Helena diminished. One Big Bend resident wryly summarized the army's role at Camp Saint Helena after 1916: "The troops at Castolon never had to cross the river into Mexico because they never saw a bandit there." W. D. Smithers, who first arrived in the Big Bend as a muleteer for the troops stationed at Glenn Springs, lamented that there was very little for the army to do after the Glenn Springs incident but "watch for bandits and play baseball." Troop activity at La Noria must have been equally unimpressive as reflected in a series of cartoons depicting the tedium of military life on the border.[22]

Excellent illustration of the cooperative effort between the U.S. Army Air Service and the U.S. Cavalry during their occupancy of the Big Bend from 1918 to 1920. *(Courtesy, Photography Collection, Harry Ransom Humanities Research Center, University of Texas at Austin)*

Glenn Springs, ca. 1918, two years after the raid. Smoke from the wax factory is still visible in the background. Note a more permanent encampment as indicated by the presence of wooden buildings in place of tents. *(Courtesy, National Archives, Washington, D.C.)*

If conditions in the Big Bend were comparatively quiescent after 1916, such was not the case farther upstream between Presidio and El Paso, where bandits were able to cross into the United States virtually at will. On Christmas Day 1917, Jesús Rentería, a member of the notorious Chico Cano band, shocked West Texans with a bold raid thirty miles north of the border. The bandits attacked the L. C. Brite ranch, located on a high rolling plateau known as the Candelaria Rim, thirty-five miles east of Marfa. Rentería and his band struck at dawn. When the fighting was over, the raiders had killed three men and stolen all of Brite's horses. The boldness that the Mexicans displayed in raiding so deep into U.S. territory gave the incident national focus. A similar raid on the Ed Nevill ranch (located 35 miles southeast of present Van Horn, Texas) in the spring of 1918 caused the army to take yet another hard look at its defenses in West Texas.

President Wilson's commitment of American troops to France in 1917 seriously reduced the number of men available to patrol the United States-Mexico border. By this time most of the members of the 5th, 6th, and 14th Cavalry units transferred to the European front. Only the 8th Cavalry, headquartered in Marfa, remained behind to defend against outlaw attacks. Under the able command of Lieutenant Colonel Langhorne, the 8th formed a thread-like barrier against Mexican incursions across the Río Grande. Though hardened by years of campaigning in Mexico and Texas, Langhorne's forces were still insufficient in number to bring an end to the raiding.

The conclusion of the First World War enabled the War Department to propose a solution to the army's border problems. On June 16, 1919, Major General Charles T. Menhor, chief of the U.S. Army Air Service, ordered the establishment of an aerial border patrol in Texas. At the general's command, twelve planes from Ellington Field in Houston and six from Kelly Field in San Antonio flew to Fort Bliss to form the 11th Aero Squadron. The pilots of this command were instructed to fly reconnaissance missions along the Río Grande from Presidio to El Paso. A second route began at Marfa, following the river through the rugged canyons of the Big Bend to Sanderson, Texas. For two years the squadron of 12-cylinder, DeHavilland–4 (DH–4) fighter aircraft—each armed with two .30 caliber machine guns—aided in the struggle against Mexican bandits.[23]

The introduction of air surveillance to the Big Bend did not diminish the importance of the cavalry, however. Indeed, reports of two missing pilots on the morning of August 10, 1919, resulted in a third expedition into Mexican territory. While on a routine mission from Marfa to Lajitas, Lieutenants Harold G. Peterson and Paul H. Davis developed engine trouble. In their search for a clear spot to land, the pilots mistook the Río Conchos for the Río Grande and landed their DH–4 aircraft in Mexico. They wandered for days on what they presumed to be the Texas side of the Río Grande. On the morning of August 16, the airmen awakened to find themselves surrounded by Mexican bandits.

Jesús Rentería, easily identified by the steel hook he wore on his artificial arm, led the outlaws. He informed Peterson and Davis that they had landed in Mexico and he intended to hold them for ransom. The next day, Colonel Langhorne received Peterson's handwritten note detailing the Mexican demands. Hoping the army would make every effort to return the two pilots to the United States, Peterson wrote, "I am in good health and spirits as I am sure the War Department will meet the ransom. If not, good-bye, as they mean business."

Although the State Department negotiated for the release of the prisoners, there was no indication that the government was prepared to meet the ransom. While Washington deliberated, a group of local ranchers sponsored $15,000 for the return of the downed pilots. Colonel Langhorne selected his most experienced officer, Captain Leonard F. Matlack, to deliver the money and escort the prisoners safely back to American soil. During the exchange, Matlack, renowned on the border as a fearless and combat-ready officer, overcame two of the Mexican captors and withdrew with both the hostages and $7,500 of the ransom money.

On August 18, 1919, Secretary of War Baker authorized Captain Matlack and the 8th Cavalry to reenter Mexico in pursuit of the bandits. Unlike the earlier interventions of Pershing and Sibley, the 8th Cavalry availed itself of aerial support from the 11th Aëro Squadron. During one reconnaissance, one of the planes spotted members of the bandit gang escaping well in advance of the pursuit column. After taking fire, the pilot guided his aircraft into a steep dive, triggered a burst from his machine guns, and scattered the horsemen below. Hours later, the cavalry arrived on the scene to confirm that the airman had, in fact, killed Rentería and three of his band.

Understandably, the Carranza government protested this latest intrusion into Mexican territory. On August 21 he demanded the War Department to recall the American troops. Colonel Langhorne, meanwhile, insisted he had informed the Mexican military commander at Chihuahua of his intent to cross the Río Grande. Apparently, local authorities voiced no objection to the crossing. Notably, after receiving reports of Rentería's death, Langhorne ordered the withdrawal of all troops from Mexico. On August 23, 1919, the combined force of cavalry and fighter support — the last American punitive expedition into Mexico — withdrew to the United States.[24]

Not unlike the days when the Plains Indians threatened the peace and security of West Texas, the Big Bend again became an armed camp after the Glenn Springs–Boquillas raids. In the twentieth century, however, the army committed men and machinery to its defense against Mexican intruders. Generally speaking, the arrival of the army to Glenn Springs after the raid did much to reduce acts of banditry along the border. From 1916 to 1921 the War Department assumed its role as guardian of the West Texas frontier with unfaltering resolution.

Increased diplomatic tension between Mexico and the United States was the price for the army's determination to secure peace on the Río Grande. In many respects, the events surrounding the Glenn Springs raid of 1916 mirrored the international complexities that stemmed from the Mexican Revolution. American reaction to the incident placed assertive interventionists in conflict with conciliatory diplomats. In most cases, the actions of the army contradicted the aims of the State Department. On three separate occasions, the army — in the performance of its duty — ignored the inherent restrictions imposed by an international boundary. In response, Mexico, a country in a desperate struggle for political identity, had no recourse but to decry its powerful northern neighbor for the blatant violations of its national sovereignty. As a consequence, President Carranza's political dilemma nearly brought the two nations to war, a situation that doubtless would have spelled disaster for an already unstable Mexican government.

By the 1920s a series of international developments helped to ease the tension that had previously existed on the Río Grande border. To begin, the interventionist policies of the Wilson administration gave way to an era of American isolationism. Republican leaders were determined to end confrontation diplomacy between Mexico and the United States. On April 1, 1920, the War Department issued General Order No. 15, which reduced the defense forces on the Río Grande to a few well-placed detachments. The United States "return to normalcy" coincided with political stabilization in Mexico. In May 1920, after nearly a decade of civil war, the Mexican Revolution entered its final stages. General Alvaro Obregón successfully ousted Carranza from power and assumed the presidency. In a gesture to normalize diplomatic relations with the United States — or perhaps because he was cognizant of his pledge to Generals Scott and Funston years earlier in El Paso — President Obregón made good his promise to police the Río Grande. Mexico's willingness to keep the international border secure enabled the United States to reduce its forces in Texas even further. The U.S. Army Air Service, meanwhile, disbanded the aerial border squadron in 1921. Finally, in 1923 political assassins brought an end to the fearsome military career of General Francisco Villa. Thus, America's commitment to ameliorate diplomatic tension with Mexico, coupled with increasing political stability within the Mexican government, enabled the War Department to bring the military occupation of the Big Bend to a conclusion.

CHAPTER EIGHT

The Fruits of the Earth

No commodity produced today, not even United States steel, holds the strategic position for commanding a big price in the world's markets for many years to come as King Cotton does.

— Neal A. Brown, 1924

For centuries, the Río Grande served as a life-giving resource to all occupants who settled within its sandy, low-lying valleys. The first arrivals to the Big Bend recognized the naturally irrigated flood plains as ideal for farming by even the most primitive methods. Most of these early inhabitants were attracted to the region surrounding the junction of the Río Grande and the Río Conchos near present Presidio, Texas. Beginning about A.D. 1000–1100 a sedentary, agricultural, pottery-making people drifted slowly down the Río Grande valley from the area near El Paso. After more than two hundred years of periodic migration, these native people eventually settled at the junction of the two great rivers.

The Spanish called this area La Junta de los Ríos upon their discovery of the Indian communities in the late sixteenth century. Indeed, the Europeans were surprised to find that the fertile valley harbored more than ten thousand sedentary Indians. The fact that a well-developed system of agriculture supported each pueblo intrigued the Spaniards even more. One priest who had accompanied the column of soldiers into Texas wrote to his superiors, "All of them were settled peoples who cultivated corn, beans, calabashes, watermelons, cantaloupes and tobacco."[1]

While the Spanish recognized the importance of agriculture in the lower Río Grande valley, the prevalence of nomadic Indians in the Big Bend precluded any significant development. Apache raiders, and later the Southern Plains Indians, kept Texas sparsely populated. In 1781 less than four thousand Spanish inhabitants were reported to occupy the entire province. Most of them were centered around San Antonio de Béxar and other military towns further east. Only a handful of isolated settlers, located along the south and east section of the Río Grande, managed to eke out a marginal existence throughout the remainder of the Spanish-Mexican period.

San Carlos (located approximately eleven miles southeast of Lajitas, Texas), was one of the early Hispanic communities that thrived on the Río Grande frontier. Originally selected as the site for one of the Spanish presidios built in 1773, a small community consisting largely of the families of soldiers developed around the fortress until its abandonment in 1789. In 1833, the Mexican government reestablished San Carlos as a military colony to protect the northern frontier. Since that time—and even to the present day—the village of San Carlos has appeared like an oasis to hundreds of travelers inching their way across miles of uninterrupted desert.

Recognized traditionally as a center of trade for Indian and Hispanic neighbors living along the Río Grande, San Carlos also gained importance as an agricultural area. When Colonel Emilio Langberg of the Mexican Army visited the village in 1851 en route to the Big Bend, he found a budding community of more than 800 people engaged in floodplain farming.[2] For the remainder of the Mexican period, the residents of this remote settlement supplied apples, peaches, figs, and a variety of fresh vegetables to militia soldiers patrolling the northern frontier. Not surprisingly, San Carlos came to be a popular stopover point for emigrating Mexican laborers bound for the mining districts of West Texas in the late nineteenth century.

Cipriano Hernández of Camargo, Chihuahua, was one of the many Mexican expatriates who crossed into the Big Bend in the 1890s. Like hundreds of laborers drawn across the border to American-owned silver mines, Hernández no doubt followed an established route into Texas. Originating in San Carlos, two well-beaten paths led the itinerant workers to the United States. The main trail skirted along the base of the Sierra de Ponce on the Mexican side of the Río Grande. At a point due south of present Big Bend National Park, the trail forked, the easternmost path leading to a crossing located at or near the present village of Santa Elena (across the Río Grande from present Castolon, Texas), and the west fork following the river upstream to Lajitas, Texas, a favorite crossover point for prospectors heading north to the Terlingua Mining District.

Hernández first arrived in Shafter, Texas (located between Presidio and Marfa), where he mined silver in the mid-1890s. In 1903 the enterprising newcomer purchased three sections of land bordering the Río

Grande in southern Brewster County. Hernández named the area Santa Helena,[3] perhaps in honor of the famous canyon overlooking the natural floodplain which he farmed. Hernández raised wheat, corn, oats, and other cereal grains which he sold to local consumers as feed for mules that hauled supplies to and from the mines. In addition, Hernández raised fresh vegetables, an equally welcome commodity in the Big Bend mining camps. Presumably in 1903, Hernández built the first permanent structure (present Alvino house) in the Castolon area.

Other Mexican nationals followed Hernández into the Big Bend. Most settled along the low-lying valleys that paralleled the Río Grande or its main tributaries. Agapito Carrasco, for example, settled a half-dozen Mexican families about one mile downstream from the Hernández place. They called the area "El Ojito" because of the natural spring which provided fresh water to the tiny community. In 1908 Ruperto Chavarría led a much larger group of immigrants to settle on the west bank of Alamo Creek, approximately two miles upriver from present Castolon. The Mexicans named this community "La Coyota."[4] In both cases the residents of these small villages utilized the sub-irrigated lands near the river to practice subsistence farming. They raised corn, beans, wheat, squash, tomatoes, and melons.

As the Mexican population increased around Castolon, Hernández enlarged his small, two-room adobe house to accommodate a small store that serviced the area. Hernández enjoyed a brisk commercial business as customers from both sides of the Río Grande frequented his place. "Don" Cipriano maintained his position as patriarch of the Castolon community until 1914, when he sold the store and all of its adjoining property to Clyde Buttrill, co-owner of a large cattle operation in the Rosillos Mountains. Hernández decided to move closer to the mining activities at Terlingua, where he and his son, Guadalupe, opened a large mercantile business in Terlingua Abaja.

The arrival of Cipriano Hernández and other Mexican immigrants to the Castolon area marked another important step toward the eventual domestication of the Big Bend. Up to this time, only a handful of soldiers representing the United States and Mexico dared venture into this ominous environment. Gradually, a steady stream of incoming pioneers — ranchers, miners, and farmers — displaced the Indian and the mounted cavalryman as the preeminent residents of the trans-Pecos region. Like their predecessors, however, each group recognized the importance of the Río Grande floodplain to their survival.

It appears that economic diversification was Clyde Buttrill's motive for buying the Hernández property. He and his older brother, Lou, already enjoyed success as cattle ranchers. It appears that Clyde realized an opportunity to produce alfalfa and other winter grains for the Buttrill's cattle operation in the Rosillos Mountains. Nonetheless, the Buttrills did not engage in the actual farming operation. According to Eunice Sublett Newman, "Buttrill did not do any of the work.... He only came down once in awhile." Instead, he employed the services of an experienced farmer well-versed in irrigation techniques and the latest farm machinery. In the spring of 1914 Buttrill hired James L. Sublett of Sweetwater, Texas, to clear his land for planting.

Sublett, a tall, raw-boned man with a walrus moustache and skin weathered brown from years of working in the hot sun, was perhaps the first man to introduce mechanized farming into the Big Bend. He had worked most of his early life for the railroad, and he understood machines. Years of experience leveling ground for the track crews, moreover, gave Sublett an invaluable expertise. Once established in the abandoned Hernández home, Sublett cleared much of the land to install the area's first pump irrigation system. Next, Sublett hired Leandro Silvas, Benjamin Sánchez, and other local Mexican laborers to plant the new fields with wheat, corn, alfalfa, and other "feed crops." Finally, his daughter Eunice recalled, Sublett brought the first wheat-threshing machine into the valley. Thus, in February 1916 Sublett entered into a partnership with Clyde Buttrill in which both men benefitted from several years of productive irrigated farming.[5]

The ensuing period of border instability, however, forced Buttrill to sell the property in 1918 to Carroll Bates, a former Texas Ranger. Bates, who showed no real interest in maintaining the farm, resold the land to Wayne Cartledge of Terlingua, Texas. Wayne Rollins Cartledge, son of a prominent Austin lawyer, was a native Texan and resident of the Big Bend since 1909. Through his father's influence, Cartledge took his first job as an accountant and manager of the Chisos Mining Company store. During the next several years, Cartledge developed a good business relationship with Howard E. Perry, the feisty little industrial tycoon who owned the Chisos Mine. In 1919 the two men formed a partnership called La Harmonía Company. With the purchase of the Castolon property that same year, Cartledge and Perry entered into a long-term involvement in commercial farming and general merchandising in the Big Bend.

James Sublett, meanwhile, formed a new business and reestablished his farm about two miles upriver from Castolon. Albert W. Dorgan, an eccentric German-born immigrant who had worked as a city planner and architect in Detroit, Michigan, was Sublett's latest associate. The two men purchased a section of land known to the local Mexican population as "Rancho Steele." Apparently, the area had been named in honor of L. V. Steele, an itinerant mining prospector who inherited the property through his marriage to the daughter of Miguel de la O, a respected Mexican rancher. Tom and Charlie Metcalf, titleholders at the time of Sublett's purchase in 1918, were eager to sell to any interested buyers.

When Sublett and Dorgan arrived at Rancho Steele, there was only a two-room adobe house standing near the base of a small hill. Tom Metcalf had lived there. Sublett hired Alvino Ybarra and Cisto Avila, two local Mexican stone masons, to help him build a home at the top of the hill, and a smaller house (known today as La Casita) for his farmhands just below it. Dorgan, meanwhile, moved about a half mile up the river, where he personally constructed an elongated rock structure for himself and his wife. Next, Sublett and Dorgan combined their engineering talents to develop an extensive irrigated farming project along the floodplain below.

It was largely Dorgan's idea that he and Sublett plant a truck garden in order to provide the Terlingua mining region with fresh vegetables. "Poppa planted anything that would grow," declared Eunice Sublett. As a result, the farm grew large enough to provide employment to a number of local Mexican families for many years. In addition to the farming operation, Sublett converted the old Metcalf house into a store which his son-in-law, Fred Spann, managed after his discharge from the army. The store was a convenient outlet for Mexican soldiers encamped on the opposite side of the Río Grande. They frequented the Sublett place to order goods and supplies that were hard to get through normal military distribution.[6]

The establishment of the Cartledge-Perry store in Castolon and the Sublett-Spann operation at Rancho Steele evidenced a steady population increase in the lower Río Grande valley. In time, the tiny Mexican communities of Terlingua Abaja, La Coyota, Castolon, El Ojito, and Buenos Aires (approximately five miles downstream from Castolon) numbered between two and three hundred residents. Virtually all of the inhabitants of this area established permanent homes and practiced some form of subsistence farming. Sublett and Cartledge, however, were the first to introduce commercial agriculture into the area. While not necessarily in competition with one another, the two entrepreneurs expanded their

businesses enough to make Castolon a viable cultivation area in the Big
Bend for years to come.

Not all farming activity was restricted to Castolon. Beginning about
1896, newly arrived Mexican immigrants employed in the mines at
Boquillas del Carmen founded the flourishing little community of San
Vicente, Texas. Named for the old presidio still visible on the opposite
side of the river, San Vicente evolved as a series of small, carefully-placed
farms along the sandy flood plains of the Río Grande. Still another area
under cultivation was present Río Grande Village (located approximately
two miles downstream from San Vicente). Brewster County records list
Jesús Estrada as the original owner of Block G–19, section 6, but in 1918
he sold the tract to a Swedish immigrant named John O. Wedin. Curiously, Wedin, an experienced wheat farmer from Kansas, made sheep his
first investment in the Big Bend. Not content with ranching, Wedin sold
his flocks just after World War I and purchased three sections of good
bottomland closer to the Río Grande.

After nearly a decade of successful irrigated wheat farming, Wedin
attracted new investors to the Río Grande Village area. In 1926 Joe H.
Graham, a prominent cattle rancher from Del Rio, Texas, bought the
Wedin place. Graham, who had recently assumed ownership of the
Buttrill ranch, saw a way to use the farm in connection with his cattle
business. In addition, Graham held interest in feed lots near Kansas City
where he fattened his stock for market. With the Wedin farm, Graham
could plant alfalfa and other grains to feed to his cattle during the winter
months. Inasmuch as Wedin had already installed an eight-inch irrigation
pump and had laid out most of the drainage system, Graham considered
the farm to be an excellent investment.

Graham and his two sons, Frank and Jeff, expanded their productive
acreage by clearing the hitherto undeveloped upper section of the farm
(present Daniels Ranch). "That whole area that is now Río Grande Village
was all fields," remarked Jeff Graham. Finally, the Grahams converted the
two adobe structures built by Wedin into a storage shed and a garage for
their machinery.[7] Thus, Joe Graham, one of the new generation of cattlemen to emerge in West Texas, used the Río Grande farm plus his feedlots
in Kansas to introduce a fully integrated ranching system into the Big
Bend. Graham revelled in his successful business until the Great Depression, when he lost the Rosillos ranch. His financial collapse in the 1930s,
moreover, forced him to subdivide his farm properties. First, he sold one
portion of the farm to Texas senator Benjamin F. Berkeley (present

Berkeley Cottage). Then, in 1937 he sold a second section to John R. Daniels of Presidio.

While John and Mary Daniels maintained the farm for approximately five more years, they did not make any significant improvements on the land. In the first place, John was not a farmer by vocation. He had spent most of his years in the Big Bend living in the Chisos Basin where he ran a small cattle operation. After many lean years in the ranching business, he decided to try his hand at floodplain farming. In 1937 the Daniels family occupied the larger structure that Wedin had built years ago and the Grahams used as a storage garage. Daniels enlarged the building to accommodate a small store for Mary, who serviced local residents living along the river.[8] For the remainder of his time in Big Bend, Daniels practiced mainly subsistence farming on his two-hundred-acre plot.

Although Joe Graham and John Daniels each established productive farms, Castolon emerged as the preeminent producer of commercial agriculture in the Big Bend. In a letter to Howard Perry dated November 28, 1922, Wayne Cartledge proposed making cotton rather than wheat, the main cash crop. "I have decided to let the farm lay idle until cotton planting time next spring," Cartledge began. He argued that while wheat was still productive, the market price had dropped significantly since 1918. Furthermore, he listed numerous mechanical difficulties involved in milling the wheat. Presenting a strong argument for his decision to switch to cotton, Cartledge informed his partner that he would encourage the local Mexican population to also make the change. "We shall have pretty lean skidding until we can make and sell some cotton," Cartledge explained.

In his decision to make a financial commitment to cotton production, Wayne Cartledge was keeping pace with prevailing economic trends visible in West Texas by the 1920s. In the 1890s, East Texas was the major cotton producer in the state. By 1910, however, cotton farming had taken firm root in the traditional stock raising counties of West Texas. One historian notes that by 1920 land speculators who "planted cotton, talked cotton, sold cotton, everything but ate cotton," began to drift into the trans-Pecos area. While the Big Bend itself remained essentially cow country, Wayne Cartledge was apparently cognizant of the economic importance that cotton had begun to assume. For this reason, he proposed to Perry that their company invest in the product.

The availability of Mexican labor, crucial to the success of any cotton-producing operation in Texas, was a second factor that influenced Cartledge's decision. He recognized that the Big Bend — in particular the

Jim Sublett's original trading post at old Castolon in 1916. Notice the rich, irrigated farm lands surrounding the structure. Santa Elena Canyon is clearly visible in the background. *(Courtesy, Photography Collection, Harry Ransom Humanities Research Center, University of Texas at Austin)*

John Daniels' farm house as it appeared shortly after the establishment of Big Bend National Park in 1944. The irrigated fields visible have since been converted into the Río Grande Village campground on the east side of the national park. *(Courtesy, National Park Service, Big Bend National Park, Texas)*

communities around Castolon and La Coyota — had a ready-made supply of inexpensive farm labor. His idea was to employ local Mexican residents as sharecroppers. "If my farm turns out well I expect to buy up the small tracts farmed by Mexicans," he wrote to Neal A. Brown, a local property owner. "Then I will rent them on shares and insist that they plant cotton." Mexicans who owned their land and were not willing to sell to La Harmonía Company were encouraged to grow cotton for sale to Wayne Cartledge at current market value.

Regarding Cartledge's proposal, Perry argued that because the nearest cotton gin was located more than two hundred miles away, profits from a tenant farming operation would be marginal at best. One solution to the problem, Perry determined, was to invest in a cotton gin. In the spring of 1923 Wayne Cartledge forwarded $450 to the Continental Gin Company of Birmingham, Alabama, as advanced payment on a Pratt-Huller cotton gin. In October Cartledge wrote to his father in Austin that he had employed forty Mexican laborers to harvest the first cotton crop. He added that the gin, after several delays for "want of lumber," was at last fully operational.[9]

The Mexican residents at Castolon responded enthusiastically to the idea of tenant farming. Cartledge's pledge to purchase all crops at current market prices guaranteed local farmers an annual income. More importantly, the presence of a fully integrated cotton operation in Castolon promised itinerant laborers an opportunity to make Big Bend a permanent home. While every member of the Castolon community maintained a family garden of corn, wheat, and vegetables, most converted the remainder of their fields to cotton.[10] In addition to local workers, Cartledge employed a sizeable labor force from Santa Elena and other villages located across the Río Grande.

Inasmuch as neither Wayne Cartledge nor any of his employees knew how to operate a cotton gin, its construction in the spring of 1923 presented La Harmonía Company with an assortment of technical problems. Initially, Cartledge relied on a member of the Department of Agriculture stationed in Castolon to advise him about how to operate the machine, with very limited results; early production figures for the first cotton harvest were a paltry three bales of cotton per day. The arrival of Richard W. Derrick to Castolon in 1924, however, led to an increase in production. Derrick, a former naval shipbuilder in Boston during World War I, knew a great deal about technical machinery. Soon after his arrival, his me-

La Harmonía Company gin mill at Castolon. Although a comparatively smaller operation than most West Texas cotton mills of the period, this gin was nonetheless an important feature of the Big Bend economy in the early decades of the twentieth century. *(Courtesy, Archives of the Big Bend, Clifford B. Casey Collection, Sul Ross State University, Alpine, Texas)*

chanical skills made him one the company's most valued employees. Derrick soon had the gin producing cotton around the clock.

Since the gin required constant supervision, Derrick trained Alvino Ybarra, one of the Mexican residents of Castolon, to keep it operating. A native of Ocampo, Coahuila, Ybarra immigrated to the Big Bend in 1914. As a young man in Chihuahua he worked as a personal servant to a wealthy San Carlos family. When the Mexican Revolution began, Ybarra, like countless other refugees, followed the familiar trail into West Texas. Once arrived in the Big Bend, Ybarra was employed at the Sublett farm. After James Sublett moved his family from Castolon in 1918, Ybarra occupied the house that Cipriano Hernández had originally built. Ybarra enlarged the structure to accommodate his own family, plus those of his two brothers who followed him from Mexico. Ybarra remained a faithful employee of the La Harmonía Company for the entire time that the cotton gin operated in Castolon.[11]

Wayne Cartledge's imaginative utilization of the Río Grande floodplain provided Big Bend residents with a viable economic alternative to ranching and mining. While not an outstanding financial success, between 150 and 200 bales of cotton were produced in the vicinity per season which were marketed in El Paso and Houston. Income from the enterprise never exceeded $1,200 per year during its twenty years of existence; nevertheless, Cartledge introduced advanced methods of farming—such as crop rotation and improved irrigation techniques—to develop perhaps the most productive farm (acre for acre) in the entire region.[12] With the installation of a gin mill, Cartledge established a fully integrated farming project that kept twenty to thirty local families actively employed. In the end, the commercial activities centered around Castolon endured years beyond the economic heyday of both the cattle and mining industries.

Cotton farming was not the only interest that Wayne Cartledge and Howard Perry pursued in Castolon. Their mercantile business increased to the point that the company soon expanded. In 1925 the army provided the two businessmen with the opportunity to increase their holdings. On January 3 the War Department announced the sale of all its military installations on the Río Grande. Included in the sale were the nine buildings at Camp Saint Helena, which the army built in 1920 but never occupied. Relying totally upon Howard Perry's sense for business, Cartledge posted a bid of $1,280 for all of the Castolon property. Despite an assessed value of $27,000, the army accepted the bid. On April 15,

1926, La Harmonía Company registered its latest acquisitions with the county clerk's office in Alpine, Texas.[13]

The Castolon store served the surrounding community in a number of ways. First, the facility took on the appearance of a frontier trading post. Cartledge acted as middleman for Mexican fur trappers who exchanged animal pelts — fox, beaver, wolf, and bobcat — for groceries and other general merchandise. La Harmonía shipped the furs to retailers, like the Finnican-Brown Company of El Paso, for a marginal profit. Second, Cartledge acted as a wholesale distributor for the sale and shipment of all candelilla wax produced in the area. Finally, the store provisioned Big Bend residents with hardware items, groceries, dry goods, medical needs — and ranch and farm supplies, which service proved to be the most profitable aspect of the Cartledge-Perry enterprise.

With the closure of the Sublett-Spann store at Rancho Steele in 1927, La Harmonía dominated the general merchandise business in Castolon. "It was a great relief to get rid of Sublett and Spann as competitors," remarked Cartledge to his senior partner. He anticipated, furthermore, that La Harmonía at last could "get reasonable prices for our goods." While the local Mexican population became dependent on the store to supply their needs, they were very often displeased with the exorbitant prices. On one occasion, Cartledge wrote to Perry to inform him of local discontent about the prices at the Castolon store. Perry countered that because "the Castolon store was subject to dangers of the border, it warranted higher prices."

Despite its shortcomings, La Harmonía was a valued institution among the local Mexican population of Big Bend. Wayne Cartledge used his influence as a successful merchant to act as legal counsel for his neighbors. He interceded on their behalf in assorted business dealings. In some cases, La Harmonía acted as a financial agent by extending personal loans to needy clients. Perhaps Cartledge's most important role was that of recorder of vital statistics within the Castolon community. Local residents depended on him to provide U.S. Immigration officials with acceptable legal proof that they were American citizens not subject to deportation. In many respects, the Cartledge-Perry enterprise came to represent the very meaning of its own name — La Harmonía; the services that the company provided to the inhabitants of the Big Bend truly promoted harmony between Mexicans and Americans living on the Río Grande.[14]

There were several causes for the decline of the cotton industry in Castolon after 1927. First, erratic price fluctuations on the domestic market forced many growers to quit raising cotton and revert to traditional crops such as wheat and corn. Prices had dropped from thirty to twenty cents per pound since La Harmonía opened for business in 1923. Also, by this time severe droughts in West Texas portended a drastic decline in future cotton production. The combination of these factors made the market as unpredictable as a "Chinese puzzle" to both Cartledge and Perry. On one occasion, Perry chided Cartledge for failing to sell their crop "before the market went to pieces." The losses that La Harmonía's farm operation sustained in 1927, in fact, caused the two men to consider dissolving the partnership and selling the business.[15]

Equally important was the loss of Mexican labor after the appearance of the U.S. Immigration Service in the Big Bend. Prior to 1928 the international border between Mexico and the United States was virtually unattended. Laborers from Santa Elena and other Mexican villages crossed freely to work on the American side. In 1928 the United States government began the strict enforcement of its immigration laws. The new border policy, therefore, made it difficult for La Harmonía to attract field hands to harvest its crops; their absence dealt a crushing blow to Texas cotton producers.

More alarming was the rate at which Mexican families who had lived in Castolon for years moved north to escape deportation. In a letter addressed to Secretary of Labor Frances Perkins, Cartledge complained of the "third degree methods used against people of Mexican extraction." He argued further that continued enforcement of the immigration laws would devastate the farming industry throughout the state.[16]

Finally, the increasingly erratic behavior of Howard Perry toward Wayne Cartledge caused an irreparable rift between them. Beginning in 1938 Cartledge was convinced that the company's farming operations had sustained too many losses. He proposed to Perry that they should sell the business, but the aging industrialist refused to discuss the matter. Instead, he accused Cartledge of poor management practices and mishandling of company funds. In a series of letters between Wayne and his father, Eugene Cartledge, Sr., the Austin lawyer instructed his son to sell before "the company's assets will be consumed with debts outstanding." He further advised Wayne to ignore Perry's wild accusations. "Perry is crazy and don't know it," the elder Cartledge advised.[17]

Just as other small businesses survived the economic catastrophe of the Great Depression, La Harmonía Company struggled through the remainder of the 1930s on federal subsidies granted through the New Deal.

Heavy losses plagued the operation, however, causing Eugene Cartledge to conclude that the situation was hopeless. In 1940 Wayne Cartledge dissolved his longstanding partnership with Perry and placed most of his Big Bend properties on the market. In 1942 La Harmonía ginned its last harvest and ceased all cotton farming activities. Finally, Wayne Cartledge turned over the management of the Castolon store — the last vestige of more than two decades of commercial activity on the Río Grande — to his son.

Throughout history the waters of the lower Río Grande stood in remarkable contrast to an otherwise unpalatable land. Its fertile valleys, like intermittent oases, offered dramatic relief to all those who settled within its boundaries. The Indians, and later the Spanish, recognized the importance of the floodplain to their existence. Their stay in the Big Bend, however, was temporary. One by one the Plains Indians, the Spanish soldiers, and the American explorers faded with the passing frontier. Their failure to overcome the challenge of the Chihuahuan desert inspired twentieth-century pioneers to combine modern scientific technology with traditional farming practices which guaranteed long-term economic survival.

Notably, the emergence of floodplain farming in the lower Río Grande valley facilitated the permanent occupation of the trans-Pecos region. Contrasted with Lubbock and other major farm areas of West Texas, Big Bend made a comparatively insignificant impact on the state's agricultural economy. Viewed in the context of local development, however, Anglo and Mexican communities utilized the Río Grande to create a viable economic climate for steady growth. The efforts of Cipriano Hernández, James Sublett, Joe Graham, Wayne Cartledge, and other adventuresome entrepreneurs combined to make the Big Bend a more livable environment. Their conscientious application of modern, irrigated farming techniques converted portions of this once uninhabitable desert into a agricultural garden. By the mid-1930s the appeal of a domesticated lower Río Grande valley captured the imagination of New Deal conservationists in Washington. One of the few remaining physical representations of a now vanished western frontier, the Big Bend stood poised in anticipation of its final occupation.

CHAPTER NINE

The Final Occupation

The area seems to be unique in many respects. It has real beauty and grandeur in and around the Chisos Mountains and the several canyons of the Río Grande, it has almost unparalleled spreads of vistas throughout ... and to the geologist will be a perpetual delight. In the somewhat limited judgement of the writer it is well worthy of national park status.

— *Bernard F. Manbey, 1935*

In 1899 the United States Geological Survey (USGS) commissioned the first successful government-sponsored navigation of the lower Río Grande. Under the able supervision of Robert T. Hill, a former Texas cowboy who learned geology in the ivy-league setting of Cornell University, the USGS team conquered the tortuous course of the canyons of the Big Bend. The following year, Hill articulated his impressions of the journey in a widely read article published in *Century Magazine.* He not only detailed the perils of boat travel down the Río Grande but also highlighted the breathtaking uniqueness of the terrain that he had witnessed. "Every aspect of the Big Bend country — landscape, configuration, rocks, and vegetation — is weird," noted the scientist. At the same time, Hill marvelled at the sheer spectacle of towering cliffs "softened by colors which camera or pen cannot reproduce."

Scarcely two years after Hill's triumphant voyage, the USGS sponsored a second expedition into the Big Bend. Unlike the Hill endeavor, the purpose of this mission was cartographic rather than exploratory. The federal government possessed no reliable map of that country other than the crude sketches that Lieutenants Echols and Hartz provided on their historic camel expeditions in the 1860s. For too long, Washington bureaucrats ignored the West Texas frontier as wild and unsettled. For this reason, the USGS assigned Arthur A. Stiles, considered one of the best topographic surveyors in the bureau, to prepare the first detailed map of the region. Stiles arrived in Terlingua in 1902 and with his youthful and talented assistant, Stuart T. Penick, proceeded to survey the area.

Like their predecessors, Stiles and Penick were impressed with the wildness and compelling beauty of the Big Bend. Armed with the traditional six-shooter and plenty of ammunition ordered through a Sears and Roebuck catalogue, the two men worked their way across the varied elevations of land, recording their observations with painstaking accuracy. First, they made note of the traditional place names — Mesa de Angila, Sierra de los Chisos, and Mariscal Canyon — that evidenced the Hispanic presence in Big Bend. To these names the two cartographers added a host of colorful descriptions of their own — Elephant Tusk, Pummel Peak, and Backbone Ridge — to testify to its unique geological character.

Although Hill's article was published in 1900 and the first reproduction of the Stiles-Penick map appeared in 1903, each focused attention on the Big Bend in later years. For example, in the 1930s Hill's narrative captured the imagination of a growing number of readers who were interested in developing Big Bend as a state park. "The cañons of the Río Grande are longest and least known," the essay began; "they have been and still are the least accessible to man, and have not hitherto been fully described." Hill's emphasis on the inspiring beauty of this geologic wonderland served to offset traditional fears about the tameless nature of the Big Bend. Added to this picturesque description, Stiles and Penick's work assured a curious public that the Big Bend was clearly "civilized." Domínguez Mountain, Roy's Peak, Pulliam's Bluff, and Ernst Valley were but a few notable indications that man had overcome the challenges of the arid West.[1]

Long before the park movement of the 1930s, however, local enthusiasts worked to bring regional and national attention to Big Bend. J. O. Langford, a native of Mississippi, where he fell victim to recurring bouts with malaria, early capitalized upon the recuperative value of the West Texas desert. In the early 1900s he moved his family to Dallas, then Midland, and finally Alpine. While living in Brewster County, he heard countless stories from longtime residents about the curative qualities of hot mineral springs found on the Río Grande. It was common knowledge that the Indians of the region frequented Boquillas Hot Springs to cure stomach ailments, rheumatic conditions, and skin diseases. Langford not only recognized the springs as a source of treatment for his own illness, but he also envisioned the long-term commercial benefits of owning such a facility.

After some investigation Langford discovered that the parcel of land containing Boquillas Hot Springs was available for purchase. On April 15, 1909, Langford bought Section 50, Block G–17, near the point where Tornillo Creek empties into the Río Grande. The following month an article appeared in the *Alpine Avalanche* announcing that Langford, owner of the hot springs near Boquillas, planned to construct a bath house and provide "accommodations for campers and health-seekers."[2] One year after Langford moved his family to the Big Bend, he hired Cleofas Navidad, who had been farming on the land for several years, to help him build the twenty-foot-square stone bath house.

For the next several years the Langford resort enjoyed widespread patronage. Mineral baths, advertised in most newspapers as "The Fountain of Youth that Ponce de León Failed to Find," sold for twenty-five cents each with blankets and towels furnished for an additional dime. Profits from the business enabled the Langfords to build a modest but comfortable stone house on a cliff overlooking the bath house and valley beyond. Business increased so much, in fact, that in 1912 Langford announced plans to enlarge the health facilities to include modern cabins for overnight patrons. The outbreak of border trouble, however, not only squelched Langford's plans for expansion, but forced him to abandon his Brewster County property in 1916 to seek refuge in El Paso.

J. O. Langford's efforts to promote the Big Bend as a regional health attraction did bring increased attention to the area, however. Advertisements for the bath house appeared in Texas newspapers from San Antonio to El Paso. Visitors seeking relief from nagging afflictions could bathe in the stately environment of the Sierra del Carmen range. Indeed, the mountainous surroundings of the Langford resort received as much publicity as the hot springs themselves. Occasionally, prominent easterners, such as industrial magnate Henry B. DuPont and his entourage, stopped at Boquillas Hot Springs to refresh themselves after a raft trip down the Río Grande. Notably, these early tourists left the Big Bend with vivid impressions of the imposing canyon country.[3]

The military presence in the Big Bend during the ensuing decade of border trouble also served to promote the area as a potential tourist haven. In addition to local militia from Texas and New Mexico, many of the soldiers stationed in the remote desert outposts of the Big Bend hailed from as far away as Pennsylvania, New Jersey, and New York. It was common practice for the national guardsmen stationed at La Noria, for example, to travel a few miles down Tornillo Creek to bathe in the abandoned hot springs. In 1916 soldier-cartoonist Sergeant Jodie P. Harris drew one illustration expressing the national guard's appreciation for the beauty and grandeur of the Big Bend despite the tedium that marked their stay along the border. Years later, the *Fort Worth Star-Telegram* published Harris's cartoon depicting an officer from Pennsylvania and one from Texas discussing their desire to see Big Bend developed into a national park.[4]

In addition, the army's introduction of aerial reconnaissance in the 1920s along the United States-Mexico border had a long-term promotional impact on the Big Bend. By the summer of 1929 the last of the army air corps patrols in West Texas were staged from a makeshift airstrip located on the Elmo Johnson property. Johnson, a slender, good-natured man with a lean, prominent face tanned from years of farming in North Texas, bought the property (located approximately sixteen miles downstream from Castolon) in August 1928. The previous owners, G. N. Graddy and W. B. Williams, were two Kentuckians whose dreams of a tobacco empire in the Big Bend never materialized. With his wife, Ada, and friend Wilfred Dudley "W. D." Smithers, photographer and journalist for the *San Antonio Light,* Johnson occupied his new home.

The proximity of Mexican revolutionaries camped just across the Río Grande alerted Johnson and Smithers to the need for military protection. No sooner had the two settlers arrived at the remote trading post when a band of armed Mexican soldiers visited Johnson's ranch in search of food and medicine. While no one sustained injury, Johnson knew he and his family could not remain there without protection. W. D. Smithers, a personal friend of Colonel Arthur G. Fisher, commanding officer of the Eighth Air Corps stationed at Fort Sam Houston, offered to approach the army with an interesting proposition. Smithers argued that Johnson's Ranch would make a good site for an emergency landing field, which the air corps wanted to establish on the Río Grande.[5]

In view of recurring incidents along the border resulting from continued instability in Mexico, Colonel Fisher welcomed the opportunity to stage aerial reconnaissance patrols out of the Big Bend. A few days later, Smithers returned to Johnson's Ranch with a truckload of oil, gas, tires, and other supplies needed to service the planes to be stationed at the proposed facility. Johnson responded enthusiastically and borrowed a road grader from the county highway department to carve out a crude landing strip, which the War Department leased for one dollar a year. On the morning of April 24, 1929, Smithers and Johnson heard in the distance the faint drone of a De Havilland DH–4 winging its way over the craggy fissures of the Río Grande canyons. On that day, Lieutenant Thad V. Foster ushered the era of aviation history into the Big Bend when he landed the first of hundreds of aircraft destined to visit the Johnson airstrip.[6]

In the ensuing years, Johnson's Ranch assumed increasing importance to America's young pilots as a place for rest and relaxation rather than as a strategic military airfield. In the first place, the Mexican Revolution entered its final stages in the 1930s. Coupled with the army air corps presence in the Big Bend, these two factors insured peace on the United States–Mexico border. For the most part, the young, mostly single airmen who visited the Big Bend during these years had nothing more to do than enjoy the cost-free recreational opportunities available to them. The visitors spent much of their time fishing, hunting, river-rafting, and consuming Ada Johnson's home-cooked meals on a regular basis. In return, the daring "fly-boys" utilized the air corps' most up-to-date machinery to give the local citizenry the thrill of a Sunday-afternoon flight.

While the stated military purpose of Johnson's Ranch was to train pilots in "cross-country navigation," and practice "open-field landings," all who participated agreed that the exercises were, for the most part, "an excuse to go hunting." For the brief period that the field remained operational, pilots representing every state in the union visited Big Bend from nearby San Antonio training bases. For those first-time visitors to the Big Bend, the haunting silhouettes of the Chisos Mountains pressed against the wide-open Texas sky were a memorable sight. One squadron leader exclaimed, "There was a wild beauty about that Big Bend area, and I remember vividly the sometimes purplish hue of the distant mountains. . . . I had never seen anything like it before."[7] After their tour-of-duty in Texas, the airmen returned home to recount the marvelous experiences they enjoyed in the isolated but captivating canyon country of the lower Río Grande.

Confident that the Big Bend would one-day become a major tourist attraction in West Texas, J. O. Langford returned to Hot Springs in 1927. His time in El Paso afforded the resourceful entrepreneur an opportunity to improve his financial status. Langford's first task was to enlarge the facilities at Hot Springs in order to accommodate overnight campers. For this purpose he built a group of small tourist cabins, each decorated with colorful wall murals depicting scenes common to the area. Next, he added a large flagstone building to serve as a post office and a general store to

One of the many improvements J. O. Langford made to his property was to build the above U.S. Post Office. For decades, Langford's bathhouse and camping units were a popular tourist attraction before the establishment of Big Bend National Park. *(Courtesy, Archives of the Big Bend, Clifford B. Casey Collection, Sul Ross State University, Alpine, Texas)*

supply visitors with groceries and other basic necessities. In effect, Langford's latest additions anticipated a new wave of tourism that automobiles and national highway construction promised to facilitate.

Others followed Langford's lead in promoting Big Bend as a tourist and outdoor recreation area. In 1929 J. J. Willis, an automobile dealer from Odessa, Texas, purchased all of the abandoned property around Glenn Springs, the site of the famous Mexican raid. In making the purchase it was not Willis's intention to homestead; rather, he planned to establish an exclusive hunting preserve for West Texas residents to enjoy. In 1932 Willis organized the Chisos Mountains Club, converting all of his twenty-five thousand acres of land into a preserve to house all game animals indigenous to the Big Bend. Willis perceived a limited organization of 150 members, each paying $500 annually for the privilege of hunting, fishing, and camping on restricted land. But although the concept was attractive, and he advertised in most of the regional newspapers, it appears that the economic downturn of the 1930s prevented its success. Still, notwithstanding that these early attempts to promote a tourist industry in the Big Bend had some limitations, Willis and Langford's efforts were significant in that both men recognized a growing interest in the region among fellow West Texans.[8]

The aesthetic, almost spiritual qualities of the Big Bend held a special appeal to visitors in the early years of the 1930s. The stock market crash of 1929 ushered in an era of economic decline that demoralized the entire nation. The extremes of poverty and massive unemployment threatened to bring a once vigorous population to a standstill. There were not many ways to escape the veil of depression that shrouded the American public. The Big Bend, however, offered a peaceful and comforting reprieve to those caught up in the turmoil of difficult times. West Texans, in particular, enjoyed the amenities that the Big Bend had to offer; many of them sought refuge there during these troubled years.

Perhaps it was the alluring quality of the region, contrasted with the distressful climate of the Great Depression, that inspired Everett Ewing Townsend. Townsend was as familiar as any man with the Big Bend. He first experienced the region in 1894 while patrolling the Río Grande on horseback from Del Rio to El Paso for the United States Customs Service. Later, as county sheriff, he helped police the territory against outlaws. In the 1930s Townsend served his Brewster County constituency as an elected representative to the state legislature. Based upon these experiences, few men matched Townsend's knowledge and commitment to the rugged canyon lands of the lower Río Grande. His personal romance with the Chisos, in fact, once led him to vow that if he could ever afford it, he would buy the famous landmark for his own personal enjoyment.

During the 43rd session of the Texas legislature in February 1933, Townsend's dream that the beauty and grandeur of Big Bend be forever preserved became a reality. Curiously, one of Townsend's political colleagues initiated the idea of creating a state park. Congressman Robert M. Wagstaff had been deeply moved after reading Robert T. Hill's inspirational article of 1899 on the exploration of the Río Grande. The essay so impressed the junior legislator from Abilene, Texas, that he approached Townsend with the idea of cosponsoring a bill for the creation of "Texas Canyons State Park." While Wagstaff, a highly skilled lawyer, articulated the details of House Bill No. 771, Townsend used his influence as a respected Texas frontiersman to introduce it before the legislature on March 2, 1933.

The bill, which set aside fifteen sections of public lands in the proximity of Santa Elena, Mariscal, and Boquillas canyons, met little opposition. Some local supporters insisted that Townsend amend the proposal to include all unused public lands in the Big Bend for park purposes. Townsend refused to consider amending the original bill without a thorough investigation by the General Land Office in Austin. Three months later, in a special session of the legislature, Townsend and Wagstaff announced that the amount of unsold public lands numbered approximately one-hundred-fifty-thousand acres. Based on their findings, the two congressmen sponsored a new bill calling for that amount of land to be set aside for the development of a state park. In addition, they changed the name of the proposed park from "Texas Canyons State Park" to "Big Bend State Park." On October 27, 1933, Governor Miriam "Ma" Ferguson signed the legislation into law.

In light of current economic conditions, supporters of the state park were jubilant over the news. Agricultural and mineral industries had by this time reached their nadir. Community boosters viewed the legislation as an opportunity to stimulate a stagnating regional economy through the promotion of tourism. The Alpine Chamber of Commerce, therefore, assumed the lead in gaining regional support for the proposed Big Bend State Park. Over a period of several years, a handful of local businessmen, school administrators, and public officials worked collectively to bring the establishment of the park to fruition.[9]

The decision to create a state park in the Big Bend made West Texas a prime target for President Franklin D. Roosevelt's New Deal program. Roosevelt responded to the Depression with a federally planned economy designed to put people back to work. One of the features of the New Deal was the Civilian Conservation Corps (CCC), established to link work relief to the conservation of natural resources. The dust storms of the 1930s, which had eroded nearly all of the farmlands in Texas as well as the Great Plains states, dramatically emphasized the need for such a program. The proposed development of Big Bend State Park conformed perfectly with the goals of the CCC program. In the federal government's view, hundreds of unemployed men between the ages of seventeen and twenty-five could be put to work building roads, trails, campsites, and reservoirs for the new facility. In May 1933, President Roosevelt approved the location of four CCC camps in West Texas, one of them in the Big Bend.

Initially, the master plan called for a camp near Santa Elena Canyon whose participants were to construct a scenic drive from the base of the Mesa de Anguila to the mouth of the famous landmark. A preliminary investigation, however, revealed that Terlingua Creek did not supply enough water for the proposed camp. Based on these findings, CCC Superintendent R. D. Morgan filed his recommendations to district headquarters. Morgan argued that because of a three-year drought, "a water supply of sufficient quantity not only for camp purposes, but also to insure a supply for the future operation of the area for public use" was required before work could be undertaken.[10] In support of Morgan's recommendation, the U.S. Army, assigned to help keep the CCC supplied, refused to establish a camp in the Big Bend until an adequate water supply was obtained to operate a sewage disposal system.

The threat to delay the CCC camp forced local park supporters into action. First, Townsend and Jim Casner, president of the Alpine Chamber of Commerce, appealed to Waddy Burnham, a Big Bend rancher who held most of the water rights in the Chisos Mountains. Burnham refused to relinquish title to any water he needed to keep his cattle alive during the recent droughts. Next, the Chamber of Commerce staged a drive for donations to sponsor a project to discover the required supply of water. Casner hired Dr. Charles L. Baker, chairman of the department of geology at Texas A&M, to determine the best location to dig a well. On Baker's instructions, Townsend supervised a handful of laborers who began digging at the foot of Pulliam Bluff on the north side of the Chisos Basin. Shortly after mid-day on April 16, 1934, the work crew struck water, enough to satisfy the needs of both the army and the CCC.[11]

Camp Sp–33–T of the Civilian Conservation Corps (CCC) in the Chisos Basin in 1935. The New Deal work relief program provided the necessary manpower for internal improvements to Big Bend State Park, which Congress designated as a federal preserve in 1944. *(Courtesy, Photography Collection, Harry Ransom Humanities Research Center, University of Texas at Austin)*

CCC boys building the present road into the Chisos Basin somewhere around Green Gulch in 1937. Casa Grande Mountain is visible in the center of the photo. *(Courtesy, Photography Collection, Harry Ransom Humanities Research Center, University of Texas at Austin)*

The effort on the part of local citizens to attract the CCC into the Big Bend underscored the importance of the role of the national government in the realization of a state park. It was one thing to pass legislation for the facility, but development demanded massive expenditures and labor acquired only through the federal largess. The movement to create Big Bend State Park coincided with Roosevelt's strategy to promote increased federal involvement in a national conservation program. Both Roosevelt and Secretary of the Interior Harold Ickes supported the creation of state and national parks as sound conservation practice. In Washington's view, the CCC became the working arm of the federal government. More important to West Texas, the CCC's commitment to make Big Bend more accessible to the American public promised long-term benefits.

Just one month after the discovery of an adequate water supply, the CCC located its first camp, designated SP–33–T, in the Chisos Basin. Over two hundred laborers, 80 percent of whom were Hispanic, converged on the Big Bend to begin work under nearly impossible conditions. Located eighty-five miles from the nearest town, the young recruits lived in tents, enduring the hardships of extreme summer temperatures and total isolation. Inasmuch as water had been found in the higher elevations, Herbert Maier, a National Park Service (NPS) employee appointed district supervisor for all CCC operations in Texas, determined the state park headquarters should be located in the basin "with its commanding view of the valley below." To make this possible, the company's first undertaking was to construct a passable road into the Chisos.[12]

With the arrival of the CCC and its proposal to make internal improvements, local residents initiated a movement to establish Big Bend as a national park. Throughout the summer and fall of 1933, Townsend deluged NPS headquarters with correspondence. He included photographs and other material extolling the virtues of the Big Bend. In January 1934 the bureau responded to Townsend by sending Roger Toll, a Park Service career man whose illustrious service record included the superintendency of Yellowstone and Mount Rainier national parks, to investigate the area. Toll's familiarity with the nation's most celebrated wilderness preserves, as well as his knowledge of the fundamental Park Service guidelines required to designate a national park, more than qualified him to make a determination on Big Bend. The aesthetic and sometimes mysterious quality of the heralded geologic attractions of the region deeply impressed Toll. He reported his unqualified endorsement of the area as a national park, saying "it gives promise of becoming one of the noted scenic spectacles of the United States."

Not all government officials shared Toll's enthusiasm. Arno Crammerer, who in August 1933 assumed the position as director of the Park Service, expressed definite reservations about the area. First, he questioned the availability of enough federal land to establish a facility worthy of national park status. Secondly, he doubted there was sufficient water to service the park.

In a letter addressed to NPS Assistant Director Conrad Wirth, Herbert Maier assured his superiors that steps had already been taken to secure more water. Regarding the availability of land, Maier noted that local ranchers "promised various parcels of land" if a national park became a reality. Confident that the area would qualify, Maier proposed that all work in the Big Bend performed under his supervision be done in such a way "as to tie in with a final master plan for a national park."

The accomplishments of the CCC during its brief stay in the Big Bend eased some of Crammerer's doubts regarding the park's elevation to national status, not the least of which was completion of the seven-mile road into the Chisos Basin. The road was a monumental achievement since neither the engineers nor the workers had the benefit of power equipment. The narrow, winding passage through Green Gulch made the employment of conventional road-making equipment impractical to use. Project supervisor R. D. Morgan reported: "In construction of this road it has been necessary to move forty thousand cubic yards of earth, five thousand yards of solid rock and to construct seventeen masonary [sic] culverts." In addition, the CCC surveyed forty-eight thousand acres of rugged terrain to determine the most suitable locations for horse trails, camp areas, and building sites.[13] With the completion of the agency's first phase of work, Crammerer recanted and proposed that Big Bend be recommended suitable for consideration as a national park.

In anticipation that Congress would approve the park, Crammerer authorized an official NPS investigation of Big Bend in the summer of 1934 to determine the location of highways, camp sites, and other improvements needed to make the proposed national park operational. He charged Herbert Maier with the completion of the report. In January 1935 Maier finished the survey and submitted his written report to Washington.

Cognizant of Crammerer's concern over the size of the park, Maier first addressed the question of land acquisition. He believed it possible for the park to comprise as many as 1.5 million acres, easily enough to qualify as a national park. "The problem of land acquisition, while complex, has indications of solution in a reasonable length of time," Maier assured his superiors. The State of Texas held outright ownership to one-hundred-fifty-thousand acres. In addition, another ninety-thousand acres had already been forfeited to the Texas State Park Board. Of the 1.2 million acres held in private ownership, Maier determined most to be submarginal lands available for purchase at a low cost per acre. Maier noted, "Much of the privately owned land is already delinquent in taxes and is likely to revert to the State."

Next, the report discussed existing transportation and the potential for tourist visitation to the park. Maier underscored the importance of Alpine and Marathon as major debarkation points for incoming railway passengers. The Southern Pacific Railroad, which ran from New Orleans to Los Angeles with connections in Houston, San Antonio, and El Paso, would bring tourists to either of the West Texas towns. From this point a bus line would deliver them to the park. To facilitate automobile traffic, U.S. Highway 90, which connected with a transcontinental highway running from Los Angeles to Savannah (present Interstate 10), would serve as the main thoroughfare into the Big Bend. Maier recommended Persimmon Gap, a natural saddle in the Santiago Mountains, as the north entrance to the park area. The western approach, meanwhile, would emanate from Van Horn, Texas, through the mining communities of Terlingua and Study Butte.

In his discussion of boundaries for the park, Maier suggested the intriguing idea of creating an international park with Mexico. "The territory on the south bank of the river is scantily populated," Maier noted. "Much of it is said to be public land and, like our own area, of no great commercial value." Maier concluded that it would not be difficult to convince the Mexican government of the advantages to both nations in promoting an international park.[14]

The prospects outlined in the Maier report provoked a series of events that led to the official establishment of Big Bend National Park. On February 5, 1935, Secretary of the Interior Ickes concurred with the NPS recommendation that Big Bend was worthy of national park status. One month later, U.S. Congressman R. Ewing Thomason of El Paso, converted to the national park movement after a brief tour of the area in 1933, introduced House Resolution 6373 calling for the conversion of Big Bend from a state facility to a federal preserve. Concurrently, Texas

Senators Tom Connally and Morris Sheppard sponsored similar legislation in the U.S. Senate. On June 20, 1935, Congress passed Public Law
No. 157 establishing Big Bend National Park; President Roosevelt endorsed the bill that same day.[15]

In his presentation before the Senate, Sheppard stressed the international potential of the park. His own infatuation with the idea caused
him to bring it to Roosevelt's attention. In a letter to the president dated
February 16, 1935, Sheppard argued that a joint effort on the part of
both governments to establish an "international peace park" in Big
Bend—similar to Waterton-Glacier International Peace Park on the
border between Alberta and Montana—would do much to improve relations between the two countries. The president forwarded Sheppard's
letter to Secretary Ickes for comment. Ickes responded favorably to the
idea, saying, if Congress authorized Big Bend National Park, Mexico
should be invited to participate in an international park effort. Thus
Ickes and Roosevelt seized an opportunity to ameliorate past differences
with Mexico through this gesture of good will.[16]

Washington's interest in improving relations with Mexico through the
creation of an international park conformed to the central diplomatic
policy of President Roosevelt toward all of Latin America. In light of an
impending war between Germany and American allies in Europe,
Roosevelt sought to strengthen political ties with the nations of the Western Hemisphere. Roosevelt's so-called "Good Neighbor Policy" was aimed
generally at Latin America. Mexico in particular became an important
target of the diplomatic appeal. That government's expropriation of all
American oil companies during the tenure of nationalist President Lázaro
Cárdenas in 1935 placed United States-Mexico relations at their lowest
level since Pancho Villa's infamous raid on Columbus, New Mexico, in
1916. As one hopeful supporter of the international park movement
noted, a cooperative effort at this time "would create ties of kindly sentiment that would multiply and become stronger between the Mexican and
American peoples, now almost unknown to each other."[17]

With Roosevelt's authorization of Big Bend National Park, the American government extended the invitation to Mexico to discuss the possibilities of an international effort. The first meeting, which took place in El
Paso, Texas, on November 24, 1935, resulted in a joint resolution to
undertake a formal investigation of the proposed project. Four months
later, Washington appointed a commission to conduct its part of the
study. Representing the United States were NPS officials Conrad Wirth,

Herbert Maier, Roger Toll, and George M. Wright, chief of the bureau's wildlife research division. Mexico appointed a similar committee that included Miguel de Quevado, director of the Department of Game and Fish, Daniel F. Galicia, chief of forestry, and his assistant, José H. Serrano.

To afford the Mexican delegation a better opportunity to determine the extent of their government's participation in the project, the United States proposed a joint tour of the Big Bend. The two commissions met in February 1936 to inspect the four hundred thousand acres in Chihuahua and Coahuila which the Mexican government intended to set aside for the international park. Upon his return to Mexico, Commissioner Galicia wrote a letter to Assistant Director Wirth reaffirming his nation's interest in the project. Nevertheless, he underscored the technical and legal difficulties facing his government which prevented any further commitments.

The plan to establish an international park seemed doomed to failure from the start. First, the commission aborted the joint inspection tour because of a freak automobile accident that resulted in the deaths of Roger Toll and George Wright. Secondly, while discussions continued for the remainder of the decade, the outbreak of World War II prevented any further negotiations. After the war, the United States tried to revive the idea, but found Mexico unwilling to resume the effort.[18]

While Washington negotiated the issues of an international park, regional officials addressed the problems associated with the creation of a national park. First, there was the question of operational development. Bernard F. Manbey, a National Park Service associate engineer based in the San Francisco office, filed an early report which argued for the focus of all work to be in the Chisos Mountains and near the park's more accessible canyons at Santa Elena and Boquillas. Accordingly, road improvements were assigned the highest priority. Manbey applauded the CCC's completion of a road leading into the Chisos Basin. Still needed, in his opinion, were two first-class approach highways from Alpine and Marathon. In addition, the park required a network of roads leading to the various attractions. "The public will demand other roads," Manbey observed, "so as to get the complete southern view of the Chisos Mountains, and enable them to visit the several Indian caves in this area."[19]

Determination of the actual physical boundary was a second consideration. Although the southern, eastern, and western periphery, coincident with the Río Grande, required no further deliberation, Park Service officials had to define the park's northern limits. For this purpose, Assistant

Director Wirth personally undertook a special investigation of the Big Bend in August 1935. Over a period of several weeks, Wirth and a party of fifteen bureau specialists examined "every area or feature of special importance in the Big Bend country." In his report to Washington, Wirth recommended that the park encompass an area of approximately 736,000 acres. In his justification of the figure, Wirth emphasized that the boundaries specified in his report were needed to adequately protect "the most comprehensive list of geological phenomena found in any one area of a similar size in the United States."[20]

Wirth's concern that the declared boundaries provide ample protection for the geologic features of the proposed park underscored the importance of the Park Service's commitment to preservation. With the creation of the National Park Service in 1916, the federal government pledged to preserve the last vestiges of primitive America "for all generations" through the establishment of national parks. In contrast with the thinking of the booster-minded citizens of West Texas, the NPS viewed the national parks as more than just a playground for curious visitors. The agency recognized the educational value of the nation's preserves as field laboratories for the enhancement of man's understanding of nature. This underlying philosophy provided the rationale needed to ensure the protection of America's natural wonders.

In the 1930s monumentalism was the preeminent force that influenced the government's determination of a national park. If scenic topography was a prerequisite to make an area worthy of national park status, Big Bend far exceeded the standard. "The variety of geologic phenomena presented in this limited area is so great," wrote geologist Carroll H. Wegemann, a member of the Wirth investigation team, "that illustrations can be found of almost every phase of the science." In time, the preservation philosophy of the National Park Service would be expanded to include the protection of living biological landscapes. For the moment, however, the geologic splendor of the Big Bend ranked it alongside Grand Teton, Zion, and other "mountain-based national parks" as being worthy of federal protection.[21]

Impressed by more than just the geological and biological attributes of Big Bend, the Park Service also acknowledged the historical significance of the region. In its effort to ascertain more information on the subject, the agency hired Walter Prescott Webb, regarded by many as the nation's foremost authority on Texas history, as a historical consultant. Herbert Maier, who recommended Webb to Director Arno Crammerer in his letter of January 8, 1937, argued that the association of such a renowned scholar was vital to the success of the Big Bend park movement. "Dr. Webb's employment," Maier asserted, "would have publicity values in arousing public opinion in support of land acquisition legislation."

Walter Prescott Webb's love affair with the Big Bend began in 1923 while doing research for his widely acclaimed history *The Texas Rangers.* His credibility as a scholar, coupled with a personal commitment to preservation of the Big Bend, made him the top candidate for the position. According to Maier, the specific goals of the project were to "nail down" outstanding historical landmarks in the proposed park area while assembling a narrative history that would "capture the spirit of the region" as only Webb could do. In accepting the appointment in March 1937, Professor Webb modestly replied "I only wish that I could convey its charm and spell to the public in written words."[22]

Webb's journey down the Río Grande in the spring of 1937 captured the imagination of a curious public. On May 16 four men in two flat-bottomed boats of specially constructed steel, appropriately christened *Big Bend* and *Cinco de Mayo,* commenced down the "rather tame but picturesque" river from Lajitas. Two days later the party began its entry into the mouth of Santa Elena Canyon. While the voyagers were never in actual danger, the Texas newspapers dramatized the event by keeping their readers in suspense with headlines that read: "Boatmen Still Unreported after Rowing into Danger Zone of the Río Grande." As local journalists reported on the "perils" the men faced in making the dangerous journey, Webb described the festive mood the members of the expedition enjoyed at the onset of the trip. "A bottle of champagne had been brought to christen the boats," Webb explained. "After much discussion, it was decided that it would be a shame to waste the champagne; it was used to toast the success of the venture."[23]

If there was some doubt as to the risk involved in Webb's navigational escapade down the Río Grande, there is no question that the event effectively promoted support for the national park movement. The wild and unspoiled beauty of Big Bend was constantly in the news throughout the media's coverage of the three-day adventure. In surviving the trip, Professor Webb and his party joined only a handful of Texas notables to conquer the formidable canyons of the lower Río Grande. Webb's subsequent reports, which greatly romanticized the adventure, were rife with lofty praises for the virtually untouched wilderness that seemed reminiscent of the nineteenth-century frontier. With the typical Webbian flair for color-

Celebrated Texas historian Walter Prescott Webb near the mouth of Santa Elena Canyon in 1937. Webb's highly publicized float trip through the canyons of the lower Río Grande attracted local and regional interest to Big Bend. The expedition also generated public support for the creation of a national park in West Texas. *(Courtesy, National Park Service, Big Bend National Park, Texas)*

ful narrative, he appealed to the adventurous spirit of his readers. Accordingly, Webb cited Robert T. Hill's lively descriptions of his own journey into the famous canyons nearly four decades earlier. In summarizing the advantages of preserving Big Bend as a national park, Webb predicted the facility would someday be as important to Texas as "Yellowstone is for Wyoming, and Carlsbad Caverns is for New Mexico."[24]

Significantly, Professor Webb's efforts to popularize the state's first prospective national park coincided with the introduction of legislation to provide for a land acquisition program. Inasmuch as Texas held no federal lands it was the responsibility of the State to assume ownership. Once accomplished, the State would convey title of all purchases to the Department of the Interior. On February 22, 1937, State Representative Coke R. Stevenson, who later became Governor of Texas, introduced House Bill 642 calling for an appropriation of $1.4 million to enable the State of Texas to purchase lands for the park. Stevenson's bill, and a companion proposal sponsored in the Senate by Senator H. L. Winfield of Fort Stockton, were resoundingly defeated. In April Stevenson resubmitted a modified version of the bill reducing the appropriation figure to $750,000. While the measure passed both houses of Congress, Texas Governor James Allred vetoed the legislation on the grounds that the special fund would worsen a strained state budget.

The governor's reluctance to sponsor a land acquisition program for the park inspired another grass-roots movement to raise money. Dr. Horace Morelock, chairman of the Local Park Committee and president of Sul Ross Teachers College in Alpine, took the lead in promoting a statewide campaign in support of the park. After logging thousands of miles in travel and writing countless requests for contributions, Morelock's efforts produced only $50,000 toward the projected goal of $1,000,000. Not easily discouraged, the Local Park Committee reorganized in January 1938. This time, however, the group solicited the assistance of Amon G. Carter, a wealthy Texas philanthropist and publisher of the *Fort Worth Star Telegram*. Under Carter's guidance, the park supporters established the Texas Big Bend Park Association.

Carter's participation, coupled with the influential publication arm of the *Star Telegram,* gave park enthusiasts a powerful vehicle with which to lobby their cause. They wasted no time in utilizing the widely read newspaper to extol the advantages of a tourist industry to the Lone Star State as well as to solicit contributions. In addition, Carter's political influence attracted several well-placed Texas politicians to align themselves with the Big Bend campaign. Foremost among the supporters were Governor-elect W. Lee "Pappy" O'Daniel, and his popular running mate, Lieutenant Governor Coke Stevenson. O'Daniel, a former radio entertainer and hillbilly band leader, pledged his offices to see through the completion of the park.

Governor O'Daniel's commitment was not entirely altruistic. On February 4, 1939, soon after the Texas chief executive assumed office, President Roosevelt addressed a letter to him that began: "As you may know, I am very much interested in the proposed Big Bend National Park in your state." The president went on to express his desire to see the park dedicated during his administration. Regarding the issue of state appropriations needed to purchase land for the facility, Roosevelt argued that the "comparatively small sum" required for the task was insignificant when compared to the benefits Big Bend would bring in return. In closing, Roosevelt assured Governor O'Daniel that he would consider passage of the required appropriations legislation at this time a personal favor.[25]

Inspired by the president's endorsement of the park, Governor O'Daniel personally oversaw a series of legislative actions that enabled Big Bend to become a reality. To begin, in April 1939 the governor helped push through the Winfield-Huffman Bill, an act that granted the Texas State Parks Board the right of public domain as well as the power to purchase lands. Secondly, in his address to the 47th Legislature in January 1941, the governor requested that the appropriations bill for land acquisition funds be given the highest priority. In this effort, Minor R. Tillotson, Region III director for the National Park Service, testified before the House Appropriations Committee. Tillotson stressed the economic advantages to the state in terms of tourist revenues that would result from the creation of the new park. On July 3, 1941, the Texas Congress voted to appropriate the $1.5 million needed for the land purchase program.[26]

With the official organization of the Big Bend Land Department in September 1941, the land acquisitions program began in earnest. The governor placed Frank D. Quinn, the executive secretary of the Texas Parks Board, in charge of the project. Appropriately, Everett E. Townsend, who had worked with great diligence to promote a national park in West Texas, was named associate administrator. In an impressive, well-coordinated effort, the agency contacted all pertinent landholders, assessed appraisals on their property, and purchased all but 13,316 of the 708,000 acres required for the park in its first year of operation.[27]

While it may appear that the land acquisition program was completed with an unusual degree of efficiency, it met considerable opposition from some local ranchers. Most West Texas cattlemen spent their life in a desperate struggle to survive the perils of an untamed frontier. In their view, no dollar value could adequately compensate them for their efforts to make Big Bend their home. One of the strongest critics, Mrs. Waddy T. Burnham, argued that the loss of their ranch destroyed her son's rightful heritage. In a doleful letter to President Roosevelt, Mrs. Burnham lamented that her son, who was fighting for his country on the beaches of Southern France, "will never feel as if he had come home." While most of the cattlemen agreed that the payment for their property was "fair and equitable," many were heartbroken to leave their homes.[28]

These disappointments notwithstanding, most Texans awaited the dedication of Big Bend National Park with great anticipation. Regional newspapers took particular pleasure in noting that the park appropriately would be located in the "Biggest County [Brewster] of the Biggest State in the Union." Some editorials publicized the increased national interest in the facility, noting that "hundreds" of tourists had already been turned away because park improvements were not yet complete. Perhaps in anticipation of a postwar tourist invasion, reporters predicted that the Big Bend could become "a vacation wonderland." Editors inquired of their readers: "If Yellowstone National Park attracted a half million visitors in one year, what can we expect from Big Bend?"[29]

Before any of the questions could be answered, it remained for the Texas State Parks Board to perform one final ceremony. On September 5, 1943, the state of Texas transferred the deed of all lands purchased in the Big Bend to Regional Director Tillotson of the Park Service. It was indeed fitting that Governor Coke R. Stevenson, who had introduced the original legislation for the land purchase program in 1937, make the presentation to the federal government in Alpine, Texas. Less than one year later, Amon G. Carter, representing the Big Bend Park Association, delivered the deed of cession to President Roosevelt and Secretary Ickes. On June 12, 1944, NPS personnel in the Region III office in Santa Fe were advised that Big Bend National Park had come under their jurisdiction as of that date. On July 5, Dr. Ross A. Maxwell, who had worked in the Big Bend as a resident geologist for almost a decade, assumed his new position as the park's first superintendent.[30]

When the Department of the Interior assumed jurisdiction over Big Bend National Park in 1944, it brought to culmination more than four

hundred years of successive occupation on the West Texas frontier. His-
torically, Indians preceded all others into the region by nearly ten millen-
nia. A network of trails etched permanently into the desert subsoil
evidenced the continuous passage of Indians through the previously unexplored canyons of the lower Río Grande centuries before the appearance
of the white man. While there is ample archeological evidence to affirm
the Indian presence in the Big Bend, there is no indication that these
early inhabitants developed communities to match those discovered
farther west. Perhaps the ruggedness of the Big Bend proved to be less
appealing to them than the area near the junction of the Río Grande and
the Río Conchos.

The white man's fascination with the trans-Pecos region began in 1535
when Alvar Núñez Cabeza de Vaca first recounted the ordeal of his West
Texas odyssey. Since that time, the overpowering attractiveness of the Big
Bend lured a curious ensemble of adventurous soldier-explorers and self-
determined pioneers to its arid domain. While the factors that motivated
each of these groups varied, they shared a common desire to occupy an
unpopulated frontier. For hundreds of years the unavoidable presence of
the Big Bend captured the imagination and the spirit of these daring
individuals. In the beginning, they viewed the Big Bend as an impregnable obstruction to the advancement of a "civilized" society. With the passage of time, however, each succeeding wave of human migration defied
the challenges of an inhospitable land to make the region more livable.

It was the relatively unspoiled beauty of the Big Bend that first attracted the attention of the federal government in the early decades of the
twentieth century. With the arrival of the National Park Service in the
1940s, preservation concepts superseded traditional land-use practices.
It was the wildness of this desert paradise that appealed to the philo-
sophical ideals of the Park Service. Early park officials, therefore, initiated a conscientious program designed to lessen the degree of man's
impact. The result was the removal of those structures that represented
human presence, and a reversion of the land to its natural state. Today,
only a handful of historic sites, weathered by the desert sun and scattered
intermittently over the vast expanse of the Chihuahuan desert, survive
as crumbling reminders of man's indomitable struggle to occupy the
Big Bend.

While government bureaucrats sought to preserve the natural beauty
of the Big Bend, West Texas boosters hoped to exploit it. They realized
the economic value of the state's first major outdoor recreational facility.

To a nostalgic American public, Big Bend stood as a symbol of a bygone frontier. Most state residents welcomed the opportunity to diversify a postwar economy through the promotion of tourism. West Texans in particular exerted an untiring effort to make the park a reality. In short, they invited the final occupation of the lower Río Grande valley. In many respects, the permanent occupation of the Big Bend began with the National Park Service takeover in 1944. In the long term, the Park Service made the most longstanding contributions to the region's final settlement. National Park Service planning and funding enabled this once isolated corner of Brewster County, Texas, to become more accessible. In the mid-1950s, under the progressive leadership of NPS Director Conrad L. Wirth, Big Bend National Park enjoyed unparalleled expansion and development. Director Wirth, an ardent supporter of the park movement from the beginning, initiated a multimillion dollar campaign for the improvement of many of the nation's parks. The "Mission 66" program, which enabled more Americans to enjoy the splendor of their federally protected preserves, lured thousands of visitors to West Texas where once only a handful dared to travel. Since the earliest recorded memories of the Big Bend, only the hardiest adventurers gazed upon the magnificent contours of the Chisos Mountains. Today, virtually anyone can stand in silence midst the timeless silhouettes of the park's most prominent landmark and witness the passage of history.

Notes

In citing works referred to several times in the notes, short titles and abbreviations have been been used. Such works have been abbreviated as follows:

AGI
Archivo General de Indias

AGN
Archivo General de la Nación

BIBE Corr.
National Park Service Records, Region III, Big Bend Correspondence File, Box 932209, National Archives and Records Administration, Federal Records Center, Denver

Casey, *Soldiers, Ranchers, and Miners*
Clifford B. Casey, *Soldiers, Ranchers, and Miners in the Big Bend* (Washington, D.C.: U.S. Dept. of the Interior, National Park Service, 1969)

Guajardo Notes
Louis Alberto Guajardo Notes, Western Americana Collection, Beinecke Rare Book and Manuscript Library, Yale Univ., New Haven, Connecticut (with box and folder numbers)

HAHR
Hispanic American Historical Review

NMHR
New Mexico Historical Review

PI
Provincias Internas

SWHQ
Southwest Historical Quarterly

WTHS
West Texas Historical and Scientific Society Publications

Yale Library
Western Americana Collection, Beinecke Rare Book and Manuscript Library, Yale Univ., New Haven, Conn.

INTRODUCTION

1. Ronnie C. Tyler, *The Big Bend: A History of the West Texas Frontier* (Washington, D.C.: U.S. Dept. of the Interior, National Park Service, 1975), 5; Charles N. Gould, "Preliminary Report of the Regional Geologist on Big Bend State Park SP–33–T," Box 794, Big Bend File, Item 1, in Walter Prescott Webb Papers, Texas State Public Library, Austin (hereafter cited as Gould Report); Ross A. Maxwell, "Big Bend National Park: A Land of Contrasts," *WTHS* 57 (June 1948): 6–18.

2. Gould Report, 4–9; Maxwell, "Land of Contrasts," 12–14: Victor H. Schoffelmayer, "The Big Bend Area of Texas: A Geographic Wonderland," *Texas Geographic Magazine* 1 (May 1937): 2.

CHAPTER ONE: FOR GOD AND KING

1. In an effort to maintain historical accuracy the original Spanish place name will be used in these early chapters whenever possible. If there is an English translation that is more commonly recognized today, it too will be designated in parenthesis with the first usage in the text. For example, La Junta de los Ríos will also be identified by its English equivalent, Presidio, Texas. In subsequent chapters dealing with the American period, however, the English placename will be used unless the Spanish is more common, e.g., San Antonio, Texas.

2. U.S. Congress, House (William H. Emory), *Report of the United States and Mexican Boundary Survey,* Ex. Doc. 135, 34th Cong., 1st sess., 1855–1856, 84 (Serial Set 862); Ronnie C. Tyler, *The Big Bend: A History of the Last Texas Frontier* (Washington, D.C.: U.S. Dept. of the Interior, National Park Service, 1975), 90; Luis Navarro García, *Don José de Gálvez y la comandancía general de las Provincias Internas del norte de Nueva España* (Seville, Spain: Escuela de Estudios Hispano-Americanos de Sevilla, 1964), 235.

3. From 1535 until well into the eighteenth century, La Junta de los Ríos became a significant target for the Spanish colonization effort in Texas. Located at the confluence of the Río Conchos and the Río Grande — two natural landmarks on the northern frontier — La Junta became a favorite stopover point for the numerous exploration parties that followed Cabeza de Vaca.

4. John Francis Bannon, *Spanish Borderlands Frontier* (Albuquerque: Univ. of New Mexico Press, 1974), 12–27; John A. Carroll, "Big Bend Country" (Ms., National Park Service, Southwest Region Office, Santa Fe, New Mexico), 3:13–14; Fanny Bandelier, *The Journey of Cabeza de Vaca from Florida to the Pacific, 1528–1536* (New York: Allerton Book, 1922); Carlysle Graham Raht, *The Romance of the Davis Mountains and Big Bend Country* (Odessa, Texas: Raht Books,

1953); C. H. Haring, *The Spanish Empire in America* (New York: Harcourt, Brace, & World, 1963), 69–81.

5. Carroll, "Big Bend Country," 3:15. For the definitive study of the War of the Gran Chichimeca see Philip Wayne Powell, *Soldiers, Indians, and Silver: North America's First Frontier War* (Tempe: Arizona State Univ. Press, 1975), 10–13; Max L. Moorhead, *The Presidio: Bastion of the Spanish Borderlands* (Norman: Univ. of Oklahoma Press, 1975), 7–11.

6. Herbert Eugene Bolton, "The Mission as a Frontier Institution in the Spanish-American Colonies," *American Historical Review* 23 (October 1917): 42–61; Bolton, "Defensive Spanish Expansion and the Significance of the Spanish Borderlands," in *The Trans-Mississippi West*, ed. James F. Willard and Colin Goodykoontz (Boulder: Univ. of Colorado Press, 1930), 1–42; Powell, *Soldiers, Indians, and Silver*, 187–205.

7. Carroll, "Big Bend Country," 3:16–20; Tyler, *Big Bend*, 23–25; J. Lloyd Mecham, "The Second Spanish Expedition to New Mexico: The Chamuscado-Rodríquez Entrada, 1581–82," *NMHR* 1 (July 1926): 267–70; Herbert Eugene Bolton, ed., *Spanish Exploration in the Southwest, 1542–1706* (New York: Charles Scribner's Sons, 1916), 168–92; J. Charles Kelley, "The Historic Indian Pueblos of La Junta de los Ríos," *NMHR* 26 (October 1952): 257–95; Joseph P. Sánchez, *The Río Abajo Frontier, 1540–1692: A History of Colonial New Mexico* (Albuquerque: Albuquerque Museum, 1987), 28–34.

8. "Accounts of the Journey Which I, Antonio de Espejo Made to the Provinces and Settlements of New Mexico, 1583," in Bolton, *Spanish Exploration*, 168–92; George P. Hammond and Agapito Rey, eds., *Expedition into New Mexico Made by Antonio de Espejo, 1582–1583, as Revealed in the Journal of Diego Pérez de Lúxan, a Member of the Party* (Berkeley: Univ. of California Press, 1929), 45–128; J. Charles Kelley, "The Route of Antonio de Espejo Down the Pecos River and Across the Texas Trans-Pecos Region," *WTHS* 7 (1937): 7–25; Sánchez, *Río Abajo Frontier*, 35–40.

9. Bannon, *Spanish Borderlands Frontier*, 92–97.

10. Ibid., 99; Carroll, "Big Bend Country," 3:23; Mendoza to viceroy, June 23, 1684, AGN, PI, vol. 37, typescript in France V. Scholes, France Vinton Scholes Papers, Archive 360, Box VII–1, Special Collections, Univ. of New Mexico, Albuquerque (hereafter cited as Scholes Papers).

11. "Itinerary of Juan Domínguez de Mendoza, 1684," in Bolton, *Spanish Exploration*, 320–43; Victor J. Smith, "Early Spanish Explorations in the Big Bend of Texas," *WTHS* 2 (1928): 59–68; Governor Don Domingo Jironza Petríz de Cruzate to viceroy, November 29, 1683, and Mendoza to viceroy, November 18, 1685, AGI, Guadalajara 138, Scholes Papers, File 1–D.

12. Bolton, *Spanish Exploration,* 320–43; Mendoza to viceroy, November 18, 1685, in Scholes Papers, Box VII–1, File 1–D.

13. Bolton, *Spanish Exploration,* 320–43; Quotes from Mendoza to viceroy, June 23, 1684, November 18, 1685, Scholes Papers. .

14. Carlos E. Castañeda, *Our Catholic Heritage in Texas, 1519–1936,* vol. 3, *The Mission Era: The Missions at Work, 1731–1761* (Austin: Von Boeckmann-Jones, 1938), 198–202; Carroll, "Big Bend Country," 4:1.

15. The viceroy of New Spain was not necessarily always a member of Spanish nobility. Therefore, if a viceroy also had a title of nobility, such as the Marqués de Casafuerte, he was referred to by that title more often than his Christian name, as in the case of Viceroy Juan de Acuña.

16. Bannon, *Spanish Borderlands Frontier,* 130–31. For a penetrating analysis of the significance of the Louisiana frontier, see Abraham P. Nasatir, *Borderland in Retreat: From Spanish Louisiana to the Far Southwest* (Albuquerque: Univ. of New Mexico Press, 1976), and Castañeda, *Our Catholic Heritage,* 3:202–3; Navarro García, *José de Gálvez,* 71–78. For the itinerary of Rivera's travels, see Guillermo Porras Muñoz, ed., *Diario y derrotero de lo caminado visto y observado en el discurso de la visita general de presidios en las Provincias Internas de Nueva España, que de orden de S.M. executó Don Pedro de Rivera, Brigadier de los Reales Ejércitos, 1724–1726* (México, D.F.: Porrúa, 1945), and Thomas H. Naylor and Charles W. Polzer, S.J., eds., *Pedro de Rivera and the Military Regulations for Northern New Spain, 1724–1729* (Tucson: Univ. of Arizona Press, 1988), 5–11.

17. For the detailed report of this expedition see "Copia del Diario de la Campaña executada de orden del Exmo Señor Marqués de Casfuerte, por Don Joseph Berroterán Capitán del Presidio de Conchos, para el reconocimiento de las Margenes del Río del Norte, en el año de 1729," AGN, Historia, vol. 52, typescript in Dunn Transcripts, Box 2Q137, File 23, 1710–1738, Eugene C. Barker Library of Texas History, Univ. of Texas, Austin (hereafter cited as Dunn Transcripts).

18. Castañeda, *Our Catholic Heritage,* 3:203–8; "Testimonio de la fundación del nuebo presidio con el título del sacramento que se ha erigido y fundado en la junta de los ríos del norte que llaman San Diego en la Nueva Vizcaya," AGI, Guadalajara 513, in Dunn Transcripts, Box 2Q147, file 84, 1735–38.

19. "Dictamen del Auditor el Marqués de Altamira, June 14, 1747," AGN, Historia, vol. 52, 127–40; Castañeda, *Our Catholic Heritage,* 3:211–13; Carroll, "Big Bend Country," 4:9–10.

20. Castañeda, *Our Catholic Heritage,* 3:214–17, says the crossing was closer to Boquillas canyon; Tyler, *Big Bend,* 34–37, places the crossing near Mariscal canyon. For a full text of the journey, see "Copia del Diario de la Campaña executada de Orden del Exmo. Señor Conde de Revillagigedo en el año de 1747 por el

Governador de Coaguila Don Pedro de Rávago y Terán para el reconocimiento de las margenes del Río Grande del Norte," AGI, Guadalajara 513 in Dunn Transcripts, Box 2Q138, File 31, 1743–50.

21. Castañeda, *Our Catholic Heritage,* 3:222–26; "Quaderno que comienza con la carta orden de Exmo. Señor Virrey y demas diligencias en esta expedición en La Junta de Los Ríos," AGN, Historia, vol. 52 in Dunn Transcripts, Box 2Q147, File 88, 1746–47.

22. Castañeda, *Our Catholic Heritage,* 3:219, 229; Carroll, "Big Bend Country," 4:15–16.

23. Bannon, *Spanish Borderlands Frontier,* 172–80; Navarro García, *José de Gálvez,* 134–43. For a full text of Rubí's report see "Dictamen que de orden del Exmo. Señor Marqués de Croix, virrey de este reino, expone el mariscal de campo Marqués de Rubí en orden a la mejor situación de los presidios para la defensa y extensión de su frontera a la gentilidad en los confines del norte de este virreinato," May 4, 1768, AGI, Guadalajara 511, in Dunn Transcripts, Box 2Q140, File 46.

24. Apparently the governor took it upon himself to move the presidio closer to a more populated area only months before Rubí's inspection; Castañeda, *Our Catholic Heritage,* vol. 4, *The Mission Era: The Passing of the Missions, 1762–1782,* 236, 247.

25. Castañeda, *Our Catholic Heritage,* 4:192–93, 223–36, 242–49; Rubí *dictamen,* May 4, 1768.

26. Navarro García, *José de Gálvez,* 215–18; *Reglamento e Instrucción para los Presidios que se han de formar en la Linea de frontera de la Nueva España Resuelto por el Rey Nuestro Señor en Cedula de 10 de septiembre de 1772,* translation in Sidney B. Brinckerhoff and Odie B. Faulk, *Lancers for the King: A Study of the Frontier Military System of Northern New Spain, With a Translation of the Royal Regulations of 1772;* Moorhead, *The Presidio,* 58–60.

CHAPTER TWO: THE POLICY OF THE IRON FIST

1. Hugo de O'Conor to Viceroy Antonio María Bucareli y Ursua, January 30, 1776, AGN, PI, vol. 88, doc. 540, on microfilm in Special Collections Library, Univ. of New Mexico, Albuquerque. A full translation of this document can be found in Mary Lu Moore and Delmar L. Beene, eds. and trans., "The Interior Provinces of New Spain: The Report of Hugo O'Conor, January 30, 1776," *Arizona and the West (AW)* 13 (Autumn 1971): 265–82.

2. There are a number of good anthropological studies of the Apache. Still considered useful are Grenville Goodwin, *The Social Organization of the Apache*

(Tucson: Univ. of Arizona Press, 1942); Edward H. Spicer, *Cycles of Conquest: The Impact of Spain, Mexico, and the United States on Indians of the Southwest, 1553–1960* (Tucson: Univ. of Arizona Press, 1962); and Henry F. Dobyns, *The Apache People* (Phoenix: Indian Tribal Series, 1971). Historical works include Jack Forbes, "The Janos, Jocomes, Mansos, and Sumas Indians," *NMHR* 32 (October 1957): 319–34.

3. Daniel S. Matson and Albert H. Schroeder, eds., "Cordero's Description of the Apache, 1796," *NMHR* 32 (October 1957): 335–56; Max L. Moorhead, *The Apache Frontier: Jacobo Ugarte and Spanish-Indian Relations in Northern New Spain, 1769–1791* (Norman: Univ. of Oklahoma Press, 1968), 200–203.

4. Marqués de Rubí, "Dictamen que de orden del Exmo. Señor Marqués de Croix, virrey de este reino, expone el mariscal de campo Marqués de Rubí en orden a la mejor situación de los presidios para la defensa y extensión de su frontera a la gentilidad en los confines del norte de este verreinato," May 4, 1768, AGI, Guadalajara 511, in Dunn Transcripts, Eugene C. Barker Library of Texas History, Univ. of Texas, Austin, Box 2Q140, File 46 (hereafter cited as Dunn Transcripts); Max L. Moorhead, *The Presidio: Bastion of the Spanish Borderlands* (Norman: Univ. of Oklahoma Press, 1975), 60–61; Frank D. Reeve, "The Apache Indians in Texas," *SWHQ* 50 (October 1946): 189–97.

5. Ernest Wallace and E. Adamson Hoebel, *The Comanches: Lords of the South Plains* (Norman: Univ. of Oklahoma Press, 1952), 3–54; Alfred B. Thomas, *Forgotten Frontiers: A Study of the Spanish Indian Policy of Don Juan Bautista de Anza, Governor of New Mexico, 1777–1787* (Norman: Univ. of Oklahoma Press, 1932), 60–61.

6. Established in 1757 as a cornerstone of defense in central Texas, Presidio de San Sabá was plagued with problems from the beginning. Poor military and administrative leadership was one cause as the unit's first commander, Captain Felipe Rábago y Terán answered charges of fraud. The demoralized troops, moreover, faced constant harassment from Comanches and Apaches until the abandonment of the presidio in 1772 and the withdrawal of its garrison to San Fernando de Austria. See Carlos E. Castañeda, *Our Catholic Heritage in Texas, 1519–1936,* 7 vols., *The Passing of the Missions, 1762–1782* (Austin: Von Boeckmann and Jones, 1938), 4:190–93.

7. David M. Vigness, "Don Hugo O'Conor and New Spain's Northeastern Frontier, 1764–1776," *Journal of the West* 6 (January 1967): 27–40.

8. O'Conor to Bucareli, January 30, 1776, AGN, PI, vol. 88, doc. 540, Luis Navarro García, *Don José de Gálvez y la commandancía general de las Provincias Internas del norte de Nueva España* (Seville, Spain: Escuela de Estudios Hispano-Americanos de Sevilla, 1964), 221–24; Don Roque de Medina to Hugo de O'Conor, May 14, 1773, AGI, Guadalajara 514, in Dunn Transcripts, Box

2Q141, File 47; "Diario de Operaciones de Don Hugo de O'Conor," October 19–November 18, 1773, AGI, Guadalajara 512, on microfilm, National Park Service, Southwest Region Office, Santa Fe, New Mexico, reel 1; Rex E. Gerald, *Spanish Presidios of the Late Eighteenth Century in Northern New Spain* (Santa Fe: Museum of Santa Fe Press, 1968), 37–69.

9. Hugo de O'Conor to Viceroy Bucareli, AGN, PI, vol. 88, doc. 540; "Diario de Operaciónes," October 19–November 18, 1773, AGI, Guadalajara 512; Hugo de O'Conor to Bucareli, May 8, 1773, AGI, Guadalajara 514, in Dunn Transcripts, Box 2Q141, File 47, Moore and Beene, "Report of Hugo O'Conor," 281, n. 28, 29.

10. O'Conor to Bucareli, AGN, PI, vol. 88, doc. 540; Navarro García, *José de Gálvez*, 235–36; James E. Ivey, "Presidios of the Big Bend Area," report (Santa Fe, New Mexico: National Park Service, Southwest Region Office, 1984), 17–30.

11. The full-length review of O'Conor's record as commandant is found in Enrique G. Flores and Francisco R. Almada, eds., *Informe de Hugo de O'Conor sobre el estado de las Provencias Internas del norte, 1771–1776* (Mexico, D.F.: Editorial Cultura, 1952), 78–93; His plan of operations may also be found in Hugo de O'Conor to Viceroy Bucareli, March 24, 1775, AGN, PI, vol. 87, doc. 5, on microfilm in Special Collections Library, Univ. of New Mexico, Albuquerque; Thomas, *Forgotten Frontiers*, 3–13.

12. Moorhead, *Presidio*, 75–79; Thomas, *Forgotten Frontiers*, 20–23; Noel Loomis, "Commandants — General of the Interior Provinces: A Preliminary List," *AW* 11 (Autumn 1969): 261–68.

13. Up to this time Spain had been unsuccessful in thwarting the Comanche challenge in Texas. Comanche attacks, in fact, forced the abandonment of Presidio San Sabá (Menard, Texas) in 1757. Perhaps recognizing past failures, the military advisors at Monclova in 1777 viewed the proposed alliance as both a sound military tactic as well as a practical necessity.

14. General Report by the Com. Gen. of the Interior Provinces, Teodoro de Croix to José de Gálvez, July 29, 1781, AGI, Guadalajara 278, typescript in Special Collections Library, Univ. of New Mexico. A full translation may be found in Alfred Barnaby Thomas, *Teodoro de Croix and the Northern Frontier of New Spain, 1776–1783* (Norman: Univ. of Oklahoma Press, 1941), 36–63, 71–243, 90–104; Moorhead, *Presidio*, 88–90; Gary Bertram Starnes, "Juan de Ugalde (1729–1816) and the Provincias Internas of Coahuila and Texas" (Ph.D. diss., Texas Christian Univ., 1971), 32–41.

15. Reeve, "Apache Indians in Texas," 196–98; For details of Anza's New Mexico campaign against the Comanches, see "Diario de la expedición que sale a practicar contra la nación Cumancha el infraescripto teniente coronel, Don Juan Bautista de Anza, governador y comandante de la provincia de Nuevo Mexico

con la tropa, milicianos e indios," translation of Anza's diary in Thomas, *Forgotten Frontiers*, 121–39; John Kessell, *Kiva, Cross, and Crown: The Pecos Indians and New Mexico* (1979; reprint, Albuquerque: Univ. of New Mexico Press, 1987), 399–407.

16. Ugalde did surprise some Mescaleros in the Sierra del Carmen, but the skirmish produced no results. Ugalde to Croix, March 9, 1783, AGI, Guadalajara 284, typescript in Guajardo Notes, Box 1, Folder 1.

17. A. B. Nelson, "Campaigning in the Big Bend of the Río Grande in 1787," *SWHQ* 39 (January 1936), 200–227; Moorhead, *Apache Frontier*, 206–20.

18. Starnes, "Juan de Ugalde," 60–90; A. B. Nelson, "Juan de Ugalde and Picax-Ande Ints-tinsle, 1787–1788," *SWHQ* 43 (April 1940): 437–64.

19. David J. Weber, *The Mexican Frontier, 1821–1846: The American Southwest Under Mexico* (Albuquerque: Univ. of New Mexico Press, 1982), 22, 107–46.

20. Ibid., 117; J. Fred Rippy, "The Indians of the Southwest in the Diplomacy of the United States and Mexico, 1848–1853," *HAHR* 2 (1919): 380–83; Carlos E. Castañeda, trans., "A Trip to Texas in 1828, José María Sánchez," *SWHQ* 29 (April 1926): 263.

21. Reeve, "Apache Indians in Texas," 200–201; Castañeda, "José María Sánchez," 263–65. Details of Mexican engagements with Comanches during this period are found in Guajardo Notes, Box 8, File 1, Box 6, File 1.

22. Castañeda, "José María Sánchez," 260–65; Weber, *Mexican Frontier*, 158–78.

23. "Itinerario de la expedición San Carlos a Monclova el viejo hecha por el Coronel D. Emilio Langberg," typescript in Guajardo Notes, Box 8, Folder 1.

CHAPTER THREE: PERFECT DESOLATION

1. Dr. Parry to Bvt. Maj. William H. Emory, November 4, 1852, William H. Emory Papers, Yale Library; Lenard E. Brown, *Survey of the United States-Mexico Boundary, 1849–1855* (Denver: U.S. Dept. of the Interior, National Park Service, 1969), 61.

2. U.S. Congress, Senate, *The Treaty Between the United States and Mexico . . .*, Ex. *Doc. 52*, 30th Cong., 1st sess., 1847–48, 43–45 (Serial 509); William H. Goetzmann, *Army Exploration in the American West, 1803–1863* (New Haven: Yale Univ. Press, 1959), 154; Norman A. Graebner, *Empire on the Pacific* (New York: Ronald Press, 1955), 70–71.

3. Goetzmann, *Army Exploration*, 4–7; Henry Putney Beers, "A History of the U.S. Topographical Engineers, 1813–1863," *Military Engineer* 34 (1942): 287; W. Turrentine Jackson, *Wagon Roads West: A Study of Federal Road Surveys and*

Construction in the Trans-Mississippi West, 1846–1869 (Berkeley: Univ. of California Press, 1952), 2; U.S. Congress, Senate, *Annual Report, Bureau of Topographical Engineers, Ex. Doc. 58,* 26th Cong., 1st sess., December 30, 1839, 10–12 (Serial 355).

4. U.S. Congress, Senate, *Report of the Secretary of War* (George W. Crawford), *Ex. Doc. 1,* 31st Cong., 1st sess., November 30, 1849, 90–91 (Serial 549).

5. The Santa Fe-Chihuahua trade, ongoing since Mexico's independence from Spain in 1821, became the envy of all the merchants along the Río Grande. For most of that time, Santa Fe and St. Louis monopolized the trade. Since the days of the Lone Star Republic, Texans hoped to establish this vital commercial link to El Paso del Norte. See David J. Weber, *The Mexican Frontier, 1821–1846: The American Southwest Under Mexico* (Albuquerque: Univ. of New Mexico Press, 1982), 125–30; Jackson, *Wagon Roads West,* 36–37; Avram B. Bender, "Opening Routes Across West Texas, 1848–1850," *SWHQ* 37 (October 1933): 116–19. Ben Leaton, who established a trading post near Presidio, Texas, in 1848, was among the first Americans to take advantage of the Chihuahua trade. A fuller discussion of Fort Leaton is in chapter 5.

6. Bender, "Opening Routes," 119–20, esp. Neighbors quote, 120, n. 19; Crawford, *Annual Report,* 91; Goetzmann, *Military Explorations,* 226.

7. Jackson, *Wagon Roads West,* 39–40; "Journal of William Henry Chase Whiting, 1849," in Ralph P. Bieber and Avram B. Bender, eds., *Exploring Southwestern Trails, 1846–1854,* vol. 2 of *The Southwest Historical Series* (Glendale, Calif.: Arthur Clark, 1938), 243–350. A summary account of this journey may also be found in Whiting's report to Gen. J. G. Totten (U.S. Congress, House, *Ex. Doc. 5,* 31st Cong., 1st sess., June 10, 1849, 281–93 [Serial 569]); U.S. Congress, Senate, Capt. Samuel G. French report to Lt. Col. Charles Thomas, Chief, Army Quartermaster Corps, *Ex. Doc. 64,* 31st Cong., 1st sess., December 21, 1849, 40–53 (Serial 562) (hereafter cited as Reports, followed by the date and page number); Bvt. 2nd Lt. William F. Smith report to Lt. Col. Joseph E. Johnston, Corps of Topographical Engineers, Reports, May 25, 1849, 4–7; Roy L. Swift and Leavitt Corning, Jr., *Three Roads to Chihuahua: The Great Wagon Roads that Opened the Southwest, 1823–1883* (Austin: Eakin Press, 1988), 86–87, 90–95.

8. Jackson, *Wagon Roads West,* 42–43; Lt. Francis T. Bryan report to Lt. Col. J. E. Johnston, Reports, December 1, 1849, 14–25. For a copy of the original handwritten report dated August 1, 1849 see "Report of a Reconnaissance from San Antonio de Béxar to El Paso del Norte, August 1, 1849," in *Letters Received by the Topographical Bureau of the War Department, 1824–1865,* National Archives Microfilm Publications, Microcopy 506, Reel 36, I–J (hereafter cited as *Letters Received*); Lt. Col. Johnston, report to Gen. George Deas, Asst. Adj. Gen., Reports, December 28, 1849, 26–28; Also in *Letters Received,* Reel 36, I–J, Capt. Samuel G. French to Lt. Col. Thomas, Reports, December 1, 1849, 50.

9. Ronnie C. Tyler, *The Big Bend: A History of the Last Texas Frontier* (Washington, D.C.: U.S. Dept. of the Interior, National Park Service, 1975), 76–77; Lt. W. F. Smith to Lt. Col. J. E. Johnston, October 26, 1850, *Letters Received,* Reel 36, I–J; Lt. Martin L. Smith to Lt. Col. Johnston, January 26, 1851, *Letters Received,* Reel 36, I–J.

10. "Whiting Journal," in Bieber and Bender, eds., *Exploring Southwestern Trails,* 258–59; Tyler, *Big Bend,* 80; Bender, "Opening Routes Across Texas," 123n.

11. The boundary between the United States and Mexico as defined in the original Treaty of Guadalupe-Hidalgo was based on J. Disturnell's 1847 map of the United States, known at the time to be in serious error. See Goetzmann, *Army Exploration,* 151; Brown, *Survey of the United States-Mexico Boundary,* 2–5; U.S. Congress, House, William H. Emory, *Notes of a Military Reconnaissance from Fort Leavenworth, in Missouri to San Diego, in California, Including Parts of the Arkansas, Del Norte, and Gila Rivers, H. Ex. Doc. 41,* 30th Cong., 1st sess., 1847–1848 (Serial 517).

12. Goetzmann, *Army Exploration,* 162–67; Brown, *Survey of the United States-Mexico Boundary,* 5–9; U.S. Congress, House, William H. Emory, *Report of the United States and Mexican Boundary Survey,* vol. 1, *Ex. Doc. 135,* 34th Cong., 1st sess., 1855–1856, 10 (Serial 861) (hereafter cited as Emory, *Report,* with volume and page numbers following).

13. Goetzmann, *Army Exploration,* 184–85; Tyler, *Big Bend,* 82–83; Emory, *Report,* 1:11–12; "Itinerario de la Expedición desde San Carlos hasta Monclova El Viejo hecha por el Coronel D. Emilio Langberg," typescript in Guajardo Notes, Box 8, Folder 1.

14. Chandler to Emory, "San Vicente to Presidio del Norte," in Emory, *Report,* 1:80–84. One of Chandler's boatmen attempted to pass through Santa Elena Canyon, but was not successful. Finding the passage impossible for boats, he recommended the detour around the canyon. Thomas Thompson to M. T. W. Chandler, October 1, 1852, Emory Papers, Box 6, File 0045.

15. Lieutenant Green refers to this site in his report as the Vado de Fleche, which historian Ronnie Tyler places "in the vicinity of present day Castolon where Terlingua Creek flows into the Río Grande." See Ronnie C. Tyler, ed., "Exploring the Río Grande: Lt. Duff C. Green's Report of 1852," *Arizona and the West* 10 (Spring 1968): 55–56. Tyler's map showing the same location in a later work places the site farther downstream from Terlingua Creek. See Tyler, *Big Bend,* 84–89. While Vado de Fleche cannot be accurately identified, the area described sounds very much like the floodplain region located just upstream from Castolon at what is today called Rancho Estelle and La Coyota. There is a river crossing to the Mexican village of Santa Elena still in use.

16. C. C. Parry to M. T. W. Chandler, November 4, 1852, Emory Papers, Box

6, File 0045; Chandler to Emory, November 4, 1852, Emory Papers, Box 6, File 0045; Chandler to Emory, November 4, 1852, in Emory, *Report,* 1:84–85; Tyler, "Exploring the Río Grande," 56–58.

17. Emory, *Report,* 1:11; C. C. Parry to Maj. Emory, November 25, 1852, Emory Papers, Box 6, File 0045; Goetzmann, *Army Exploration,* 194–95.

18. For a good history on the establishment of Fort Davis, see Robert M. Utley, *Fort Davis National Historic Site, Texas* (Washington, D.C.: U.S. Dept. of the Interior, National Park Service, 1965); see also Barry Scobee, *Fort Davis, Texas: 1580–1960* (El Paso: Hill Printing, 1963).

19. Army experiments with camels in Texas were part of a larger plan to use them throughout the West. See Harlan D. Fowler, *Camels to California* (Palo Alto: Stanford Univ. Press, 1950); U.S. Congress, Senate, Lt. Edward L. Hartz to Maj. David H. Vinton, *Diary, Ex. Doc. 2,* 36th Cong., 1st sess., 1859–1860, 422–41 (Serial 1024).

20. Casey, *Soldiers, Ranchers, and Miners,* 22–25; U.S. Congress, Senate, Bvt. 2nd Lt. William H. Echols, *Report of Reconnaissance West of Camp Hudson, Ex. Doc. 1,* 36th Cong., 2d sess., 1860–1861, 36–50 (Serial 1079).

CHAPTER FOUR: THE DOCTRINE OF HOT PURSUIT

1. J. Fred Rippy, "The Indians of the Southwest in the Diplomacy of the United States and Mexico, 1848–1853," *HAHR* 2 (1919): 363–64; U.S. Congress, Senate, *The Treaty Between the United States and Mexico . . . , Ex. Doc. 52,* 30th Cong., 1st sess., 1847–1848, 431–36 (Serial 509).

2. There appears to have been a second crossing into Mexico known as the Chisos Ford which was said to have been located just east of Mariscal Canyon. Texas anthropologists T. N. Campbell and William Field, who have done the most extensive research on the Comanche Trail, were unable to discover any physical evidence of this crossing. For further details see, T. N. Campbell and William T. Field, "Identification of Comanche Raiding Trails in Trans-Pecos Texas," *West Texas Historical Association Yearbook* 44 (October 1968): 128–44.

3. Ibid., 128–44; The best firsthand description of the east branch of the trail is in U.S. Congress, Senate, Lt. Edward L. Hartz to Maj. David B. Vinton, *Diary of Lieutenant Edward L. Hartz, Ex. Doc. 2,* 36th Cong., 1st sess., 1859–1860, 422–41 (Serial 1024).

4. U.S. Congress, House, Sec. of War, *Annual Report, Ex. Doc. 5,* 31st Cong., 1st sess., 1849–1850, 188 (Serial 565); Robert M. Utley, *Frontiersmen in Blue: The United States Army and the Indian, 1848–1865* (Lincoln: Univ. of Nebraska Press,

1967), 70–74; Rippy, "Indians in United States-Mexican Diplomacy," 377–78, 384–87, 391–94.

5. Robert M. Utley, *Fort Davis National Historic Site, Texas* (Washington, D.C.: U.S. Dept. of the Interior, National Park Service, 1965), 11; Barry Scobee, *Fort Davis, Texas: 1586–1960* (El Paso: Hill Printing, 1963), 43–52.

6. David J. Weber, *The Mexican Frontier, 1821–1846: The American Southwest Under Mexico* (Albuquerque: Univ. of New Mexico Press, 1982), 115–21; Rippy, "Indians in United States-Mexican Diplomacy," 380–83.

7. E. S. Parker, Commissioner of Indian Affairs to J. D. Cox, Sec. of the Interior, April 26, 1871, in *Letters Received by the Office of the Adjutant General, Main Series, 1861–1889* (Washington, D.C.: National Archives Microfilm Publications), Microcopy 619, reel 799 (hereafter cited as *Letters Received by AGO*); Kenneth W. Porter, "The Seminole In Mexico, 1850–1861," *HAHR* 31 (February 1951): 1–4; A. M. Gibson, *The Kickapoos: Lords of the Middle Border* (Norman: Univ. of Oklahoma Press, 1963), chaps. 1–4.

8. Guajardo Notes, Box 8, Folder 1; Porter, "The Seminole in Mexico, 1850–1861," 8–36; Gibson, *Kickapoos,* 179–92.

9. Robert M. Utley, *Frontier Regulars: The United States Army and the Indian, 1866–1891* (Bloomington: Univ. of Indiana Press, 1973), 163–68; Kenneth Wiggins Porter, "The Seminole-Negro Indian Scouts, 1870–1881," *SWHQ* 55 (January 1952): 321–24; Bvt. Col. J. C. DeGress to Brig. Gen. H. Clay Wood, Asst. Adj. Gen., Texas Dept., March 17, 1870, in *Letters Received by AGO, 1861–1870,* reel 799; Lt. Col. William Shafter, Commander, Fort Duncan, to Asst. Adj. Gen., January 27, 1873, reel 800; Article II of the Treaty between the United States and the Seminole Nation, March 21, 1866, reel 800.

10. Lt. Col. William Shafter, Commander, Fort Clark to Asst. Adj. Gen., January 27, 1873, *Letters Received by AGO, 1861–1870,* reel 800; Porter, "The Seminole Negro Indian Scouts," 324–25; Edward S. Wallace, "General John Lapham Bullis: Thunderbolt of the Texas Frontier," *SWHQ* 55 (July 1951): 77–85. For the most comprehensive evaluation of the black soldier on the western frontier, see William H. Leckie, *The Buffalo Soldiers: A Narrative of the Negro Cavalry in the West* (Norman: Univ. of Oklahoma Press, 1967); U.S. Congress, House, *The Texas Border Troubles, Misc. Doc. 64,* 45th Cong., 2d sess., 1877–1878, 187–91 (Serial 1820); Utley, *Frontier Regulars,* 344–49.

11. Lt. Gen. Philip Sheridan to Sec. of War William Belknap, May 22, 1873, *Letters Received by AGO, 1861–1870,* reel 799. For the official report on MacKenzie's raid from the Mexican point of view, see *Informe de la Comision Pesquisidora de la Frontera del Norte al ejecutivo de la Nacion, 1873,* Guajardo Notes, Box 8, Folder 2, 23–32.

12. Sworn testimony of Eustaquio Garza, June 20, 1874 in *Letters Received by*

AGO, 1861–1870, reel 800. Lt. Bullis admitted to crossing the border with his scouts on four separate occasions between 1873 and 1877; see U.S. Congress, House, *Texas Border Troubles, Misc. Doc. 64,* 45th Cong., 2d sess., 1877–1878, 187–204 (Serial 1820); Robert Utley, " 'Pecos Bill' on the Texas Frontier," *American West* 6 (January 1969): 4–13, 61–62; Leckie, *The Buffalo Soldiers,* 150–55.

13. Utley, *Frontier Regulars,* 359–65; Leckie, *The Buffalo Soldiers,* 210–29; William H. and Shirley A. Leckie, *Unlikely Warriors: General Benjamin Grierson and His Family* (Norman: Univ. of Oklahoma Press, 1984), 258–68.

14. Lt. Bullis related this incident, which occurred in 1877, in his testimony before the House Committee on Military Affairs. While it was not a significant encounter with the Apaches, it did give the Seminole scouts some early knowledge of the territory that is today Big Bend National Park. See U.S. Congress, House, *Ex. Doc. 64,* 45th Cong., 2d sess., 1877–1878, 191 (Serial 1820); Leckie, *The Buffalo Soldiers,* 154–55.

15. Capt. Smither's detailed report dated December 20, 1884, is found in *Letters Received by AGO,* Microcopy 689, reel 317; Maj. Gen. J. M. Schofield to Brig. Gen. Stanley, Commander, Dept. of Texas, December 16, 1884, *Letters Received, 1881–1889,* reel 317; Eddie J. Guffee, "Camp Peña Colorado, Texas, 1879–1893" (Master's thesis, West Texas State Univ., 1976), 74–79.

16. Brig. Gen. Stanley to Thomas M. Vincent, Asst. Adj. Gen., January 2, 1885, in Record Group 393 ((hereafter cited as RG–393), *Letters of United States Commands, Fort Davis, Texas, 1867–1891* (copies on file at Fort Davis National Historic Site, Fort Davis, Texas); Lt. Charles H. Grierson to Col. Benjamin H. Grierson, February 22, 1885, in Benjamin H. Grierson Papers, 1827–1941, Southwest Collection, Texas Tech Univ., Lubbock (copy on file at Fort Davis National Historical Site, Fort Davis, Texas); *Department of War. Returns of U.S. Military Posts, 1880–1916,* Fort Davis, Texas, reel 298, Camp Peña Colorado, Texas, reel 901 (Washington, D.C.: National Archives Microfilm Publications); Guffie, "Camp Peña Colorado," 75–79; Leckie and Leckie, *Unlikely Warriors,* 239–40.

17. Gen. Crook's order's found in Asst. Dept. Com. to Com., Camp Peña Colorado, Texas, June 10, 1885, RG–393, Fort Davis File; Post Returns, Camp Peña Colorado, Texas, 1886, reel 901; 2nd. Lt. Cunningham to Post Adj., Fort Davis, Texas, RG–393, Fort Davis; Porter, "Seminole Negro Indian Scouts," 332–33; Wallace, "General John Lapham Bullis," 84–85.

CHAPTER FIVE: NO WINNERS, ONLY SURVIVORS

1. 2nd Lt. J. M. Cunningham to Post Adjutant, Fort Davis Texas, RG–393, *Letters of United States Military Commands, Fort Davis, Texas, 1867–1891,* copy on

file at Fort Davis National Historic Site, Fort Davis, Texas; Walter Prescott Webb, *The Great Plains* (1931; reprint, Lincoln: Univ. of Nebraska Press, 1981), 207–12; Robert M. Utley, "Longhorns of the Big Bend" (Santa Fe, New Mexico: National Park Service Report, Southwest Region, 1962), 1–8.

2. Webb, *Great Plains,* 212; Leavitt Corning, Jr., *Baronial Forts of the Big Bend: Ben Leaton, Milton Faver, and Their Private Forts in Presidio County* (Austin: Trinity Univ. Press, 1967), 19–41; *Texas Historic Forts: Part I, Fort Leaton* (Austin: Univ. of Texas School of Architecture Report, 1968), 6–10.

3. "Journal of William Henry Chase Whiting, 1849," in Ralph P. Bieber and Avram B. Bender, eds., *Exploring Southwestern Trails, 1846–1854,* vol. 2, *The Southwest Historical Series* (Glendale: Arthur Clark, 1938), 284–87; Corning, *Baronial Forts,* 37–38.

4. Webb, *Great Plains,* 212–13; Corning, *Baronial Forts,* 43–50; Henry T. Flecher, "From Longhorns to Herefords: A History of Cattle Raising in Trans-Pecos Texas," *Voice of the Mexican Border* 1 (October 1933): 61; Utley, "Longhorns of the Big Bend," 8–22; W. D. Smithers, *Early Trail Drives in the Big Bend* (El Paso: Texas Western Press, 1979), 4–9; Roy L. Swift and Leavitt Corning, Jr., *Three Roads to Chihuahua: The Great Wagon Roads That Opened the Southwest, 1823–1883* (Austin: Eakin Press, 1988), 117–18.

5. Utley, "Longhorns of the Big Bend," 23–24; Carlysle Graham Raht, *The Romance of the Davis Mountains and Big Bend Country* (Odessa, Texas: Raht Books, 1963), 157–58; Virginia A. Wulfkuhle, "The Buttrill Ranch Complex, Brewster County, Texas: Evidence of Early Ranching in the Big Bend," Report, Office of the State Archeologist (Austin: Texas Historical Commission, 1984), 31; Webb, *Great Plains,* 220–24.

6. Charles Judson Crane, *The Experiences of a Colonel in the Infantry* (New York: Knickerbocker Press, 1923), 13–15; Wulfkuhle, "The Buttrill Ranch Complex," 33; St. Clair Griffin Reed, *A History of the Texas Railroads and of Transportation Conditions under Spain and Mexico and the Republic and the State* (Houston: St. Clair Publishing, 1941), 190–98.

7. Walter E. Weyl, "Labor Conditions in Mexico," *Bulletin of the Bureau of Labor* 38 (January 1902): 71; Victor Clark, "Mexican Labor in the United States," *Bulletin of the Bureau of Labor* 78 (September 1908): 475–78; Mark Reisler, *By the Sweat of Their Brow: Mexican Immigrant Labor in the United States, 1900–1940* (New York: Greenwood Press, 1976), 165–69.

8. Virginia Madison, *Big Bend Country of Texas* (Albuquerque: Univ. of New Mexico Press, 1955), 111–13.

9. John E. Gregg, "The History of Presidio County" (Master's thesis, Univ. of Texas, Austin, 1933), 72; Fletcher, "From Longhorn to Herefords," 66; Wulfkuhle, "The Buttrill Ranch Complex," 37–39, 42.

10. Fort Davis, established in 1871, was the original county seat of Presidio County. In 1885 Marfa became the new seat of government. In 1887 Presidio County was subdivided into four smaller jurisdictions, Jeff Davis, Foley, Buchel, and Brewster. Present Big Bend National Park is included in the southern portion of Brewster County; Alpine, Texas, is the county seat.

11. Casey, *Soldiers, Ranchers, and Miners,* 150–52; Ronnie C. Tyler, *The Big Bend: A History of the Last Texas Frontier* (Washington, D.C.: U.S. Dept. of the Interior, National Park Service, 1975), 127; J. B. Gillett, "The Old G4 Ranch," *Voice of the Mexican Border* 1 (October 1933): 82–83.

12. Casey, *Soldiers, Ranchers, and Miners,* 154; Carey McWilliams, *North From Mexico: The Spanish Speaking People of the United States* (1949; reprint, New York: Greenwood Press, 1968), 151–56; Totsy Nelle Hitchcock, "Some Big Bend Personalities, 1895–1925" (Master's thesis, Sul Ross State College, 1966), 14, 20–24, 74–75.

13. Fletcher, "From Longhorn to Herefords," 66; Gerald D. Nash, *The American West in the Twentieth Century: A Short History of an Urban Oasis* (1973; reprint, Albuquerque: Univ. of New Mexico Press, 1977), 68; Bill Burnham, interview with author, Fort Stockton, Texas, June 2, 1985.

14. Hitchcock, "Some Big Bend Personalities," 40–42, 81–82; Bill Burnham, interview with author, Fort Stockton, Texas, June 2, 1985; Fred Rice, Jr., interview with author, Hamilton, Texas, June 6, 1985; Julia Moss, interview with author, Alpine, Texas, May 1, 1985.

15. McWilliams, *North From Mexico,* 162–64; Fred Rice, Jr., interview with author, Hamilton, Texas, June 6, 1985; Simon Celaya, interview with author, Alpine, Texas, May 31, 1985.

16. One year Wilson hired a professional to live in the Chisos and trap mountain lions. In that year, Bill Sloan trapped fifty-two of the animals. Most were captured crossing Mount Emory, the highest point in the Chisos range. Bill Burnham, interview with author, Fort Stockton, Texas, June 2, 1985.

17. Simon Celaya, interview with author, Alpine, Texas, May 31, 1985; Casey, *Soldiers, Ranchers, and Miners,* 161–67, 172–76; Nash, *The American West in the Twentieth Century,* 161–64; Hallie Stillwell, interview with author, Alpine, Texas, November 10, 1984.

CHAPTER SIX: THE RAINBOW SEEKERS

1. Robert T. Hill, "Running the Cañons of the Río Grande," *Century Illustrated Monthly Magazine* 51 (November 1900–April 1901): 382. U.S. Census figures for the year 1900 show Brewster County as having a total population of 2,356, a

232 percent increase over the 1890 census. Presumably, mining was responsible for the increase. U.S. Bureau of the Census, 1900 Census, vol. 1, Census of Population, Texas, p. *liv.*

2. Documentary evidence indicates that financial bankruptcy of the garrison's quartermaster unit in part forced the abandonment of Presidio San Vicente in 1781. Moreover, the fact that the presidio experienced these financial difficulties strongly suggests that the so-called Lost Mine never existed. See General Report by the Com. Gen. of the Interior Provinces, Teodoro de Croix to José de Gálvez, July 29, 1781, Archivo General de Indias, Guadalajara, 278. Typescript of this document in Special Collections Library, Univ. of New Mexico, Albuquerque. For references to the legend of the Lost Mine, see Richard B. Stolley, "Mysterious Maps to Lost Gold Mines," *Life Magazine* 56 (June 1964): 90–98; Ross A. Maxwell, *The Big Bend of the Río Grande: A Guide to the Rocks, Geologic History, and Settlers of the Area of Big Bend National Park* (Austin: Bureau of Economic Geology, Univ. of Texas, 1968), 51.

3. Luis Alberto Guajardo, "La Mina de la Sierra de Los Chisos," Guajardo Notes, Box 6, Folder 2; see also "Itinerario de la expedicion desde San Carlos a Monclova el viejo hecha por el Coronel D. Emilio Langberg," in Guajardo, Box 8, Folder 1.

4. Marvin D. Bernstein, *The Mexican Mining Industry, 1890–1950: A Study of the Interaction of Politics, Economics, and Technology* (New York: State Univ. of New York Press, 1964), 21–22, 60; Guajardo Notes, Box 6, Folder 2.

5. Isaac F. Marcosson, *Metal Magic: The Story of the American Smelting & Refining Company* (New York: Farrar, Straus and Co., 1949), 190; Carlysle Graham Raht, *The Romance of the Davis Mountains and Big Bend Country* (Odessa, Texas: Raht Books, 1963), 283; Foley County Records of Deed, 2:199, Brewster County Courthouse, Alpine, Texas; *Alpine Avalanche,* September 14, 1951.

6. Raht, *Romance of the Davis Mountains,* 283; *Commissioner's Court Minutes,* Brewster County, 33:367, Brewster County Courthouse, Alpine, Texas; Census reports for Brewster County in 1910 show a population increase from 2,356 to 5,220. Mining and internal improvements were, in part, the cause for this increase, U.S. Bureau of Census, 1910 Census, vol. 1, Census of Population, Texas; Ernesto Gallego, interview with author, May 1, 1985, Alpine, Texas.

7. Mary Antoine Lee, "A Historical Survey of the American Smelting and Refining Company in El Paso, 1887–1950" (Master's thesis, Texas Western College, 1950), 41–46; Marcosson, *Metal Magic,* 190; Brewster County Records of Deed, 54:92, Brewster County Courthouse, Alpine, Texas.

8. Maxwell, *Big Bend of the Río Grande,* 42–43; Ronnie C. Tyler, *The Big Bend: A History of the Last Texas Frontier* (Washington, D.C.: U.S. Dept. of the Interior,

National Park Service, 1975), 138; Farmer Jennings to Hallie Stillwell, August 27, 1947, a copy of the original letter in possession of the author.

9. There are many conflicting stories about how cinnabar was first discovered in the Big Bend. Clifford Casey, the foremost authority on local history in the area, cites Kleinman's discovery as one of the earliest. See Casey, *Soldiers, Ranchers, and Miners*, 211–16. Kenneth Ragsdale, a more recent scholar of mining in the Big Bend, says "it is impossible to cite the date and location of the first quicksilver recovery." See Kenneth Baxter Ragsdale, *Quicksilver: Terlingua and the Chisos Mining Company* (College Station: Texas A&M Univ. Press, 1976), 13–14.

10. Virginia Madison and Hallie Stillwell, *How Come It's Called That? Place Names in the Big Bend Country* (Albuquerque: Univ. of New Mexico Press, 1958), 54; Kathryn B. Walker, "Quicksilver in the Terlingua Area" (Master's thesis, Sul Ross State College, 1960), 22–23; Madison, *Big Bend Country*, 178–79.

11. Ragsdale, *Quicksilver*, 22–30, 36–39; Isidro García, interview with Vidal Davila, Jr., October 24, 1979, Castolon, Texas.

12. Clifford Casey lists Chisos Mine production figures for the years 1903–1920 at 92,341 flasks. These statistics drop to 45,523 flasks for the years 1920–1940.

13. C. A. Hawley, "Life Along the Border," *West Texas Historical and Scientific Society Publications* 20 (1964): 16–17; Simon Franco, interview with Vidal Davila, Jr., October 14, 1979, Alpine, Texas.

14. Ragsdale, *Quicksilver*, 46–47, 56–58; Vicente Molinar, interview with author, May 31, 1985, Alpine, Texas. Others living in the area listed as freighters for the Chisos Mining Company include Leandro Silvas, Ignacio Rentería, Chonito Ybarra, Cisto Silvas, and Antonio Franco. See Wayne R. Cartledge Collection, Box 5, File 153, Archives of the Big Bend, Sul Ross State Univ., Alpine, Texas (hereafter cited as Cartledge Collection).

15. Hawley, "Life Along the Border," 18–19; Howard E. Perry to the Chisos Mining Company, June 23, 1908, Chisos Mining Company Papers, Manuscript Collection, Texas Archives Division–Texas State Library, Austin; Cartledge Collection.

16. *Alpine Avalanche*, August 19, 1904; Casey, *Soldiers, Ranchers, and Miners*, 223–28.

17. Experienced miners worked a ten-hour day for $1.50 per day. Auxiliary labor worked the same number of hours for a salary that ranged from $1.00 to $1.25 per day. All labor except for Burcham, the foreman, and the brick kiln specialist were Mexican nationals. See Casey, *Soldiers, Ranchers, and Miners*, 244–49.

18. Ibid. 244–49; Simon Franco, interview with Vidal Davila, Jr., October 14, 1979, Alpine, Texas.

19. Carey McWilliams, *North from Mexico: The Spanish Speaking People of the United States* (1949; reprint, New York: Greenwood Press, 1968), 139–40; Casey, *Soldiers, Ranchers, and Miners,* 211–16; Ragsdale, *Quicksilver,* 13–14.

CHAPTER SEVEN: WINGS AND SADDLES

1. Michael C. Meyer and William L. Sherman, *The Course of Mexican History* (New York: Oxford Univ. Press, 1979), 498–505; Ronnie C. Tyler, "Notes and Documents: The Little Punitive Expedition in the Big Bend," *SWHQ* 78 (January 1975): 272.

2. J. O. Langford with Fred Gibson, *Big Bend: A Homesteader's Story* (Austin: Univ. of Texas Press, 1952), 144–51; Tyler, "Little Punitive Expedition," 273.

3. For a comprehensive study of the wax industry in Big Bend, see Curtis Tunnell, "Wax, Men, and Money: A Historical and Archeological Study of Candelilla Wax Camps along the Río Grande Border of Texas" (Austin: Texas Historical Commission, 1981); Clifford B. Casey, "The Candelilla Wax Industry in the Big Bend Country" (Alpine, Texas: Sul Ross State Univ., 1970).

4. J. Kilpatrick, Sr. to Hon. W. R. Smith, May 26, 1915, Adj. Gen. Doc. File, Record Group 94, Box 7644, File 2294479, National Archives, Washington, D.C. (hereafter cited as AGO File); W. R. Smith to Lindley M. Garrison, Secretary of War, June 5, 1915, AGO File, Box 7644, File 2294479; Tyler, "Little Punitive Expedition," 275.

5. Gov. Ferguson to Pres. Wilson, June 11, 1915, AGO File, Box 7644, File 2264551. The troop shortage that Funston referred to were elements of the 13th and 15th Cavalry originally stationed on the Río Grande but later reassigned to the Philippine Islands to put down a native insurrection against American occupation forces. See Funston to Gov. Furguson, July 1, 1915, AGO File, Box 7644, File 2264551.

6. Gen. Funston to Gov. Ferguson, July 1, 1915, AGO File, Box 7644, File 2264551; Brig. Gen. Tasker Bliss, a member of the Army General Staff, agreed that the problem in Texas was a civil not a military matter. Somewhat more sympathetic to the governor's plea than Funston, Bliss pointed out that financial difficulty had forced the reduction of the Texas Rangers from four companies to one. This left only twelve men to patrol a 250 mile-long border in Big Bend. See Brig. Gen. Tasker Bliss to Army Chief of Staff, June 22, 1915, AGO File, Box 7644, File 229906.

7. Lindley M. Garrison to Pres. Wilson, June 22, 1915, AGO File, Box 7644, File 229906; Meyer and Sherman, *Course of Mexican History,* 540–41; Michael C. Meyer, "The Mexican-German Conspiracy of 1915," *The Americas* 23

(July 1966): 76–89; Clarence C. Clendenen, *The United States and Pancho Villa: A Study in Unconventional Diplomacy* (Ithaca: Cornell Univ. Press, 1961).

8. Lindley M. Garrison to Pres. Wilson, June 22, 1915, AGO File, Box 7644, File 229906; Gen. Funston to Adj. Gen. of the Army, AGO File, Box 7644, File 228742. Quote cited in Tyler, "Little Punitive Expedition," 277.

9. Payne and Deemer rode with a smaller group of bandits ahead of the main body. Alvarez, meanwhile, took several more prisoners, who managed to turn on their captors, arrest the colonel, and take him back to Boquillas to face charges for the raids. See W. D. Smithers, "Bandit Raids in the Big Bend Country," *WTHS* 63 (September 1963): 82; Capt. C. D. Wood, "The Glenn Springs Raid," *WTHS* 63 (September 1963: 65–71; Clifford B. Casey, "Glenn Springs, Texas," report, Resource Management Division, Big Bend National Park, Texas, 1969, 28; Tyler, "Little Punitive Expedition," 277–81.

10. Gen. Funston to Adj. Gen., May 7, 1916, AGO File, Box 8132, File 2398805; George Carothers to Sec. of State, May 8th, 1916, *Records of the Department of State Relating to the Affairs of Mexico,* National Archives Microfilm Publications, M–256, Reel 53, Washington, D.C., 256-53 (hereafter cited as RDS); Funston to Adj. Gen., May 17, 1916, AGO File, Box 8132, File 2377632. The casualties at Glenn Springs were as follows: Killed — Pvts. William Cohen, Stephen J. Coloe, and Hudson Rodgers; Wounded — Sgt. Charles E. Smyth, Pvts. Frank Defrees, Roscoe C. Tyres, and Joseph Birch. All were of Troop "A," 14th Cavalry; see Lt. Col. William A. Raborg, "The Villa Raid on Glenn Springs," report, Big Bend National Park, Texas, 1954, 7–8.

11. Raborg, "Villa Raid," 3–5; Col. Sibley to Com. Gen., Southern Dept., June 13, 1916, AGO File, Box 8132, File 2377632; Stuart W. Cramer, Jr., "The Punitive Expedition from Boquillas," *U.S. Cavalry Journal* 28 (October 1916): 208–15.

12. Funston to Adj. Gen., May 17, May 19, 1916, AGO File, Box 8132, File 2377632; Col. Sibley's full report of the operations of the punitive expedition in Col. Sibley to Com. Gen., Southern Dept., June 13, 1916, AGO File, Box 8132, File 2377632.

13. James L. Rogers to Sec. of State, April 28, 1916, RDS, reel 53; Gens. Hugh L. Scott and Frederick Funston to Sec. of War, May 3, 1916.

14. Gens. Scott and Funston to Sec. of War, May 3, 1916, Scott and Funston to Sec. of State, May 8, 1916, and summary of agreement in Scott to Sec. of War, May 9, 1916, RDS, reel 53.

15. Gen. Scott to Sec. of War, May 10, 1916, RDS, reel 53; U.S. Consul James Rogers to Sec. of State, May 7, 1916; Carranza to Eliseo Arredondo, May 8, 1916; Gens. Scott and Funston to Adj. Gen., May 11, 1916, AGO File, Box 8132, File 2394312.

16. George Carothers to Sec. of State, May 12, 1916, Scott and Funston to Sec. of War, May 8, 1916, James L. Rogers to Sec. of State, May 7, 1916, and Newton D. Baker to Gov. Hunt of Arizona, May 1, 1916, RDS, reel 53.

17. Smithers, "Bandit Raids," 82; quote cited in Tyler, "Little Punitive Expedition," 281.

18. Parker to Sec. of State, May 23, 1916, and copy of *El Democrata* in Rogers to Sec. of State, May 9, 1916, RDS, reel 53.

19. William Blocker to Sec. of State, May 11, 1916, John Silliman to Sec. of State, May 10, May 15, 1916, and James Rogers to Sec.of State, May 23, 1916, RDS, reel 53.

20. Gen. Funston to Adj. Gen., May 22, 1916, RDS, reel 53; Tyler, "Little Punitive Expedition," 290–91; W. D. Smithers, interview with Vidal Davila, Jr., El Paso, Texas, January 16, 1980. Notably, the 8th Cavalry, headquartered in Marfa, was under the command of Lt. Col. George Langhorne, promoted for his action against the Glenn Springs raiders.

21. James Sheire and Robert V. Simmonds, *Historic Structure Report: Castolon Army Compound, Big Bend National Park, Texas* (Denver: U.S. Dept. of the Interior, Denver Service Center, 1973), 8–10, 16–24; Casey, *Soldiers, Ranchers, and Miners,* 48–52.

22. W. D. Smithers, interview with Vidal Davila, Jr., El Paso, Texas, January 16, 1980; Jodie P. Harris, "Protecting the Big Bend—A Guardsman's View," *SWHQ* 78 (January 1975): 292–302.

23. Smithers, "Bandit Raids," 84–93; Stacy C. Hinkle, *Wings Over the Border: The Army Air Service Armed Patrol of the United States-Mexico Border, 1919–1921* (El Paso: Texas Western Press, 1970), 6–17.

24. A full account of the Peterson-Davis incident is found in Stacy C. Hinkle, *Wings and Saddles: The Air and Cavalry Punitive Expedition of 1919* (El Paso: Texas Western Press, 1967); Smithers, "Bandit Raids," 101.

CHAPTER EIGHT: THE FRUITS OF THE EARTH

1. J. Charles Kelley, "The Historic Indian Pueblos of La Junta de los Ríos," *NMHR* 27 (October 1952): 258–78; W. Eugene Hollon, *The Great American Desert: Then and Now* (1966; reprint, Lincoln: Univ. of Nebraska Press, 1975), 40–41.

2. Population figures for Texas in 1781 are found in General Report by the Commandant of the Interior Provinces, Teodoro de Croix to José de Gálvez, July

19, 1781, AGI, Guadalajara 278, typescript of the original in Special Collections Library, Univ. of New Mexico, Albuquerque; Colonel Langberg was clearly impressed with the hardy inhabitants of Villa de San Carlos on his visit in 1851. See "Itinerario de la expedición desde San Carlos a Monclova el viejo hecha por el Coronel D. Emilio Langberg," in Guajardo Notes, Box 8, Folder 1.

3. Santa Helena, Texas, remained the official name of the area until 1914 when it was changed to Castolon. Today the Mexican village of Santa Elena is across the river from Castolon.

4. "La Coyota" consisted of about nine families including those of Ruperto Chavarría, Atelano Pando, Tiburcio García, Tiburcio Ramírez, Tomás Domínguez, Juan Silvas, Sabino Estorga, Patricio Domínguez, and Mario Ramírez. Casey, *Soldiers, Ranchers, and Miners;* United States-Mexico International Boundary Commission, Water Diversion Census, report, 1940, 8–12, 52–54; Mateo Ybarra, interview with author, April 30, 1985, Alpine, Texas.

5. Casey, *Soldiers, Ranchers, and Miners,* 31–32; Virginia A. Wulfkuhle, "The Buttrill Ranch Complex, Brewster County, Texas: Evidence of Early Ranching in the Big Bend," Office of the State Archeologist Report (Austin: Texas Historical Commission, 1984); Isidro García, interview with Vidal Davila, Jr., October 24, 1979, Castolon, Texas; Eunice Sublett Newman, interview with author, May 31, 1985, Alpine, Texas.

6. Casey, *Soldiers, Ranchers, and Miners,* 32–33; Mateo Ybarra, interview with author, April 30, 1985, Alpine, Texas; Eunice Sublett Newman, interview with author, May 31, 1985; Wayne Cartledge to Howard E. Perry, June 10th 1927, Cartledge Collection, Appendix 1, Chisos Mining Correspondence, folder 1, Archives of the Big Bend, Sul Ross State Univ., Alpine, Texas.

7. Clifford B. Casey, "The Boquillas-Hot Springs Area," report, History File, Big Bend National Park, Texas, 1970; Wulfkuhle, "The Buttrill Ranch Complex," 67–69; Jeff Graham, interview with author, June 1, 1985, Alpine, Texas.

8. U.S. Customs officials suspected John Daniels of engaging in illicit cattle trading with Mexicans across the border. Perhaps this may have influenced his decision to abandon ranching and practice farming. Ross Maxwell, interview with author, June 6, 1985, Austin, Texas; Susan Godbold, "Mary Coe Daniels, Woman of the West," paper, Marfa Historical Society, Marfa, Texas, 1969, 9–11; Ross Maxwell to Regional Director, January 22, 1945, BIBE Corr.

9. Carey McWilliams, *North from Mexico: The Spanish-Speaking People of the United States* (1949; reprint, New York: Greenwood Press, 1968), 169–73; Casey,

Soldiers, Ranchers, and Miners, 104–5; Cartledge Collection: Wayne Cartledge to Howard Perry, November 28, 1922, Appendix I; Cartledge to N. A. Brown, March 13, 1923, Box 2, File 43; La Harmonía Company to Continental Gin Company, April 4, 1923, Box 4, File 126; Wayne Cartledge to Eugene Cartledge, Sr., September 18, 1923, Box 3, File 87.

10. In addition to the families living in La Coyota that are listed above, others from Castolon engaged in cotton production included Alvino and Jorge Ybarra, Lázaro Hinojos, Amado Leyba, Francisco and Juan Silvas, Baldomiano and Guadalupe Avila, Florentino García, Nacasio Chacón, and Juan Medina. Mateo Ybarra, interview with author, April 30, 1985, Alpine, Texas.

11. Isidro García, interview with Vidal Davila, Jr., October 24, 1979; Mateo Ybarra, interview with author, April 30, 1985.

12. Casey, *Soldiers, Ranchers, and Miners,* 103–5; Wayne Cartledge to J. C. Wilson, Pres., Texas Cotton Industries, February 17, 1942, Cartledge Collection, Box 2, Folder 52.

13. Actually, Cartledge and Perry first leased the abandoned army barracks at Camp Saint Helena for $1.00 in December 1923. When the army announced the sale of the properties in January 1925, the two men were enthusiastic about the prospects for owning the buildings. Cartledge Collection: Capt. L. H. Palmer, U.S. Army Quartermaster Corps, to Wayne Cartledge, December 12, 1923; Lt. F. D. Wheeler to Cartledge, January 3, 1925; Capt. Palmer to Cartledge, May 5, 1925, Box 6, File 196; La Harmonía Company inventory of property, April 15, 1926, Box 2, File 61.

14. W. D. Smithers, "The Border Trading Post," *WTHS* 18 (1961): 42–45; Casey, *Soldiers, Ranchers, and Miners,* 78–85; Cartledge to Perry, June 10, 1927, July 8, 1927, and Perry to Cartledge, July 16, 1927, Cartledge Collection, Appendix I.

15. Cartledge Collection: Wayne Cartledge to Eugene Cartledge, Sr., January 10, 1927; Eugene Cartledge, Sr., to Wayne Cartledge, January 16, 1927, Box 3, File 87; Wayne Cartledge to Howard Perry, June 10, 1927, Appendix I.

16. Isidro García, interview with Vidal Davila, Jr., October 24, 1979, Castolon, Texas; Mateo Ybarra, interview with author, April 30, 1985, Alpine, Texas; Cartledge Collection: Wayne Cartledge to Harry E. Hull, Com. Gen. of Immigration, August 22, 1930; Cartledge to Sec. of Labor Frances Perkins, October 7, 1937; Cartledge to Sec. of State Cordell Hull, July 2, 1940, Box 15, File 467.

17. Wayne Cartledge to Eugene Cartledge, Sr., May 27, 1938, and Eugene Cartledge, Sr., to Wayne Cartledge, April 15, 1940, July 25, 1940, Cartledge Collection, Box 3, File 88.

CHAPTER NINE: THE FINAL OCCUPATION

1. Robert T. Hill, "Running the Cañons of the Río Grande," *Century Illustrated Monthly Magazine* 61 (November 1900–April 1901): 371–80; Virginia Madison and Hallie Stillwell, *How Come It's Called That?: Place Names in the Big Bend Country* (Albuquerque: Univ. of New Mexico Press, 1958), 15–33; for a comprehensive analysis of the image of the West in nineteenth-century writings, see Henry Nash Smith, *Virgin Land: The American West as Symbol and Myth* (Cambridge: Harvard Univ. Press, 1950), chaps. 8–9.

2. Clifford B. Casey, "The Boquillas-Hot Springs Area," report, History File, Resources Management Division, Big Bend National Park, Texas, 1970, 20–24; Benjamin Levy, *Hot Springs, Big Bend National Park: Historic Structures Report, Part I* (Washington, D.C.: U.S. Dept. of the Interior, National Park Service, Office of Archeology and Historic Preservation, 1968), 5–8; *Alpine Avalanche*, May 20, 1909.

3. *Alpine Avalanche*, July 25, 1912; J. O. Langford with Fred Gipson, *Big Bend: A Homesteader's Story* (Austin: Univ. of Texas Press, 1952), 81–86. It is noteworthy that Mr. Langford dedicated the above autobiography to Henry DuPont. Levy, *Hot Springs*, illus. 10–11.

4. Ronnie C. Tyler, *The Big Bend: A History of the Last Texas Frontier* (Washington D.C.: U.S. Dept. of the Interior, National Park Service, 1975), 189–90; other cartoons may be found in Jodie P. Harris, "Protecting the Big Bend: A Guardman's View," *SWHQ* 78 (January 1975): 292–302.

5. Kenneth Baxter Ragsdale, *Wings Over the Mexican Border: Pioneer Military Aviation in the Big Bend* (Austin: Univ. of Texas Press, 1984), 141–46; W. D. Smithers, interview with Vidal Davila, Jr., El Paso, Texas, January 16, 1980.

6. The revolt of Gen. José Gonzalo Escobar, prompted by the assassination of Pres. Alvaro Obregón on July 17, 1928, was the latest in a series of armed insurrections against the Mexican government. The army's main concern was the protection of the international border against invasion. See Baxter, *Wings Over the Mexican Border*, 3–13, 69–72; W. D. Smithers, interview with Vidal Davila, Jr., El Paso, Texas, January 16, 1980.

7. Ragsdale, *Wings Over the Mexican Border*, 137–40, 176. Some of the young officers who visited Johnson's Ranch in these early years went on to assume important positions in the United States Armed Forces. Most notable were Gens. Nathan F. Twining, later to become chairman of the Joint Chiefs of Staff, and Jonathan M. Wainwright, the hero of Bataan. Ragsdale, *Wings Over the Mexican Border*, 73.

8. Langford, *Homesteader's Story*, 152–54; Levy, *Hot Springs*, 20–21; Clifford B.

Casey, "Glenn Springs, Texas," report, History File, Resources Management Division, Big Bend National Park, Texas, 1969, 12–14.

9. Clifford Casey and Lewis Saxton, "The Life of Everett Ewing Townsend," *WTHS* 17 (1958): 53–55; John Robert Jameson, "Big Bend National Park of Texas: A Brief History of the Formative Years, 1930–1952" (Ph.D. diss., Univ. of Toledo, 1974), 10–12. The principal local leaders in the promotion of Big Bend State Park and later Big Bend National Park were James E. Casner, an Alpine businessman; Dr. W. Horace Morelock, president of Sul Ross Teachers College; Dr. Benjamin F. Berkeley, a former state senator; and Brewster County Judge Roy B. Slight.

10. Ross A. Maxwell, "History: Big Bend National Park," report, History File, Resources Management Division, Big Bend National Park, Texas, 1957; Casey and Saxton, "Life of Everett Ewing Townsend," 32–35; R. D. Morgan to CCC Regional Headquarters, n.d., Box 230, CCC Projects File, *Records of the Branch of Recreation, Land Planning, and State Cooperation. Project Reports on CCC Projects in State and Local Parks, Texas,* Record Group 79, National Archives (hereafter cited as RG–79).

11. The well-digging crew consisted of Ira H. Hector, W. T. McClure, Vicente Molinar, Nicolás Moreno, and Andreas Molinar; Vicente Molinar, interview with author, May 31, 1985, Alpine, Texas; Maxwell, "History of Big Bend National Park," 19.

12. Established in 1916 as a branch of the Department of the Interior, the National Park Service had previous experience in park development. For this reason, Secretary Ickes placed the bureau in charge of all projects that fell under the category of State Emergency Conservation Work. See Conrad Wirth, *Parks, Politics, and the People* (Norman: Univ. of Oklahoma Press, 1980), 103, 118; Herbert Maier to NPS, Washington, D.C., September 15, 1934, RG–79, Box 445.

13. Jameson, "Big Bend National Park of Texas," 13–16; Herbert Maier to Conrad Wirth, February 18, April 9, 1934, BIBE Corr.; Morgan report, RG–79, Box 230, CCC Projects.

14. "Report of the Big Bend Area, Texas," January 1935, in Big Bend Scrapbook, Box 2Q439, Item 1, Eugene C. Barker Library of Texas History, Univ. of Texas, Austin; Jameson, "Big Bend National Park of Texas," 16–18.

15. Maxwell, "History of Big Bend National Park," 20–21; Casey and Saxton, "Life of Everett Ewing Townsend," 58–60; Jameson, "Big Bend National Park of Texas," 18–21.

16. Casey and Saxton, "Life of Everett Ewing Townsend," 60–61; Sec. Harold Ickes to Pres. Roosevelt, February 27, 1935, BIBE Corr., Box 932209, Big Bend International File.

17. Michael C. Meyer and William L. Sherman, *The Course of Mexican History*

(New York: Oxford Univ. Press, 1979), 603–4, quoted from E. E. Townsend as cited in Casey and Saxton, "Life of Everett Ewing Townsend," 62.

18. Daniel F. Galacia to Conrad Wirth, April 3, 1936, in "Report on the Conference with Mexican Representatives Relative to the Proposed Big Bend International Park and Other Border Areas," November 14, 1935, BIBE Corr.

19. Manbey's recommendations are found in "Report on Suggested Park Boundary, Engineering Requirements and General Notes," August 1935, BIBE Corr.

20. Conrad Wirth, "Boundary Line Report: Big Bend National Park Project, Texas," report, History File, Resources Management Division, Big Bend National Park, Texas, 1935.

21. Alfred Runte, *National Parks: The American Experience* (Lincoln: Univ. of Nebraska Press, 1979), 109–14. Quote from Carroll H. Wegemann as cited in Wirth, "Boundary Line Report."

22. Herbert Maier to Director, National Park Service, January 8, 1937; BIBE Corr.; Maier to Walter P. Webb, April 26, 1937, Box 794, Big Bend File, in Walter Prescott Webb Papers, Texas State Library, Austin (hereafter cited as Gould Report); Webb to Maier March 19, 1937, BIBE Corr.; John R. Jameson, "Walter Prescott Webb, Public Historian," *The Public Historian* 7 (Spring 1985): 47–49.

23. The other three men who made the journey included Thomas V. Skaggs, a local entrepreneur from Lajitas; Joe Lane, an experienced riverman; and U.S. Border Patrol Officer James W. Metcalfe. See Walter Prescott Webb, "Through Santa Helena Canyon," Gould Report; *Fort Worth Star Telegram,* May 18, 1937.

24. Based on his successful venture, Webb joined a small but elite group of explorers that included Robert T. Hill, Jim McMahon (a local trapper who later escorted Hill), Presidio county surveyors E. L. Gage and John T. Gano, and Captain Charles Nevill of the Texas Rangers. See E. E. Townsend "Passages Made Through the Canyons of the Río Grande," Gould Report; and Walter Prescott Webb, "The Big Bend of Texas," NPS Press Release, April 18, 1937, History File, Resources Management Division, Big Bend National Park, Texas. Although Webb wrote two articles for the National Park Service, he failed to produce the historical narrative of Big Bend that he was contracted to write. See Jameson, "Walter Prescott Webb," 52.

25. Franklin D. Roosevelt to Gov. W. Lee O'Daniel, February 4, 1939, BIBE Corr.

26. Jameson, "Big Bend National Park of Texas," 28–48; James G. Anderson, "Land Acquisition in the Big Bend National Park of Texas" (Master's thesis, Sul Ross State College, 1967), 26–37.

27. For a comprehensive breakdown and analysis of the land acquisitions program from September 1, 1941, to September 30, 1942, see Anderson, "Land Acquisitions," chap. 4. Other local residents besides Townsend appointed to the Big Bend Land Department were Pink Phelps, an experienced title expert from Alpine, and Robert Cartledge of Terlingua, an auditor and field guide. Anderson, "Land Acquisitions," 57–58. It is interesting to note that nearly 4,000 acres of the unpurchased lands remaining in 1942 belonged to the Cartledge family. These properties, which included all of the present structures at Castolon, did not revert to the park until 1957. Anderson, "Land Acquisitions," 87.

28. Mrs. W. T. Burnham to Pres. Roosevelt, March 5, 1945, cited in Jameson, "Big Bend National Park of Texas," 58; Bill Burnham, interview with author, June 2, 1985, Fort Stockton, Texas; Hallie Stillwell, interview with author, November 10, 1984, Alpine, Texas.

29. "Tourists Are Eager to Visit Big Bend," *Texas Parade Magazine,* 1938, copy in RG–79, Box 439, Big Bend File; *Dallas News,* September 29 and March 17, 1940.

30. Supt. Maxwell's staff included Harry P. Linder, Clerk; Oren P. Senter, Park Ranger; and Upton J. Edwards, Laborer. Maxwell, "History of Big Bend National Park," 31–33.

Selected Bibliography

Archival Collections

Adjutant General's Office (Texas) Records, 1838–1889. 9 vols. Eugene C. Barker Library of Texas History, Univ. of Texas, Austin.

Archivo General de Indias, 1511–1850. Dunn Typescripts. Eugene C. Barker Library of Texas History, Univ. of Texas, Austin.

Archivo General de la Nación, 1538–1849. Dunn Typescripts. Eugene C. Barker Library of Texas History, Univ. of Texas, Austin.

U.S. Department of the Interior. National Park Service, Recreation, Land Planning and State Cooperation Division. General Files, Texas. Record Group 79. Washington, D.C.: National Archives and Records Administration.

U.S. Department of the Interior. National Park Service Records, Region III. Big Bend Correspondence File. Denver: Federal Archives and Records Center.

U.S. Department of State. Dispatches from U.S. Consuls in Piedras Negras, Mexico, 1868–1906. Washington, D.C.: National Archives Microfilm Publications. Microcopy 299. Rolls 1–5.

U.S. Department of State. Records of the Department of State Relating to Internal Affairs of Mexico, 1910–1929. Washington, D.C.: National Archives Microfilm Publications. Microcopy 274. Roll 53.

U.S. Department of War. Letters Received by the Topographical Bureau of the War Department and by Successor Divisions in the Office of the Chief Engineers, 1824–1865. Washington, D.C.: National Archives Microfilm Publications. Microcopy 506. Roll 36, I–J.

U.S. Department of War. Letters Received by the Office of the Adjutant General, Main Series, 1822–1860. Washington, D.C.: National Archives Microfilm Publications. Microcopy M–567. Roll 601.

U.S. Department of War. Letters Received by the Office of the Adjutant General, Main Series, 1861–1870. Washington, D.C.: National Archives Microfilm Publications. Microcopy M–619. Rolls 799–800.

U.S. Department of War. Letters Received by the Office of the Adjutant General, Main Series, 1881–1889. Washington, D.C.: National Archives Microfilm Publications. Microcopy M–689. Roll 317.

U.S. Department of War. Office of the Adjutant General Document File. Record Group 94. Washington, D.C.: National Archives and Records Administration.

U.S. Department of War. Records of United States Army Commands. Southern Department Mexican Revolution, Reports of Border Conditions, 1913–1916. Record Group 393. Washington, D.C.: National Archives and Records Administration.

U.S. Department of War. Letters of United States Army Commands, Fort Davis, Texas, 1867–1891. Record Group 393. Washington, D.C.: National Archives and Records Administration.

U.S. Department of War. Returns from United States Military Posts, 1800–1916. Washington, D.C.: National Archives Microfilm Publications. Microcopy M–617. Rolls 297–98, 901.

Manuscript Collections

Aldrich, Roy Wilkinson. Papers. Eugene C. Barker Library of Texas History, Univ. of Texas, Austin.

Big Bend National Park. Resources Management Correspondence File. Big Bend National Park, Texas.

Big Bend National Park. Resources Management History File. Big Bend National Park, Texas.

Big Bend National Park. Land Acquisition Papers. Archives of the Big Bend, Sul Ross State Univ., Alpine, Texas.

Big Bend Scrapbook. Eugene C. Barker Library of Texas History, Univ. of Texas, Austin.

Cartledge, Wayne R. Wayne R. Cartledge Papers. Archives of the Big Bend, Sul Ross State Univ., Alpine, Texas.

Casey, Clifford B. Clifford B. Casey Papers. Archives of the Big Bend, Sul Ross State Univ., Alpine, Texas.

Chisos Mining Company Papers. Texas State Library, Austin.

Emory, William H. William H. Emory Papers. Western Americana Collection, Beinecke Rare Book and Manuscript Library, Yale Univ., New Haven.

Guajardo, Luis Alberto. Luis Alberto Guajardo Notes. Western Americana Collection. Beinecke Rare Book and Manuscript Library, Yale Univ., New Haven.

Hill, Robert T. Robert T. Hill Papers. Eugene C. Barker Library of Texas History, Univ. of Texas, Austin.

Scholes, France V. France V. Scholes Papers. Special Collections Library, Univ. of New Mexico, Albuquerque.

Smithers, W. D. Wilfred D. Smithers Collection. Harry Ransom Humanities Research Center, Univ. of Texas, Austin.

Walthall, Harris. Harris Walthall Collection. Resources Management History File. Big Bend National Park, Texas.

Webb, Walter P. Walter P. Webb Papers. Texas State Public Library, Austin.

Unpublished Material

Anderson, James G. "Land Acquisition in the Big Bend National Park of Texas." Master's thesis, Sul Ross State Univ., Alpine, Texas, 1967.

Cain, Virginia Alice. "A History of Brewster County, 1535–1934." Master's thesis, Sul Ross State Teacher's College, Alpine, Texas, 1935.

Carroll, John. A. "The Big Bend Country: A Regional History." Paper, National Park Service Library, Southwest Region Office, Santa Fe, 1969.

Casey, Clifford B. "The Boquillas Hot Springs Area." Paper, National Park Service, Resources Management History File, Big Bend National Park, Texas, 1970.

————. "The Candelilla Wax Industry in the Big Bend Country." Paper, National Park Service, Resources Management History File, Big Bend National Park, Texas, 1970.

————. "Glenn Springs, Texas." Paper, National Park Service, Resources Management History File, Big Bend National Park, Texas, 1969.

Daniel, James M. "The Advance of the Spanish Frontier and the *Despoblado*." Ph.D. diss., Univ. of Texas, Austin, 1955.

Davila, Vidal Jr. "Research and Management of Historic Structures in Big Bend National Park." Paper presented at the Second Annual Chihuahuan Desert Symposium, Alpine, Texas, October 1983.

Garrison, L. A. "A History of the Proposed Big Bend International Park." Paper, National Park Service, Resources Management History File, Big Bend National Park, Texas, 1953.

Godbold, Susan. "Mary Coe Daniels, Woman of the West." Paper, Marfa Historical Society, Marfa, Texas, 1969.

Gregg, John E. "The History of Presidio County." Master's thesis, Univ. of Texas, Austin, 1933.

Guffee, Eddie J. "Camp Peña Colorado, Texas, 1879–1893." Master's thesis, West Texas State Univ., 1976.

Hitchcock, Totsy N. "Some Big Bend Personalities, 1895–1925." Master's thesis, Sul Ross State Univ., Alpine, Texas, 1966.

Ivey, James. "Presidios of the Big Bend Area." Report, National Park Service, Southwest Region Office, Santa Fe, 1984.

Jameson, John Robert, Sr. "Big Bend National Park of Texas: A Brief History of the Formative Years, 1930–1952." Ph.D. diss., Univ. of Toledo, Toledo, Ohio, 1974.

Lee, Mary Antoine. "A Historical Survey of the American Smelting and Refining Company in El Paso, 1887–1950." Master's thesis, Texas Western College, El Paso, 1950.

Liles, James E. "Notes on the Legend of the Lost Mine." History File, Big Bend National Park, Texas, n.d.

Maxwell, Ross A. "History: Big Bend National Park." Report, National Park

Service, Resources Management History File, Big Bend National Park, Texas, 1951.

Raborg, William A., Lt. Col. (Ret.). "The Villa Raid on Glenn Springs." Paper. Resources Management History File, Big Bend National Park, Texas, 1954.

Starnes, Gary Bertram. "Juan de Ugalde and the Provincias—Internas of Coahuila and Texas." Ph.D. diss., Texas Christian Univ., Fort Worth, 1971.

Walker, Kathryn B. "Quicksilver in the Terlingua Area." Master's thesis, Sul Ross State College, Alpine, Texas, 1960.

Weedin, Teresa J. "Historic Ruins Along Middle Tornillo Creek, Big Bend National Park, Texas." Paper, Dept. of History, Sul Ross State Univ., Alpine, Texas, 1975.

Government Documents and Public Records

Brown, William E., and Roland H. Wauer. *Historic Resources Management Plan: Big Bend National Park.* Washington, D.C.: U.S. Dept. of the Interior, National Park Service, 1968.

Brewster County. *Records of Deed.* Brewster County Courthouse, Alpine, Texas.

Casey, Clifford B. *Soldiers, Ranchers, and Miners in the Big Bend.* Washington, D.C.: U.S. Dept. of the Interior, National Park Service, 1969.

Brewster County. *Commissioner's Court Minutes.* Brewster County Courthouse, Alpine, Texas.

Echols, William H. *Report of Reconnaissance West of Camp Hudson.* 36 Cong., 2d sess., 1860–1861. S. Exec. Doc. 1. Serial 1078.

Emory, William H. *Report of the United States and Mexican Boundary Survey.* 2 vols. 34 Cong., 1st sess., 1855–1856. H. Exec. Doc. 135. Serial 862.

———. *Notes of a Military Reconnaissance from Fort Leavenworth, in Missouri to San Diego, in California, Including Parts of the Arkansas, Del Norte, and Gila Rivers.* 30th Cong., 1st sess., 1847–1848. S. Exec. Doc. 7. Serial 505.

Foley County. *Records of Deed.* Brewster County Courthouse, Alpine, Texas.

International Boundary Commission Records. Water Division Census, 1940.

Levy, Benjamin. *Historic Structures Report: Hot Springs, Big Bend National Park, Texas. Part One: Historical Data.* Denver: U.S. Dept. of the Interior, National Park Service, 1968.

Report of the Texas State Parks Board, 1941–1953. Big Bend National Park Land Aquisition Papers. Archives of the Big Bend, Sul Ross State Univ., Alpine, Texas.

Sheire, James, and Robert V. Simmonds. *Historic Structure Report: Castolon Army Compound, Big Bend National Park, Texas.* Denver: U.S. Dept. of the Interior, National Park Service, 1973.

Texas Historic Forts: Part I, Fort Leaton. Austin: Univ. of Texas School of Architecture, 1968.

Tunnell, Curtis. *Wax, Men, and Money: A Historical and Archeological Study of*

Candelilla Wax Camps along the Río Grande Border of Texas. Texas Historical Commission Report, Austin, Texas, 1981.

U.S. Bureau of Census. *1900 Census. Vol I: Census of Population, Texas.* Washington, D.C.: Government Printing Office, 1901.

U.S. Bureau of Census. *1910 Census. Vol. I: Census of Population, Texas.* Washington, D.C.: Government Printing Office, 1911.

U.S. Congress. Senate. *Annual Report, Bureau of Topographical Engineers.* 26 Cong., 1st sess., 1839–1840. S. Exec. Doc. 58. Serial 355.

U.S. Congress. Senate. *Report of the Secretary of War.* 31st Cong., 1st sess., 1849–1850. S. Exec. Doc. 1. Serial 549.

U.S. Congress. Senate. *Report of Lieutenant W. H. C. Whiting's Reconnaissance of the Western Frontier of Texas.* 31st Cong., 1st sess., 1849–1850. S. Exec. Doc. 64. Serial 562.

U.S. Congress. Senate. *Reports of Reconnaissance of Routes from San Antonio to El Paso.* 31 Cong., 1st sess., 1849–1850. S. Exec. Doc. 64. Serial 562.

U.S. Congress. Senate. *The Treaty Between the United States and Mexico.* 30th Cong., 1st sess., 1847–1848. S. Exec. Doc. 52. Serial 509.

U.S. Congress. House. Committee on Military Affairs. *The Texas Border Troubles.* 45th Cong., 2d sess., 1877–1878. H. Misc. Doc. 64. Serial 1820.

U.S. Department of the Interior. *Report of the Big Bend Area, Texas.* Washington, D.C.: National Park Service, State Park ECW, District III, 1935.

U.S. Immigration Commission. *Reports of the Immigration Commission, Immigrants in Industries.* Vol 25. Washington, D.C.: Government Printing Office, 1911.

U.S. Secretary of War. *Annual Report.* 31st Cong., 1st sess., 1849. H. Exec. Doc. 5. Serial 565.

Utley, Robert M. *Fort Davis National Historic Site, Texas.* Washington, D.C.: U.S. Dept. of the Interior, National Park Service, 1965.

————. *Longhorns of the Big Bend.* National Park Service Report. Southwest Region Office. Santa Fe, New Mexico, 1962.

Wirth, Conrad L. *Boundary Line Report: Big Bend National Park Project, Texas.* Washington, D.C.: U.S. Dept. of the Interior, National Park Service, 1935.

Wulfkuhle, Virginia. *The Buttrill Ranch Complex, Brewster County, Texas: Evidence of Early Ranching in the Big Bend.* Office of the State Archeologist Report, Texas Historical Commission, Austin, 1984.

Newspapers

Alpine Avalanche. Alpine, Texas. 1900–1950.
Dallas Morning News. Dallas, Texas. 1930–1950.
Fort Worth Star Telegram. Fort Worth, Texas. 1930–1950.
San Angelo Standard-Times. San Angelo, Texas. 1930–1950.
San Antonio Light. San Antonio, Texas. 1930–1940.

Maps

Map of Big Bend, Texas, and Bordering Mexican States. From Ronnie C. Tyler. "Notes and Documents: The Little Punitive Expedition in the Big Bend." *Southwestern Historical Quarterly* 78 (January 1975): 273.

Map of Big Bend, Texas. Chisos Mountains Quad. By Arthur A. Stiles and Stuart T. Penick, U.S. Geological Survey, 1903. National Archives and Records Administration. Cartographic Division, Record Group 57.

Map of the Eastern Apaches. From Max Moorhead. *The Apache Frontier: Jacobo Ugarte and Spanish-Indian Relations on the Northern Frontier, 1769–1781.* Norman: Univ. of Oklahoma Press, 1968. 201.

Map of the Geography of the Big Bend Region. By Bureau of Economic Geology, Univ. of Texas, Austin.

Map of General Benjamin Grierson's Area of Operations in West Texas, 1880. From William H. Leckie and Shirley A. Leckie. *Unlikely Warriors: General Grierson and His Family.* Norman: Univ. of Oklahoma Press, 1984. 273.

Map of Mexican Border Conflict, 1870–1886. From Robert M. Utley. *Frontier Regulars: The United States Army and the Indian, 1866–1891.* Bloomington: Univ. of Indiana Press, 1973. 348.

Map of Military Operations in West Texas, 1884. National Archives and Records Administration. Cartographic Division. Record Group 393, Texas Dept.–1.

Map of Presidial Line, 1776. From Mary Lu Moore and Delmar L. Beene. "The Interior Provinces of New Spain: The Report of Hugo O'Conor, January 30, 1776." *Arizona and the West* 13 (Autumn 1971): 275.

Map of Terlingua Quicksilver District. From Kenneth Baxter Ragsdale. *Quicksilver: Terlingua and the Chisos Mining Company.* College Station: Texas A&M Press, 1976.

Map of Texas and Part of New Mexico, 1857. By Bureau of Topographical Engineers. Archives of the Big Bend, Sul Ross State Univ., Alpine, Texas.

Map of West Texas Trails, 1849–1880. From Robert M. Utley. *Fort Davis National Historic Site, Texas.* Washington, D.C.: U.S. Dept. of the Interior, National Park Service, 1965.

Books

Bannon, John Francis. *The Spanish Borderlands Frontier.* Albuquerque: Univ. of New Mexico Press, 1974.

Bernstein, Marvin D. *The Mexican Mining Industry, 1890–1950: A Study of the Interaction of Politics, Economics, and Technology.* New York: State Univ. of New York Press, 1964.

Bieber, Ralph P., and Avram B. Bender, eds. *The Southwest Historical Series.* Vol. 2, *Exploring Southwestern Trails, 1848–1854.* Glendale: Arthur Clark, 1938.

Bolton, Herbert Eugene, ed. *Spanish Exploration in the Southwest, 1542–1706.* New York: Charles Scribner's Sons, 1916.

Brinckerhoff, Sidney B., and Odie B. Faulk, eds. and trans. *Lancers for the King: A Study of the Frontier Military System of Northern New Spain, With a Translation of the Royal Regulations of 1772.* Phoenix: Arizona Historical Foundation, 1965.

Brown, Lenard E. *Survey of the United States-Mexico Boundary, 1849–1855.* Washington, D.C.: U.S. Dept. of the Interior, National Park Service, 1969.

Casey, Clifford B. *Mirages, Mysteries, and Reality, Brewster County, Texas: The Big Bend of the Río Grande.* Hereford, Texas: n.p., 1972.

Casteñeda, Carlos E. *Our Catholic Heritage in Texas, 1519–1936.* 7 vols. Austin: Von Boeckmann and Jones, 1938.

Clendenen, Clarence C. *The United States and Pancho Villa: A Study in Unconventional Diplomacy.* Ithaca: Cornell Univ. Press, 1961.

Corning, Leavitt, Jr. *Baronial Forts of the Big Bend: Ben Leaton, Milton Faver, and Their Private Forts in Presidio County.* Austin: Trinity Univ. Press, 1967.

Crane, Charles Judson. *The Experiences of a Colonel in the Infantry.* New York: Knickerbocker Press, 1923.

Dobyns, Henry F. *The Apache People.* Phoenix: Indian Tribal Series, 1971.

Fowler, Harlan D. *Camels to California.* Palo Alto: Stanford Univ. Press, 1950.

García, Luis Navarro. *Don José de Gálvez y la comandancia general de las Provincias Internas del norte de Nueva España.* Sevilla: Escuela de Estudios Hispano Americanos de Sevilla, 1964.

Gerald, Rex E. *Spanish Presidios of the Late Eighteenth Century in Northern New Spain.* Sante Fe: Museum of Santa Fe Press, 1968.

Gibson, A. M. *The Kickapoos: Lords of the Middle Border.* Norman: Univ. of Oklahoma Press, 1963.

Goetzmann, William H. *Army Exploration in the American West, 1803–1863.* New Haven: Yale Univ. Press, 1959.

Gonzales Flores, Enrique, and Francisco R. Almada, eds. *Informe de Hugo O'Conor sobre el estado de las Provincias Internas del Norte, 1771–1776.* Mexico, D.F.: Editorial Cultura, 1952.

Goodwin, Grenville. *The Social Organization of the Apache.* Tucson: Univ. of Arizona Press, 1942.

Graebner, Norman A. *Empire on the Pacific.* New York: Ronald Press, 1955.

Hollon, W. Eugene. *The Great American Desert: Then and Now.* 1966. Reprint. Lincoln: Univ. of Nebraska Press, 1975.

Hammond, George P., and Agapito Rey, eds. *Expedition into New Mexico Made by Antonio de Espejo, 1582–1583, as Revealed in the Journal of Diego Pérez de Luxan, a Member of the Party.* Berkeley: Univ. of California Press, 1929.

Haring, C. H. *The Spanish Empire in America.* New York: Harcourt, Brace & World, 1963.

Hinkle, Stacy C. *Wings and Saddles: The Air and Cavalry Punitive Expedition of 1919.* El Paso: Texas Western Press, 1967.

————. *Wings Over the Border: The Army Air Service Armed Patrol of the United States-Mexico Border, 1919–1921.* El Paso: Texas Western Press, 1970.

Jackson, W. Turrentine. *Wagon Roads West: A Study of Federal Road Surveys and Construction in the Trans-Mississippi West, 1846–1869.* Berkeley: Univ. of California Press, 1952.

Kessell, John L. *Kiva, Cross, and Crown: The Pecos Indians and New Mexico.* 1979. Reprint. Albuquerque: Univ. of New Mexico Press, 1987.

Langford, J. O., with Fred Gipson. *Big Bend: A Homesteader's Story.* Austin: Univ. of Texas Press, 1952.

Leckie, William H. *The Buffalo Soldiers: A Narrative of the Negro Cavalry in the West.* Norman: Univ. of Oklahoma Press, 1967.

————, and Shirley A. Leckie. *Unlikely Warriors: General Grierson and His Family.* Norman: Univ. of Oklahoma Press, 1984.

Madison, Virginia. *The Big Bend Country of Texas.* Albuquerque: Univ. of New Mexico Press, 1955.

————, and Hallie Stillwell. *How Come It's Called That?: Place Names in the Big Bend Country.* Albuquerque: Univ. of New Mexico Press, 1958.

Marcosson, Issac F. *Metal Magic: The Story of the American Smelting & Refining Company.* New York: Farrar, Straus and Co., 1949.

Maxwell, Ross A. *The Big Bend of the Río Grande: A Guide to the Rocks, Geologic History, and Settlers of the Area of Big Bend National Park.* Austin: Bureau of Economic Geology, Univ. of Texas, 1968.

McWilliams, Carey. *North from Mexico: The Spanish Speaking People of the United States.* 1949. Reprint. New York: Greenwood Press, 1968.

Meyer, Michael C., and William L. Sherman. *The Course of Mexican History.* New York: Oxford Univ. Press, 1979.

Moorhead, Max L. *The Apache Frontier: Jacobo Ugarte and Spanish-Indian Relations in Northern New Spain, 1769–1791.* Norman: Univ. of Oklahoma Press, 1968.

————. *The Presidio: Bastion of the Spanish Borderlands.* Norman: Univ. of Oklahoma Press, 1975.

Nasatir, Abraham P. *Borderland in Retreat: From Spanish Louisiana to the Far Southwest.* Albuquerque: Univ. of New Mexico Press, 1976.

Nash, Gerald D. *The American West in the Twentieth Century: A History of an Urban Oasis.* 1973. Reprint. Albuquerque: Univ. of New Mexico Press, 1977.

Nash, Roderick. *Wilderness and the American Mind.* New Haven: Yale Univ. Press, 1967.

Porras, Muñoz Guillermo, ed. *Diario y derrotero de lo caminado visto y observado en el discurso de la visita general de presidios en las Provincias Internas de Nueva España, que de orden de S.M. executó Don Pedro de Rivera, Brigadier de los Reales Ejércitos, 1724–1726.* Mexico: n.p., 1945.

Powell, Philip Wayne. *Soldiers, Indians, and Silver: North America's First Frontier War.* Tempe: Arizona State Univ. Press, 1975.

Ragsdale, Kenneth Baxter. *Quicksilver: Terlingua and the Chisos Mining Company.* College Station: Texas A&M Univ. Press, 1976.

―――. *Wings Over the Mexican Border: Pioneer Aviation in the Big Bend.* Austin: Univ. of Texas Press, 1984.

Raht, Carlysle Graham. *The Romance of the Davis Mountains and Big Bend Country.* Odessa, Texas: Raht Books, 1963.

Reed, St. Clair Griffen. *A History of the Texas Railroads and of Transportation Conditions under Spain and Mexico and the Republic and the State.* Houston: St. Clair Publishing, 1941.

Reisler, Mark. *By the Sweat of Their Brow: Mexican Immigrant Labor in the United States, 1900–1940.* New York: Greenwood Press, 1976.

Runte, Alfred. *National Parks: The National Experience.* Lincoln: Univ. of Nebraska Press, 1979.

Sánchez, Joseph P. *The Río Abajo Frontier, 1540–1692.* Albuquerque: Museum of Albuquerque, 1987.

Scobee, Barry. *Fort Davis, Texas: 1586–1960.* El Paso: Hill Printing, 1963.

Spicer, Edward H. *Cycles of Conquest: The Impact of Spain, Mexico, and the United States on the Indians of the Southwest, 1553–1960.* Tucson: Univ. of Arizona Press, 1962.

Smith, Henry Nash. *Virgin Land: The American West as Symbol and Myth.* Cambridge: Harvard Press, 1950.

Smithers, W. D. *Early Trail Drives in the Big Bend.* El Paso: Texas Western Press, 1979.

Swift, Roy L., and Leavitt Corning, Jr. *Three Roads to Chihuahua: The Great Wagon Roads That Opened the Southwest, 1823–1883.* (Austin: Eakin Press, 1988.

Thomas, Alfred B. *Forgotten Frontiers: A Study of Spanish-Indian Policy of Don Juan Bautista, Governer of New Mexico, 1777–1787.* Norman: Univ. of Oklahoma Press, 1932.

―――. *Teodoro de Croix and the Northern Frontier of New Spain, 1776–1783.* Norman: Univ. of Oklahoma Press, 1941.

Tyler, Ronnie C. *The Big Bend: A History of the Last Texas Frontier.* Washington, D.C.: U.S. Dept. of the Interior, National Park Service, 1975.

Utley, Robert M. *The International Boundary United States and Mexico: A History of Frontier Dispute and Cooperation, 1848–1963.* Washington, D.C.: U.S. Dept. of the Interior, National Park Service, 1964.

―――. *Frontiersmen in Blue: The United States Army and the Indian, 1848–1865.* Lincoln: Univ. of Nebraska Press, 1967.

―――. *Frontier Regulars: The United States Army and the Indian, 1866–1891.* Bloomington: Univ. of Indiana Press, 1973.

Wallace, Ernest, and E. Adamson Hoebel. *The Comanches: Lords of the South Plains.* Norman: Univ. of Oklahoma Press, 1952.

Weber, David J. *The Mexican Frontier, 1821–1846: The American Southwest Under Mexico.* Albuquerque: Univ. of New Mexico Press, 1982.

Webb, Walter Prescott. *The Great Plains.* 1931. Reprint. Lincoln: Univ. of Nebraska Press, 1981.

Wirth, Conrad L. *Parks, Politics, and the People.* Norman: Univ. of Oklahoma Press, 1980.

Articles

Beers, Henry Putney. "A History of the U.S. Topographical Engineers, 1813–1863." *Military Engineer* 34 (1942): 270–90.

Bender, Avram B. "Opening Routes Across West Texas, 1848–1850." *SWHQ* 37 (October 1933): 116–35.

Bolton, Herbert Eugene. "Defensive Spanish Expansion and the Significance of the Spanish Borderlands." In *Trans-Mississippi West*, ed. by James Willard and Colin Goodykoontz. Boulder: Univ. of Colorado Press, 1930, p. 1–42.

———. "The Mission as a Frontier Institution in the Spanish-American Colonies." *American Historical Review (AHR)* 23 (October 1917): 42–61.

Campbell, T. N., and William T. Field. "Identification of Comanche Raiding Trails in Trans-Pecos Texas." *West Texas Historical Association Year Book* 44 (October 1968): 128–44.

Casey, Clifford B. "The Big Bend National Park." *WTHS* 13 (June 1948): 32–35.

Castañeda, Carlos, trans. "A Trip to Texas in 1828, José María Sánchez." *SWHQ* 29 (April 1926): 249–88.

Clark, Victor. "Mexican Labor in the United States." *Bulletin of the Bureau of Labor* 78 (September 1908): 466–522.

Cramer, Stuart W., 1st Lt. "The Punitive Expedition from Boquillas." *U.S. Cavalry Journal* (October 1916): 200–27.

Domínguez de Mendoza, Juan. "Itinerary of Juan Domínguez de Mendoza, 1684." In *Spanish Explorations in the Southwest, 1542–1706,* ed. by Herbert Eugene Bolton. New York: Charles Scribner's Sons, 1916, 320–43.

Espejo, Antonio de. "Accounts of the Journey Which I, Antonio de Espejo Made to the Provinces and Settlements of New Mexico, 1583." In *Spanish Exploration in the Southwest, 1542–1706,* ed. by Herbert Eugene Bolton. New York: Charles Scribner's Sons, 1916, p. 168–92.

Fletcher, Henry T. "From Longhorn to Herefords: A History of Cattle Raising in Trans-Pecos Texas." *Voice of the Mexican Border* 1 (October 1933): 61–69.

Forbes, Jack D. "The Janos, Jocomes, Mansos, and Sumas Indians." *NMHR* 32 (October 1957): 319–34.

Gillett, James B. "The Old G4 Ranch." *Voice of the Mexican Border* 1 (October 1933): 82–83.

Harris, Jodie P. "Protecting the Big Bend—A Guardsman's View." *SWHQ* 78 (January 1975): 292–302.

Hawley, C. A. "Life Along the Border." *WTHS* 20 (1964): 7–86.

Hill, Robert T. "Running the Cañons of the Río Grande." *Century Illustrated Monthly Magazine* 51 (November 1900–April 1901): 371–87.

Jameson, John R. "Walter Prescott Webb, Public Historian." *The Public Historian* 7 (Spring 1985): 47–52.

Kelley, J. Charles. "The Route of Antonio de Espejo Down the Pecos River and Across the Texas Trans-Pecos Region." *WTHS* 7 (1937): 7–25.

———. "The Historic Indian Pueblos of La Junta de los Ríos." *NMHR* 26 (October 1952): 257–95.

Loomis, Noel. "Commandants-General of the Interior Provinces: A Preliminary List." *Arizona and the West (AW)* 11 (Autumn 1969): 261–68.

Matson, Daniel S., and Albert H. Schroeder, eds. "Cordero's Description of the Apache, 1796." *NMHR* 32 (October 1957): 335–56.

Maxwell, Ross A. "Big Bend National Park: A Land of Contrasts." *WTHS* 13 (June 1948): 6–18.

Mecham, J. Lloyd. "The Second Spanish Expedition to New Mexico: An Account of the Chamuscado-Rodríquez Entrada of 1581–82." *NMHR* 1 (July 1926): 265–91.

Moore, Mary Lu, and Delmar L. Beene, eds. and trans. "The Interior Provinces of New Spain: The Report of Hugo O'Conor, January 30, 1776." *AW* 13 (Autumn 1971): 265–82.

Meyer, Michael C. "The Mexican-German Conspiracy of 1915." *The Americas* 23 (July 1966): 76–89.

Nelson, A. B. "Campaigning in the Big Bend of the Río Grande in 1787." *SWHQ* 39 (January 1936): 200–227.

———. "Juan de Ugalde and Picax-Ande Intstinsle, 1787–1788." *SWHQ* 43 (April 1940): 437–64.

Porter, Kenneth W. "The Seminole in Mexico, 1850–1861." *HAHR* 31 (February 1951): 1–36.

———. "The Seminole-Negro Indian Scouts, 1870–1881." *SWHQ* 55 (January 1952): 358–77.

Reeve, Frank D. "The Apache Indians in Texas." *SWHQ* 50 (October 1946): 189–219.

Rippy, J. Frederick. "The Indians of the Southwest in the Diplomacy of the United States and Mexico, 1848–1853." *HAHR* 2 (1919): 363–96.

Saxton, Lewis H., and Clifford B. Casey. "The Life of Everett Ewing Townsend." *WTHS* 17 (1964): 1–68.

Schoffelmayer, Victor H. "The Big Bend Area of Texas: A Geographic Wonderland." *The Texas Geographic Magazine* 1 (May 1937): 1–25.

Smith, Victor J. "Early Spanish Explorations in the Big Bend of Texas." *WTHS* 2 (1928): 59–68.

Smithers, W. D. "Bandit Raids in the Big Bend Country." *WTHS* 63 (September

1963): 75–105.

———. "The Border Trading Posts." In *Pancho Villa's Last Hangout on Both Sides of the Río Grande in the Big Bend Country*. Alpine, Texas: Sul Ross State Univ., n.d., 41–59.

Townsend, E. E. "Rangers and Indians in the Big Bend Region." *WTHS* 6 (1935): 43–48.

Tyler, Ronnie C. "Notes and Documents: The Little Punitive Expedition in the Big Bend." *SWHQ* 78 (January 1975): 271–91.

———. "Exploring the Río Grande: Lt. Duff C. Green's Report of 1852." *AW* 10 (Spring 1968): 43–60.

Utley, Robert. " 'Pecos Bill' on the Texas Frontier." *American West* 6 (January 1969): 4–13, 61–62.

Vigness, David M. "Don Hugo O'Conor and New Spain's Northwestern Frontier, 1764–1776." *Journal of the West* 6 (January 1967): 27–40.

Wallace, Edward S. "General John Lapham Bullis: Thunderbolt of the Texas Frontier." *SWHQ* 55 (July 1951): 77–85.

Weyl, Walter E. "Labor Conditions in Mexico." *Bulletin of the Bureau of Labor* 38 (January 1902): 1–94.

Whiting, William Henry Chase. "Journal of William Henry Chase Whiting, 1849." *Exploring Southwestern Trails, 1846–1854*, ed. by Ralph P. Bieber and Avram B. Bender. Vol. 2, *The Southwest Historical Series*. Glendale: Arthur Clark, 1938.

Wood, C. D. "The Glenn Springs Raid." *WTHS* 63 (September 1963): 65–71.

Personal Interviews

Burnham, Bill. Interview with author. Fort Stockton, Texas, June 2, 1985.
Celaya, Simon. Interview with author. Alpine, Texas, May 31, 1985.
Franco, Simon. Interview with Vidal Davila, Jr. Alpine, Texas, October 14, 1979.
Gallego, Ernesto. Interview with author. Alpine, Texas, May 1, 1985.
García, Isidrio. Interview with Vidal Davila, Jr. Castolon, Texas, October 24, 1979.
Graham, Jeff. Interview with author. Alpine, Texas, June 1, 1985.
Maxwell, Ross A., Dr. Interview with author. Austin, Texas, June 6, 1985.
Molinar, Vicente. Interview with author. Alpine, Texas, May 31, 1985.
Moss, Julia. Interview with author. Alpine,Texas, May 1, 1985.
Newman Sublett, Eunice. Interview with author. Alpine, Texas, May 31, 1985.
Rice, Fred Jr. Interview with author. Hamilton, Texas, June 6, 1985.
Smithers, W. D. Interview with Vidal Davila, Jr. El Paso, Texas, January 16, 1980.
Stillwell, Hallie. Interview with author. Alpine, Texas, November 10, 1985.
Ybarra, Mateo. Interview with author. Alpine, Texas, April 30, 1985.

Index